CHANGED MEN

CULTURAL FRAMES, FRAMING CULTURE
Robert Newman, Editor
Justin Neuman, Associate Editor

CHANGED MEN

VETERANS IN AMERICAN POPULAR CULTURE AFTER WORLD WAR II

ERIN LEE MOCK

UNIVERSITY OF VIRGINIA PRESS
Charlottesville and London

The University of Virginia Press is situated on the traditional lands of the Monacan Nation, and the Commonwealth of Virginia was and is home to many other Indigenous people. We pay our respect to all of them, past and present. We also honor the enslaved African and African American people who built the University of Virginia, and we recognize their descendants. We commit to fostering voices from these communities through our publications and to deepening our collective understanding of their histories and contributions.

University of Virginia Press
© 2024 by the Rector and Visitors of the University of Virginia
All rights reserved
Printed in the United States of America on acid-free paper

First published 2024

1 3 5 7 9 8 6 4 2

Library of Congress Cataloging-in-Publication Data
Names: Mock, Erin Lee, author.
Title: Changed men : veterans in American popular culture after World War II / Erin Lee Mock.
Description: Charlottesville : University of Virginia Press, 2024. | Series: Cultural frames, framing culture | Includes bibliographical references and index.
Identifiers: LCCN 2024002380 (print) | LCCN 2024002381 (ebook) | ISBN 9780813950945 (hardback) | ISBN 9780813950952 (paperback) | ISBN 9780813950969 (ebook)
Subjects: LCSH: World War, 1939–1945—Veterans—United States. | Veterans in popular culture. | Veterans—Public opinion. | Popular culture—United States—History—20th century. | Masculinity—United States—History—20th century. | United States—Civilization—1945– | BISAC: PERFORMING ARTS / Film / History & Criticism | LITERARY CRITICISM / Subjects & Themes / Culture, Race & Ethnicity
Classification: LCC D810.V42 U665 2024 (print) | LCC D810.V42 (ebook) | DDC 305.9/06970973—dc23/eng/20240205
LC record available at https://lccn.loc.gov/2024002380
LC ebook record available at https://lccn.loc.gov/2024002381

Cover art: Submarines service poster, USA, 1940s. (© The Advertising Archives/Bridgeman Images)
Cover design: Susan Zucker

For Juanita and Leroy, Rosemary and Lewis

CONTENTS

Acknowledgments | ix

Introduction: "His Blood Is Up" — 1

Prologue: Before We Pick Up Where We Left Off — 41

1. "It Was Easy": Postwar Paperbacks and the Veteran Killer — 59

2. "Do We Become What We Do?": Glenn Ford and Van Heflin in Hollywood — 94

3. Getting Comfortable: Hugh Hefner's *Playboy* in the 1950s — 133

4. The Horror of "Honey, I'm Home!": 1950s Domestic Sitcoms in the Twilight Zone — 172

Conclusion: The "Loving Little Stoic" Speaks — 207

Notes | 229

Bibliography | 239

Index | 263

ACKNOWLEDGMENTS

Writing a book, like any honest endeavor, is not a solitary process. I appreciate everyone who participated.

First, I thank Angie Renee Hogan, Fernando Campos, and Wren Morgan Myers at the University of Virginia Press, as well as Frank Episale, for their stewardship and attention to detail. The Department of English at the CUNY Graduate Center awarded me the Calder Dissertation Fellowship and the Doctoral Students Council supported my trip to the UCLA Film and Television Archive. David Newton, Meg Pearson, and Kimily Willingham helped me get funding for trips to the New York Public Library of the Performing Arts, the Paley Center, and the Steven Schwartzman Library. The staff at these institutions provided me invaluable research assistance.

Ideally, one's academic path involves many mentors, and here too I was fortunate. My dissertation supervisor, Marc Dolan, helped me wrangle my reveries. The late Morris Dickstein came to my rescue. Gary Giddins forced me to rethink my assumptions about the postwar period. Heather Hendershot could not have been a better mentor. I am humbled by the care she has given my work over the years; she applied the rigor and integrity she shows in her own work to mine for which I'll be forever grateful.

My gratitude extends well beyond my official mentors. Lewis and Jerolyn Mock are the rare nonacademic parents of an academic who never questioned my choice. Gwendolyn Beetham and Julia E. Kohn related to me from across vast disciplinary divides. Conversations with Keisha Bolden, Michelle DuQuesnay, and the members of Blackwell-Bolt and the Electric Think Tank helped me focus in the early stages. Jessica Wells Cantiello knows this book better than anyone except me. I thank Adam Bolt: without him, I would not have written this book because I wouldn't have known that I needed to. And Brooks E. Hefner, my academic big brother, answered the questions I didn't know I needed to ask and his counsel was unfailingly right-on.

Nicholas B. Bussey, honey, you're the most honest and the finest man in the world. And I couldn't have done what I had to do if I hadn't always known that I could trust you.

CHANGED MEN

INTRODUCTION

"HIS BLOOD IS UP"

William Wyler's Oscar-winning *The Best Years of Our Lives* (1946) is, without question, the defining Hollywood text of post–World War II veteran reintegration. Its brilliance lies in its triple-protagonist structure: the film suggests that there are many ways, all difficult, for veterans to "come home." Directed by a veteran, written by a veteran, filmed by a veteran, and produced by a crew of mostly veterans—though two of the three major actors were not—it shows remarkable compassion for the three servicemen, even as they drink, argue, and run away from home. The film's treatment of their loved ones is more ambivalent: two out of three of the men's lovers simply cannot understand their returning partners, but one embraces her injured sweetheart with open arms. Also, some in their community (the fictional Boone City) do not truly appreciate the men's service to their country. In the 1940s, *The Best Years of Our Lives* received critical acclaim and achieved widespread popularity—it had the biggest box office grosses since 1939's *Gone with the Wind* (Victor Fleming). And, as the Korean War ended, some critics suggested that Americans should watch the film again in order to better understand the current moment. What Wyler, his crew, and his contemporaries viewed as "highly authentic"—Wyler claimed it was "written by events that imposed a responsibility on us to be true"—many critics now write off as false or soft-pedaled. The film is "proud of itself," "stifling[ly] pious," and, for some, "a horse-drawn truckload of liberal schmaltz."[1] Even while in agreement with these negative assessments, many other recent critics justify the film's drawbacks. David Thomson, for example, claims that any harder-edged film would never have made it through censors and MGM Studios, which is a fair assessment.[2] In fact, Goldwyn struck a riot from the script, and the film's violence comes at the expense of a window, not a human being.[3]

Philip Beidler astutely interprets the film in contrast to depictions of the Vietnam War:

> [W]e have sat through waves of astringent depictions of the returned veteran—*The Deer Hunter, Coming Home, First Blood, In Country, Born on the Fourth of July*—invariably troubled albeit necessary exercises in national self-examination. Yet perhaps if we have learned through our passage out of the Vietnam era that there actually is more than one kind of national experience of war, so perhaps we may now see that there is also more than one way to make a film that bravely confronts the problems of return, especially to an America once flushed with victory and not without reason deeming itself the geopolitical hope of a new order of history. (29–30)

Post–World War II America did not want or need *Apocalypse Now* or *Jarhead*, and every era creates the popular culture it needs. As critic Gary Giddins puts it, "Popular art listens, absorbs, reflects, harangues, and can, in troubled times, console."[4] If it does all of those things, it does not do them all in equal measure at all times, and each medium, let alone each work on its own, does not always do all of these things at once. *The Best Years of Our Lives* defines our ideas of post–World War II reintegration because it had to—a generation of men had returned from "the good war." However, *The Best Years of Our Lives* is just one example of the ways in which popular culture managed this war's troubled aftermath.

It is easy to understand why World War II has been considered "the good war" both during the conflict and ever since. The United States was attacked by Japan, the Nazis were waging not just war but genocide, and the US military had strong and relatively harmonious relations with its Allies. The Axis were fighting for things that seem incontrovertibly "bad," so the war against them is rationally positioned as "good." And, of course, the Allies won it. But there is so much more at stake in making World War II "the good war." The notion that the lives lost and the pain suffered during a war is "in vain" if the war is not a good one remains salient in America after Vietnam, Iraq, and Afghanistan, though a very small number of Americans have served in any post–World War II conflict. Moreso, the myth of "the good war" had such currency around World War II because of its broad importance: the myth was fundamental to the maintenance of very basic social order in a nation of veterans. Simply because of the number of men who returned from fighting and the carnage they wrought, saw, and felt, maintaining the war's "goodness" was a national priority. It would never again be as crucial to put a positive face on a war.

Veteran reintegration was a key issue in American life in the 1940s and 1950s because of the vastness of that era's veteran identity. Because so many Americans associate the postwar period with the GI Bill, heightened prosperity, strong civic spirit, and growing families, one might imagine of this enormous transition, "it was easy." But how could it have been? The return of sixteen million service members to their families and communities was a migration on an enormous scale and one of the most sudden and large-scale culture clashes in American history. In numbers alone, it was three times the Great Migration, thirty times the number of Americans who traveled the Oregon Trail, four times Irish immigration to America during the whole of the nineteenth century, one hundred and sixty times the number of Native Americans relocated during Andrew Jackson's Indian Removal. Because so many more Americans served in some capacity, the reintegration of World War II and Korean War vets was radically more diasporic than any of these movements.

No community in America, and nary a family, was isolated from this dramatic repopulation. And repopulation it was: though some had brief furloughs, many World War II veterans served "the duration," which was often several years, some overseas throughout. Others came home earlier with injuries or served stateside, but the dispersal of trained military throughout the United States in 1945 and 1946 was indeed a resettlement, and it created a uniquely expansive veteran diaspora, spread over soil untouched by the war. The explosive growth of the suburbs exacerbated this expansion. According to Michael Bennett, "Starting in 1950, almost all the nation's cities lost population while the suburbs gained sixty million new residents."[5] This was the result of a nationwide housing shortage, which many feared would anger veterans who had dreamed of coming home to own their own houses, but would be forced to live with family, roommates, or in collective housing. Rapid suburbanization was a response to fears of veterans. Ultimately, the isolation of men from one another further served efforts to tame the veteran.[6]

This reintegration of veterans followed a home front population shuffle, which led many Americans out of rural areas into places where war-related labor was more plentiful. This was especially true for African Americans, 1.5 million of whom left their hometowns (especially in the South) for better-paying defense work.[7] Unfortunately, their newfound economic prosperity was not often met by social equality, with housing conditions a particular concern. Black veterans and their families moved to the suburbs in the postwar period as did whites, though their reasons for doing so and the places they landed differed in many cases.

For many reasons, this is an American story. World War II's place in American history is different from its place in other national histories. Unlike the other major players in the second World War, the American military had not been involved in so long a conflict in nearly eighty years. Never had so many Americans—both the total number and the percentage of the eligible population—served in any conflict. 1954 marks the year in which there were more veterans in the American population than ever before. Though our military remained inexcusably segregated until the war in Korea and prejudice was widespread, the racial, ethnic, regional, class, professional, and religious mixing that took place created a definition of masculinity was broader than it had been before. Until the war, American men shared biological traits and were frequently "heads" of their families, but they often shared little else in common, which made it both more difficult and less necessary to solidify an aggregate conception of American manhood. After the war, not only did so many men share a war past, they shared the experience of coming home and, in many cases, the movement away from their hometowns shortly after their return to the United States. Region, neighborhood, class, and ethnicity weakened as marketing categories during the war, leading to an unprecedentedly homogenous national popular culture.

During wartime, Hollywood studios, radio networks, magazine and book publishers, among others, considered the major demographic divide to be military/civilian, not class, race, or region. By the time men returned from service, shared popular culture was as much a given as shared experience. While discrete American masculinities defined by race, ethnicity, class, region, profession, and sexual orientation have always had traction, shared veteran identity created a coterminous collective masculinity, which included a wide-ranging set of expectations, definitions of good and bad behavior, "natural" impulses and emotions, appropriate goals, relationships, and boundaries. It is fair to say that World War II created American masculinity in the twentieth century. And a definition of masculinity defined in battle is a frightening one, frightening by necessity. Though the war and shared veteran culture and experience invented this new masculinity, many aspects of it are what David Glover calls "the refurbishing of already existing masculine forms."[8] According to Ellen Herman, while "predisposition" was the dominant concept in the nineteenth century, "by 1940 large-scale socioeconomic events like the depression had moved the concept away from a narrow, genetic meaning and neo-Freudians . . . were stressing the power of culture to shape and reshape human behavior."[9]

In most periods of American history, some men were assumed to be inherently violent, and this group was typically isolated by class, ethnicity, race, or region. One of the many differences between the post–World War II version of masculinity and those that preceded it is that it came to seem that not just some, but all men were predisposed to violence because so many seemed to have proven themselves capable of such. Furthermore, this idea persisted throughout the remainder of the twentieth century. However, elements of American masculinities as old as the country itself are perennially reanimated when met with events.

BRAVE MEN

After the bombing of Pearl Harbor, many Americans were eager for war. But after the first ten months of the conflict, many questioned that initial spirit: were American troops really ready to fight the more experienced and brutal Axis warriors? Early on, Americans seemed too far behind their allies and opponents to participate successfully, and morale understandably ebbed. It's far more satisfying, if no differently brave or patriotic, to vanquish the enemy than to march naively into a bloodbath. In response to this flagging spirit, journalists and propagandists worked to assure Americans back home that the men were getting better all the time. Ernie Pyle was the country's most renowned war journalist, and no one celebrated American competence on the battlefield more than he. In his famous piece "Brave Men, Brave Men," he tells of returning to the front after an absence to find that American troops were no longer out of their depth.

> The most vivid change is the casual and workshop manner in which they now talk about killing. They have made the psychological transition from the normal belief that taking human life is sinful, over to a new professional outlook where killing is a craft. To them now there is nothing morally wrong about killing. In fact it is an admirable thing.... His blood is up. He is fighting for his life, and killing now for him is as much a profession as writing is for me.... Say what you will, nothing can make a complete soldier except battle experience.[10]

Frightening as this description may be, it was almost certainly a comfort as well for home front Americans. Consider how, amid otherwise violent language, Pyle returns many times to words like "workshop," "professional," "craft," and "profession." The men are becoming efficient at their jobs.

After his own visit, President Franklin Roosevelt agreed that American troops had matured, telling listeners to his Fireside Chat, "On my trip, I saw hundreds of thousands of soldiers. Young men who were green recruits last autumn have matured into self-assured and hardened fighting men. They are in splendid physical condition. They are mastering the superior weapons that we are pouring out of our factories. The American people have accomplished a miracle."[11] It was a miracle of transformation: according to Pyle, Roosevelt, and much of the media, the military was now made up of experienced, competent professionals. They measured their competence by their hardness and their ability to kill and, specifically, to kill without moral qualms or metaphysical discomfort. And we, the American people, had accomplished this miracle.

This particular definition of American competence—and, thus, the indication that Americans might prevail—was necessitated by Office of War Information (OWI) campaigns that painted the enemies as incomparable sadists and torturers of soldiers and civilians. As the war went on, the images of the Japanese and the Nazis got scarier. Early portrayals of the Japanese military showed them as subhuman and incompetent, but after several Allied defeats, the soldier was remodeled into what John Dower calls "the Japanese superman," who was "possessed of uncanny discipline and fighting skills ... a uniquely formidable and contemptible foe who deserved no mercy and virtually demanded extermination."[12] American media—sometimes government-sponsored, but just as often not—cataloged Japanese atrocities and featured images of Japanese soldiers bayoneting and disemboweling children. After some deliberation, the United States government eventually allowed the news media to cover the Bataan Death March, a decision which made a considerable impact on public opinion of the Pacific War. Because the Japanese were portrayed as not just sadists, but regimented and effective sadists, businesslike murder was incumbent upon American soldiers trying to defeat them.

Americans were also expected to disregard a lifetime of indoctrination in American ethics. Eugene B. Sledge, an American veteran of the Pacific Theater, recalls this being put quite bluntly: "Our drill instructor at boot camp would tell us, '. . . Don't hesitate to fight the Japs dirty. Most Americans, from the time they're kids, are taught not to hit below the belt. It's not sportsmanlike. Well, nobody has taught the Japs that, and war ain't a sport. Kick him in the balls before he kicks you in yours.'"[13] It was crucial for American troops to distinguish sporting spirit from battlefield professionalism, opponents from enemies. Exaggerating or emphasizing ethnic and national difference was one potent way of doing so.

Peggy Terry remembers that these notions were just as prevalent among American civilians: "We were just ready to wipe [the Japanese] out. They sure as heck didn't look like us. They were yellow little creatures that smiled when they bombed our boys."[14] The image of Hitler in the media was, as Michael Birdwell puts it, "evil incarnate" and Nazi officers received similar treatment.[15] American media may have dehumanized Germans less than the Japanese, using overtly racist descriptions like Terry's, but, when asked to describe Germans (not just Nazis), Americans selected two adjectives: "hardworking" and "warlike."[16] In light of their description as "warlike," the choice of "hardworking" is ominous: it is no wonder that Pyle and Roosevelt praised American soldiers for becoming workers themselves.

But not all anti-Nazi propaganda portrayed them as hardworking warriors; some images presented them in savage terms too, eating the meat off the bones of Allied troops. Roosevelt himself described the Germans to the American public: "We must not underrate the enemy. He is powerful and cunning—and cruel and ruthless. He will stop at nothing that gives him a chance to kill and to destroy. He has trained his people to believe that their highest perfection is achieved by waging war. For many years he has prepared for this very conflict—planning, and plotting, and training, arming, and fighting. We have already tasted defeat. We may suffer further setbacks. We must face the fact of a hard war, a long war, a bloody war, a costly war."[17] In John Morton Blum's words, both the Nazis and the Japanese together were viewed as "brutal, dangerous foes, destroyers of the peace, enemies of mankind."[18]

A bitter irony of war propaganda is that its message boomerangs. If the Japanese and the Germans were that evil, it stands to reason that Americans had to descend to their level, or at least come close, in order to win the war. If American soldiers were rising to the challenges of combat with the Germans and the Japanese, American civilians were, in this respect, reassured. They ought to have been. Underestimated by the Axis, American troops went on to many remarkable successes in the remaining years of World War II. Of course, the terms by which American civilians were reassured resonated differently as the end of the war came nearer. Americans may have felt safer that their men would survive and win the war; later, the skills they had developed would prove both inappropriate and frightening in the context of civilian life. Our men, Pyle claimed, had changed fundamentally. We should be proud of them, but we should know that they are bloodthirsty and competent killers. The story of postwar America is the story of a country trying to recover from that message in order to open its arms to sixteen million people trained to kill. And the story of how those people coped with coming home.

COMING HOME

Worries about reintegration were animated almost from the war's beginnings but reached a fever pitch well before VJ Day. In his Fireside Chat on July 28, 1943, Roosevelt argued that it was never too early to worry about the welfare of veterans on their return, saying: "We must, this time, have plans ready—instead of waiting to do a hasty, inefficient, and ill-considered job at the last moment. I have assured our men in the armed forces that the American people would not let them down when the war is won." Indeed, he had begun plans for the GI Bill months beforehand, fearing riots if veterans were disillusioned on their return. All of these messages would remind listeners of the veterans' riots after World War I, including the Bonus Army protests.[19]

Americans had to wish for their soldiers to fight to the death and come home, but also to realize that this coming home after fighting to the death (or being trained to do so) would be difficult. As the war was coming to an end, journalists (including Pyle) began to suggest that these veterans were, in fact, victims of the government they served rather than fortunate recipients of wartime morale and postwar veterans' benefits.

Meanwhile, mainstream advice and "sociological" literature about veteran reintegration blossomed. Historian Dixon Wechter's *When Johnny Comes Marching Home* (1944) and sociologist and World War I veteran Willard Waller's *The Veteran Comes Back* (1944) were two significant books in this emerging genre.[20] Both writers cautioned that reintegration would have its hardships, but their predictions and advice differed dramatically by degree. Though he suggested ways to smooth the process, Wechter concluded with optimism: "About Johnny one thing is sure. As he went forth, so he will return: friendly, generous, easygoing, brave, the citizen-soldier of America" (558). By contrast, Waller's perspective was alarmist:

> [Veterans] are the principal social problem of the coming years. Like no other group, the veterans command our minds and hearts today. The kind man pities them. The just man feels guilty toward them. The informed man fears them.
>
> NOT TO PLAN NOW, IS TO PLAN DISASTER
>
> We know from past experience that we must not be caught unprepared. The veterans will descend upon us with frightening suddenness. (260)

He continued:

> The cost of solving the veteran problem will undoubtedly be high. The cost of not solving it will be immensely higher. If we neglect our veterans, we shall pay for our heartlessness in a thousand different ways. Not one of us will be able to escape the impact on our own personal lives of the mass misery of millions of maladjusted veterans. . . . If, in the years immediately after the war, we do not give the veterans what they need and have a right to have, they will in later years force us to pay a heavy price for our thrift. (304)

Wechter and Waller's predictions were both resonant and reflective of their time of publication, but their variance illuminates the coexistence of multiple strands of thought about veterans as the war came to an end. The writers' variance likely emerged from their biographies and training. As a professor of English and history, Wechter discoursed on the history of American involvement in armed conflict, marveling at the suffering, but also at the resilience of Americans at war since the Revolution. He documented the difficulties of reintegration at a distance and so found it easy to conclude that war is essentially an inevitable part of American life and a part of history that can be effectively reabsorbed time and again. He cautioned civilians against taking extreme positions on the veteran—"Idealists expect him to return deeply purified and spiritualized by his experience. Pessimists say that he will come home a rake, a thief, and probably a killer"—urging a middle ground (10). He hoped that American girls could "cure" men of "new and degenerate ideas" about sex but suggested that these ideas were more performance than reality, a "veneer" like much of military life: "Escape for months and years from petticoat government—of mothers, sweethearts, wives—has likely given him a certain veneer. . . . [Vices] belong to the cult of roughing it; their self-indulgence is often a way of relaxing nerves and tempers. Civilians seldom guess how quickly this veneer is put on, in another milieu how willingly rubbed off. Traces may remain, however, for some time." Men indulged in vices while away from women; women and the comforts of home would provide them with more wholesome methods of relaxation. And, if only traces of this "veneer" remained for some time, they would eventually be "rubbed off."

As a veteran, Waller vehemently disagreed that these traces would simply wear off, saying that, "every soldier who returns to civilian life is still mentally and nervously organized for war—a condition that requires something more active than the passage of time for its cure" (113). His message on every page was vigilance and activity. Waller discussed World War I frequently as a veteran of that conflict, a credential prominently displayed on the cover of the book. His argument was that he knew what it meant to be a veteran, and so he knew just how dangerous it would be to have them surrounding civilians in such unprecedented numbers. His insight into the veteran psyche echoed Pyle and Roosevelt's descriptions of American men at war: "To meet the other hardnesses of army life, there arise other kinds of fitness. The necessity of preparing to be a killer engenders in the soldier an almost prideful attitude toward murder and its instruments. When a soldier and civilian meet, the soldier sometimes says and more often thinks, 'I could kill you. One smash of a gun butt would splatter your brains all over the sidewalk.

And I know several sure-fire ways of killing you with my bare hands'" (83). Note that Waller does not say "having killed" but says "preparing to be a killer" will provoke this line of thinking. This is common in the texts about veteran reintegration: warning families of non-combatants not to get too comfortable. Waller also trumpeted his training as a social scientist, and his solutions to the problems he anticipated ranged from individual compassion to the creation of national think tanks. He believed that colleges, universities, and social workers should offer open courses on dealing with veterans: "It is not enough for the psychiatrist to know that the shell-shocked veteran has a tendency toward explosive aggression; *everybody must know it in order to understand how to live with and treat such a man*" (emphasis in original) (306).

In Wechter's formulation, the veteran is, at bottom, friendly and generous. To Waller, violence is the default mode and war the permission slip: "for most men, war becomes a perfect excuse for killing" (46). Indeed, it is "the attitudes and controls of civilian life" that keep him from killing before the war, but in wartime "the soldier must kill, must make a study of the art of killing. . . . Perhaps he comes to enjoy killing" (124, 42).

Waller's soldier is, however, conflicted: drawn toward killing, he also longs for the civilization in which he has come of age and felt at home. His natural, instinctual violence and lust compete with the social taboos which have kept him from acting out on these impulses; the military, and specifically the comradeship that supports violence and sexual immorality, "weakens these taboos" (124). If these taboos, attitudes, and controls are not reasserted, Waller argues "many veterans [will] become criminals, just how many we do not know, since the subject has never been studied as thoroughly as it deserves to be" (124).

Waller helpfully argues that the future of the United States is not hopeless. As a veteran, he offers civilians a choice: accommodate these returning potential murderers, rapists, and criminals, or face the consequences. Unsurprisingly, much of American culture in the postwar era responded by accommodating them. Waller could create such a terrifying vision of the veteran because he was one himself. Wechter's guilt may have interfered with his ability to represent the worst-case scenarios; in this respect, he is like many civilians of his time.

Despite his lighthearted conclusion, Wechter is not entirely a Pollyanna. He does worry about political unrest: "the average veteran, friendly, hearty, and something of a 'joiner,' is particularly susceptible to manipulation by the unscrupulous. This has been proved time and again" (115). But, on the whole, he is confident that reintegration is mostly a matter of time. The issue of political unrest comes up in Waller's book as well, and both argue that Americans must show support for veterans and appreciation for their service to the country consistently, unflaggingly, and enthusiastically. Failure to do so could demoralize veterans (Wechter) or outright provoke them to a level of violence that could utterly destroy American society (Waller).

RACE IN WARTIME AND AFTER

Among their many predictions about veteran discontent, both Wechter and Waller sympathetically argue that Black soldiers will have good reason to revolt if their service is not sufficiently appreciated when they return.[21] Wechter and Waller thusly indicate an intriguing by-product of this emerging collective (veteran) masculinity: many traits long associated with Black masculinity were incorporated into broader discussions of men, which invariably focused on white men—a category which was rapidly expanding. While Black men bore and continue to bear the burden of these biases far more than others, the "Black brute" stereotype which characterized Black men as raging amoral violent rapists shared a great deal with negative stereotypes of veterans and, later, men in general. Race does indeed fit into the picture, but as part of a spectrum: Black veterans had specific concerns related to their unjust treatment, but their behavior was imagined to be similar to and similarly provoked by the war.

One fascinating matter of the postwar period is that some of the assumptions once applied to Black men came to be applied to men in general in ways that would previously have been unthinkable: historians have noted that Black soldiers were critical to the war effort and that their return only heightened their justified sense of grievance against the US government and white American society. The postwar period was deeply invested in the notion of the man, a notion from which Blacks were frequently excluded, but a notion for which their prewar stereotypes were rather prototypical. After the war, an essentialism of gender coexists with the essentialism of race, incorporating non-Black men into a pre-existing discourse of male savagery, theretofore primarily concerning Black men and, in wartime, the Japanese.

This point is not to argue that Black men and white men were then seen as equal or interchangeable by any means, but that many of the assumptions made about Black men extended to include men of other races, including whites, and also that many of the assumptions placed upon Black men during the postwar period were those associated with men as a group. The divisions between races on the question of masculinity changed enormously, such that "breadwinning" in the post-Depression era became a way to deflect fears of male violence. Given that government policies like the GI Bill served a lower percentage of Blacks, and given rampant discrimination elsewhere, Black men were deprived of opportunities to prove themselves equal to "controlling" themselves. Interestingly though, the media seemed eager to offer images of Black men who were "under control" in ways that were sometimes deeply unsatisfying.

Chester Himes's *If He Hollers Let Him Go* (1945) articulates this strangeness when protagonist Bob Jones, a rightly angry Black man who has been (as often was the case) wrongly accused of raping a white woman, is sent off to war as a substitute for prison. The substitution is telling: take that violence and turn it against the "Japs." The novel explicitly argues that Bob's rage is a direct result of the racism he experiences rather than an inborn trait and that this rage is something that is pre-existing and can be "tapped into" by the US government, even though that government is one he abhors and holds responsible for many of his own problems and for other injustices he witnesses.

Of course, Richard Wright's *Native Son* (1940), which came out a year before the United States entered World War II and which predates *If He Hollers* by five years, presents protagonist Bigger Thomas as a "scapegoat" who commits crimes essentially because that is what's expected of him. The experiences of racism and poverty and the accompanying presumption of guilt have prepared the way for Bigger to murder the daughter of the white couple he works for and then rape and murder his own girlfriend. His lawyers suggest that his crimes were inevitable—he is a Black man. In *Native Son* and *If He Hollers*, few characters ever question the inevitability of Black male violence. (It is worth noting that both novels feature prominent Black female characters, not one of whom shows any violent tendencies.) During Reconstruction, the notion of the Black man as "savage" and "violent" was key to the legislation's undoing, related to the 4,000 lynchings that took place between Reconstruction and World War II, and frequently perpetuated. Both Himes and Wright effectively complicate this idea, suggesting that it is racism (and the poverty which often attends it), not race itself, which inculcates violent impulses in Black men. Just as white masculinity began to be associated with some version of the stereotypes long applied to Black men, the definition of Black masculinity shifted to authorize their subordination. As Stephen Tuck put it, "by the outbreak of World War II . . . the brute was replaced by the fool."[22] Novelist Ralph Ellison argued that, at least since *Birth of a Nation*, those types were a "twin screen image of the Negro as bestial rapist and grinning, eye-rolling clown."[23] These representations called into question whether Black men could be as "professional" and battlefield-competent as those that Pyle and Roosevelt described.

The stories of Black men and women appear in every chapter of this book, but are not and cannot be tossed in casually. It is impossible to understand the role of Black Americans in this book without considering the complexity of their situations in wartime and in the postwar period. They shared a great deal in common with Americans of other races during and after wartime, but their experiences were also unique. Without question, Black men served honorably and contributed significantly to the war effort. Their heroism is in no way diminished by acknowledging that they did so in numbers beneath their proportion of the population. This disparity was largely due to military policy, rather than a lack of patriotism. Black men were discouraged from volunteering. Once they volunteered, they were turned down much more often than they were accepted. When they served, they served for shorter tours.

There was considerable discord generally, but specifically among Black Americans, over this discrepancy, much of it falling along class lines. Walter White and the NAACP as well as religious leaders fought hard for Black men's inclusion from the war's beginning.[24] White and other leaders demanded the full desegregation of the Armed Forces, that Black men participate in the war in numbers consistent with their share of the population, and that Black men be equally involved in combat operations. Mostly white representatives of the military responded with some agreement in principle but were not entirely willing to be proactive: current policies and practices were certainly unjust, but they could not be expected to solve a "social issue" like racism in the United States in the midst of a war of this scope. In other words, Black Americans were told to *wait* for this small measure of justice, a refrain of anti-Black racism which Julius B. Fleming Jr. recently termed "Black patience."[25]

Much to the chagrin of elite Black leaders, many Black men agreed with the mostly white military leadership that it was not the time for desegregation. Only a minority wished to be in integrated units, which, while disappointing to many Black leaders, seems rational. After all, integration could mean placing their lives in the hands of racists. Even off the battlefield, fears of interracial violence on base were well-founded.

Much of the Black press echoed White's viewpoints, stressing that their readers were patriotic, willing and eager to serve, and up to any battlefield challenge. These publications encouraged their readers to enlist and prove their patriotism and celebrated Black men's combat triumphs. Understandably though, Black men and their families were divided over their increasing exposure to combat, another dispute which tended to fall along class lines. All families of servicemen faced this dilemma, but it stands to reason that people who felt their country's persecution most deeply and its hypocrisies most directly may have been less interested in risking their own or their loved ones' lives to defend it.

Many scholars have pointed out that the civil rights movement may have been in reaction to white Americans' underappreciation of Black men's service, but civilian Black men may also have been frustrated that, left out of the war effort, they were left out of the benefits and attendant upward mobility that policies like the GI Bill provided.[26] Though Black men were underrepresented, the GI Bill was instrumental in the development of a more sizable Black middle class. Latino servicemen of the working class also experienced this upward mobility, as did white men of lesser means.[27] If Black men had been allowed full participation, the American middle class might look different today.

Japanese Americans, of course, faced a very particular set of prejudices: while they were first barred from service, they were eventually included, though often in separate units and under immense scrutiny, sometimes even while their families lived in internment camps on American soil.[28] So, while Latinos, Native Americans, citizens of Jewish, Irish, Italian, Polish descent, and most Asian ethnicities were involved and integrated with "nonethnic" whites as never before, race and ethnicity mattered deeply for the simple numbers of enlistees accepted. The military and media representations of this diversity urged Americans home and abroad to see interethnic battlefield brotherhood as a new normal.[29] The Korean War military was integrated, and both Blacks and Japanese Americans (unsurprisingly in this conflict), served in numbers consistent with their populations. By the time the United States became involved in the war in Vietnam, Black men volunteered in numbers above proportional representation, likely in part to avail themselves of the economic advantages accrued to the veterans of earlier conflicts.

Even at a time of prevalent racism and ethnic bias, the US government expected men of various backgrounds to serve. Catholics and Jews fought along with Protestants and Mormons; some of these were meeting religious others for the first time. Married men with children were initially exempt, but hundreds of thousands enlisted and, eventually, married fathers were also subject to the draft. Many men originally classified as 4-F (mentally or physically unfit to fight) were reconsidered when numbers ran low. Younger men and older men joined twenty- and thirty-somethings as the conflict progressed. They lived with strangers who, over the years, became buddies, lovers, rivals, even brothers.

SEX AT WAR

They didn't simply get to know each other, but met people from all over the world and were exposed to them in ways they may not have chosen or imagined when the war began: the dispatch of sexual urges over years of separation by gender changed American sexual mores forever. As Alan Petigny argued, "the sexual revolution actually began during World War II."[30] Thousands of teenaged GIs had their first sexual experiences with women and men whose languages they could not understand. The long-married, too, found comfort in the arms of others: French sex workers or Japanese "comfort women," Samoan "welcomers," California khaki-whackies, and the men in their own units. Women also reached out for companionship and sex in ways they may not have dared outside of wartime. Extramarital, interracial, interethnic, and homosexual erotic contact flourished, along with a new frankness about masturbation. Within years of American men's return to the United States, Alfred P. Kinsey released his famous report *Sexual Behavior in the Human Male* (1948), a veritable "Pandora's box," which revealed that more than a third of American men had had homosexual experiences and nearly half had had "sexual reactions" to other men.[31] More than half of men had had extramarital sex with other women and nearly one-quarter "responded sexually" to sadomasochism. The reaction to this information was mixed. As Miriam Reumann points out, women's publications were among the many to suggest that women "face the reality" of men's changed sexuality, but this was not always simple: experts and intellectuals from Wechter and Waller to Lionel Trilling believed that these experiences, expectations, and impulses could be modulated, re-channeled, and possibly even tamed.³² Americans needed to strike a balance between expression and repression, and soon.

Many critics blame the influence of Freud—if not Freud himself—for a cultural obsession with sexuality which enabled Kinsey's research and which, later, entrenched pseudo-scientific ideas of sexual difference. Indeed, Freud is an inescapable part of post–World War II American culture, but so too were widespread and simplified ideas of "psychiatry" and "psychology," which meant different things at different times and, in many cases, consisted primarily of cultural buzzwords, but which incorporated some of the new discoveries of battlefield psychiatrists that writer Penny Coleman isolates with Freudian and post-Freudian theories. As Louis Menand puts it, "Freudianism managed to coexist in the cultural imagination with trends in psychiatry and intellectual life with which it was partly and sometimes wholly incompatible."³³ The unfocused quality of Americans' love affair with Freud should not diminish its importance, and his thesis on "penis envy" barely scratches the surface of his meaning to postwar Americans. Freud insisted on profound gender divisions, but he and his followers grappled with more than gender and sexuality, and also used concepts of gender and sexuality in service of other inquiries. One of these was war trauma.

PSYCHOANALYZING WAR TRAUMA

In *Beyond the Pleasure Principle,* Freud considers the psychic "situation" of war. He argues that a new psychic structure—what he calls the "war superego"—might develop in wartime. In peacetime, the superego, of course, adheres to the demands of authority, including morality. The war superego does the same in wartime, but with a fundamentally different set of "moral" demands. If the superego in peacetime creates guilt in those who break rules, it might create guilt for soldiers who, for example, do not kill or do not kill enough. The war superego is structured just like the peacetime superego—the superego is always the internalized "rules"—but, when the rules are different, the war superego actually offers a temptation to the id because the two, for the first time, overlap. Suddenly, the things that the superego had prohibited, it now enables. For some, a "peace superego" emerges, which reinstates the values of the prewar peacetime superego. This creates war neurosis. For others, this dual superego does not exist: the war superego simply replaces the peacetime superego, protecting the soldier from battle neurosis. The creators of the postwar environment then, for these men, must work especially hard to reestablish the particular superego—or conscience—that the civilian world needs them to have. Freud's many followers attempted to convert, specify, refine, and adapt his theories of war trauma after World War II. Simmel argued that it was not the development of a war superego or peace superego that caused or exacerbated war trauma. In fact, they said, the danger was in the lack of responsibility—essentially, the disappearance of any superego—which led men to return to an "oral-receptive" experience of the world. Because superior officers gave the orders, the superego developed since childhood was simply expunged, allowing instinct to "follow orders" with psychic as well as legal impunity.

It is difficult to resolve a psychic dilemma like war because of the confluence of individual and group psychic phenomena. The soldier combines in a single body the deepest components of group and individual psyche: an id, ego, and superego to each. Unsurprisingly then, shortly after the above writing on war trauma, Freud attempted to deal with "group psychology" in his essay, "Group Psychology and the Analysis of the Ego," using the concept of the "primal horde":

> The dwindling of the conscious individual personality, the focusing of thoughts and feelings into a common direction, the predominance of the emotions and of the unconscious mental life, the tendency to the immediate carrying out of intentions as they emerge—all this corresponds to a state of regression to a primitive mental activity, of just such a sort as we should be inclined to ascribe to the primal horde. We must conclude that the psychology of the group is the oldest human psychology; what we have isolated as individual psychology, by neglecting all traces of the group, has only since come into prominence out of the old group psychology, by a gradual process which may still, perhaps, be described as incomplete.[34]

How a man manages to experience conflict at the level of the self *and* coherence at the level of the group became a fundamental source of confusion for postwar Americans.

Another of Freud's theories of trauma attempted to explain just how the traumatized could resume individuality when the group has disassembled.

The traumatized, according to Freud and followers including postwar psychoanalysts Otto Fenichel, Ernst Simmel, and Melanie Klein, finds himself on a psychic loop in which he returns to his trauma—mentally, figuratively, or literally—again and again, reliving the pain. In his essay, "Remembering, Repeating, and Working Through," Freud called this exception to the pleasure principle "repetition compulsion." In an attempt to understand why a person would return time and again to a harmful experience, he suggested that these repeats might be attempts to gain "mastery" of the events in which he felt passive.

According the Fenichel, a member of Freud's "Inner Ring" writing about war trauma in 1946, this "repetition compulsion" could be divided in two: first, Freud's notion of repetition-to-master; second, repetition to express the repressed.[35] To use the analysts' example, a child who is spanked may, as an adult, wish to spank or be spanked in her erotic life in order to "gain mastery" over the spanking event. However, a soldier's trauma is different and has a dangerous—Freud says "demonic"—character. In the traumatic event, the soldier is passive because his commanding officer ordered the kill. In order to gain mastery, he must himself make the choice to act out.

The actual symptoms of war trauma, Fenichel argued, suggest a sort of "ramping up" to a bid for mastery:

> We see two sets of spontaneous attempts at recovery that seem to be actually contradictory: a) attempts to get distance and rest, to collect energy, as it were, for the task of belated mastery: the stopping of or decrease in ego functions and the undoing of differentiations, a withdrawal toward a fresh start for the reconstruction of the collapses equilibrium; b) attempts at belated discharges.... The first set could be called the quieting-down method, the second the stormy method—both aimed at the same end of belated mastery. Therapy can and should imitate both ways.[36]

In other words, even therapy for war trauma ought to offer a mixture: equal parts repression and expression. Without the latter part of this equation—this stormy part—Fenichel warned of "persons whose sexual instinct has undergone a sadomasochistic distortion, and who have an immense (conscious or unconscious) interest in all dangerous, extraordinary, cruel, and 'thrilling' events. The more an interest of this kind is repressed, the more likely it is that a trauma may unconsciously give the feeling: 'Now, my sexual fantasies are becoming real at last.'"[37] Not only did repression and expression have to coexist, they had to coexist because analysts were never quite sure whether war brought out the pre-existing violent and sexual impulses in men or originated them. One thing was clear: America seriously needed safe forms of expression. Postwar popular culture was designed—consciously and unconsciously—to achieve this therapeutic aim. What was achieved, however, was a culture-wide repetition compulsion, through which Americans worked to gain mastery over fears of veterans by remaking *men* as monsters.

FROM MORALE CULTURE TO THE REPRESSION-EXPRESSION CONUNDRUM

This repression-expression conundrum is the defining ethos of postwar America, oriented as it was around veteran reintegration. This conundrum appeared on nearly every cultural front. Though an ideal response to war, this conundrum was also a logical outgrowth of earlier modes of American culture, which have been identified by Ann Douglas and Morris Dickstein.

Douglas argues that what she calls "terrible honesty"—a serious reckoning with "awful truth" and "brutal reality"—defined the 1920s in American culture.[38] Regarding the next decade, Dickstein suggests that, after the market crash, a kind of "dancing in the dark"—fluid movement between a "democratized elegance" of escapism and sincere recognition of the day's dire circumstances—created the culture of the Depression. During the relatively short period of wartime, what I call "morale culture"—a popular culture which was often not just escapist, but hysterically so, based on the belief that mitigating the pain of war was the most important job of culture—became the way of managing a nation at war.

Survival through distraction is the essence of morale culture, begun in wartime and not easily or simply concluded in its aftermath. During wartime, enormous amounts of money and effort went into making sure that spirits were up. As war correspondent Quentin Reynolds put it, "Entertainment, all phases of it—radio, pictures and live—should be treated as essential."[39] It was even thought of as preventative of breakdown.[40] Roosevelt himself was so keenly aware of the importance of morale that he started building an organizational apparatus to support it even before the US became involved in World War II. In 1941, immediately after instituting the draft, he and

Secretary of War Henry L. Stimson arranged to meet with the heads of the Salvation Army, Young Men's Christian Association (YMCA), Young Women's Christian Association (YWCA), National Catholic Community Service, National Travelers Aid Association and the National Jewish Welfare Board. Roosevelt and Stimson requested that the organizations band together to organize entertainment for American servicemembers in coordination with the War Department. This organization would be called United Services Organization, or the USO. As soon as the war began, the USO began opening centers across the United States anywhere they could get space, including "churches, barns, railroad cars, museums, castles, beach clubs, and log cabins."[41] These centers hosted dances, screened movies, and offered refreshments. In areas without centers, some women would travel many miles to "provid[e] friendly diversion" for servicemen.[42]

More well known than the centers were the camp shows featuring Hollywood stars and recording artists including the Andrews Sisters, Fred Astaire, Jack Benny, Bing Crosby, Judy Garland, Laurel and Hardy, Lena Horne, Al Jolson, the Marx Brothers, Frank Sinatra, and, most famously, Bob Hope. Many of these USO performers entertained troops in the Korean War as well. The camp shows were often huge entertainment extravaganzas, but other times more intimate performances for only hundreds—rather than thousands—of soldiers. The USO negotiated with Actors' Equity, the Screen Actors Guild, and the musicians' union so that performers could work longer hours, in subpar conditions, and make drastically less money for their country, and the organization worked directly with United Artists and Warner Bros. to make films for and about the USO.[43] In short, the USO was a coordinated effort of government, charity and service organizations, labor unions, big business, and individuals: it was all hands on deck in a time of war.

All hands included those of Black Americans too, both men and women. The Stage Door Canteen, a recreation venue in New York City administered by the American Theatre Wing (ATW), had zero tolerance for racial and ethnic segregation.[44] ATW documents show that the organizers worked to include Black, Jewish, and Italian performers and also responded swiftly to any suggestion of prejudice in the performances themselves or among the guests. The ATW expanded Canteens beyond New York City, but made clear that they would not install such venues in regions in which segregation was practiced, legally or otherwise. Hostesses too were of different races and ethnicities. In fact, the ATW sought to employ Black hostesses specifically to meet what they saw as the needs of African American servicemen. While the Hollywood Canteen was in some ways segregated, this policy was not as consistent as many believe. *Hollywood Canteen,* the motion picture, took pains to show that all ethnicities were welcome, including "our own colored boys." White women were allowed to refuse dances with men of other races, but mixed-race dancing was allowed as policy and Black entertainers, including Black women, appeared.

Black women were involved in their own activism, some of which also centered around "morale," but with more overtly political aims. During World War II, they had to work to make sure that Black servicemen had access to the morale materials available to others. They set up service clubs and dances in segregated regions and worked to ensure that Black servicemen were receiving packages from home. Of longer lasting importance, Black women pushed for—and ultimately achieved—the integration of Americas' armed forces.

Of course, the USO and Canteens were not the only morale efforts. Book and magazine publishers, booksellers, librarians, and authors, catered to servicemen too, largely through the Council on Books in Wartime. The Council also worked with the OWI and the Department of Defense to distribute their Armed Services Editions (ASEs). The ASEs ranged from bestsellers to classics, were sized to fit military pockets, and were hugely popular with servicemen who read them aloud and tore them in half in order to share. Magazines were also sized, designed, and priced with servicemembers in mind and the military started its own *YANK: The Army Weekly,* a magazine specifically catering to enlisted men that famously featured cartoons and pin-ups.

Food and drink were also part of morale. The temperance movement saw the war as an opportunity to renew their efforts, but Stimson and his military leaders strongly opposed legislation that would limit or ban alcoholic beverages. The public just as strongly agreed that fighting men deserved to drink. And, even as sugar was rationed on the home front, many used what they had to send homemade cookies and candy to the servicemen. As Weaks-Baxter, Bruun, and Forslund describe, "the cookie was a powerful domestic metaphor" and recipes and model care packages were swapped among women and distributed by businesses to encourage sweets for servicemen.[45]

Domestic metaphors—and direct invocations of home—were rampant in morale materials. As Steven Cohan argues, in the 1940s and 1950s, "'home' stood for the utopian myth of a coherent, homogenous popular culture."[46]

Nowhere was this truer than in USO, CBW, OWI and other DOD-affiliated entertainment materials, nearly all of which claimed that they were "bringing home" or "a piece of home" to "our boys." Of course, these organizations revised existing content but they also produced new content geared specifically to men serving overseas—hardly a piece of the "home they once knew." In this way, pop-culture makers and the people they influenced came to equate "showbiz," entertainment, recreation, and even morale itself with the concept of home. Home was not the place of making a living or riding the bus; home was cookies, movies, romance, and sex. If the equation of morale with home had gotten Americans through the war, some version of this same equation seemed necessary for recovering from it.

Morale culture remained a vigorous celebration of home and entertainment in the postwar era, even as the promises of home had begun to look exaggerated. So, postwar popular culture was a negotiation of this recreation patriotism and its inevitable disappointments. In the words of Greil Marcus, postwar Americans "exchanged real life for an idea of normal life."[47] This does not mean that postwar Americans were living a fantasy, just that they were working with reality and popular culture in tandem, trying desperately to blend them seamlessly. More than that, they *knew* they were doing it. As Norman Rockwell said, defending his work against charges that it was not adequately "realistic": maybe the world was not how he portrayed it, but "it should be."[48] As Waller and Roosevelt warned, pulling the rug out from beneath a nation of veterans was clearly a recipe for disaster.

GENDER AND MORALE CULTURE

Wartime "morale culture" created a gendered division of patriotic labor, in which women provided morale for men who needed it. Women's roles during wartime were, for the most part, not what we in the twenty-first century wish they had been. Relatively few women worked in defense plants or otherwise in "men's jobs" and even fewer served as WACs or nurses. So few women served as nurses or in defense plants that it became a national security issue. Roosevelt took to the State of Union address and many Fireside Chats to urge women to sign up, to little avail.[49] In desperation, he even threatened to institute a women's draft (which Congress prevented). The image of Rosie the Riveter informs (and is even emblazoned upon the cover of) many discussions of women's World War II participation, but that image was part of a government propaganda campaign designed to entice women into defense jobs, rather than an accurate image of most wartime American women. The image would not have been necessary had it been a reflection of reality. It would not have existed if it had been.[50] Women of all races and classes continued to face discrimination both when applying for jobs and once they got them. Women's absentee rates were so high that, once they got the jobs, many did not keep them. And, certainly, many women's partners overseas were uncomfortable with or even panicked or enraged by the idea of their wives in a male-dominated workforce and asked that they live on allotment. Women were more active in the workforce during and immediately after the war than they had been before, but their entry was more trickle than flood. Their collars, too, were more pink than blue. Of course, women contributed en masse to the war effort, but they often did so in ways that are less amenable to a narrative of gender overthrow, even a gradual one. White women were more active in the paid workforce than they had been, but primarily in jobs that had always been female-dominated, especially secretarial, administrative, and service jobs. Many Black women who were already in the workforce as domestic workers were able to find other work in those administrative jobs but were more likely than white women to work in defense plants, making significantly more money than they had before.[51] Of course, women who wished to palliate men's anxiety about the possibility of "Dear John" letters or infidelity might simply stay home altogether. In fact, many women, especially mothers, saw staying home for their men as part of their service to the war effort. After all, keeping up the GIs' morale was the most important job anyone on the home front could do.

Whether employed outside the home or not, many women spent hours each day on wartime work.[52] One of their most important tasks was writing their partners, brothers, friends, neighbors, and others in the service. They compiled care packages, wrote poetry, stories, and songs, collected inspirational quotes and prayers, drew pictures and cartoons, and set up photo shoots for themselves, their girlfriends, and their children. Women's magazines and pamphlets trained women to write good-enough letters and send good-enough pictures, explaining that, "Letters should be as much like your best moments as possible," and, "If you pout, if you sulk, if you complain, it will sadden him for days and yield you no profit."[53] Black women's efforts were at times painfully underappreciated. In the Black press, Black women were accused of "letting down" their men for not supply ample letters and pin-ups.[54] McEuen puts it, "From all quarters, women were reminded that the war would be won or lost based on their attitudes."[55]

They managed the family budget carefully, so that they could buy war bonds and plan for a future home, car, education, vacations, and children.[56] They cooked for, prayed with, and comforted others who had lost sons, brothers, fathers, and husbands. Many young women without partners devoted their evenings to distracting men on their way to basic training, on furlough, or back with injuries. Some women actively polished their appearances, then danced, cooked, and went to the picture show, holding hands (or much more) with the servicemen who needed something to come home to and a little comfort on the cusp of battle. Some even married and had children—the Baby Boom is marked most accurately beginning in 1943—out of a sense of duty, rather than romantic love.[57] Many partnered women also spent hours on beauty regimens, so that they could welcome their men home looking just as beautiful as the day they parted. Sex appeal—and sometimes sex itself—was patriotism.

Women's roles during the war were a preamble to those they would occupy after. They made men comfortable, kept their spirits up, offered them all sorts of simple pleasures, and worked hard so that their men would not lash out, misbehave, become neurotic, or have to think about anything but their mission. They embodied, both literally and figuratively, morale culture. Men's mission once home was to recover from the war—to put it behind them—so women's was to facilitate this process. Waller describes women's appropriate behavior after their men's return:

> The wife or mother of a veteran will not be able to delegate her function to a social worker, nor will she wish to do so. If she can gain an understanding of his condition, she may be able to help him along the road to recovery. She must try to learn, as well as she can, being a woman and a civilian, what it feels like to be a veteran, and she must thoroughly realize that the boy who comes back is not the boy who went away. She must give him time to find his bearings again, to rest and recover; she must make him feel secure again, must tolerate his outbursts, and forbear to lecture him for his eccentricities and strange habits. Above all, she must give him lavish—and undemanding—affection, for part of his emotional maladjustment arises from his love-starved condition. But this love she gives him must expect no immediate return from the man whose sickness is his soul. (288)

Waller demands that women be nurses, psychotherapists, objects of sexual desire and scorn and perhaps violence for an indefinite period, and to flag is to fail. Unsurprisingly, in the postwar era, sociologists determined that women who reported domestic violence took an average of ten years to do so; they "tolerated his outbursts" for a decade, perhaps hoping they would simply pass with time. Women who reported it received a variety of responses from authorities, including assertions that the man's violence could strengthen the family.[58]

Many argue now and argued at the time that the postwar period saw a crisis in masculinity, one aspect of which was the (at least imagined) domination of men by women. *Look* magazine's 1958 issue, called "The Decline of the American Male," highlighted an essay by military historian and journalist J. Robert Moskin in which he claimed that experts "fear that the American male is now dominated by the American female. The scientists worry that in the years since World War II, he has changed radically and dangerously."[59] It's not hard to see how women's hyper-consciousness of and attempts at reining in men's behavior and beliefs might seem "domineering," even if the outcome was not that women were dominant. Women's role was anything but a small one: they were to make surviving the war worth the sacrifice. This was not just an enormous and profound charge, it was an impossible feat and it required little less than sainthood. They were to deny themselves everything in service of veterans' recovery, not only "tolerat[ing] outbursts," but responding without expectation of anything in return. As custodians of men's mental health and morale, their jobs were not complete until the war was over in the minds and heart of men. And, of course, it never was.[60]

MOVING ON: PTSD AND REINTEGRATION

The cultural frenzy to assert that the war was over, that the country and therefore its citizens were "moving on" with faith and gusto, makes sense given the very experience of trauma. As Michael Roth points out in *Memory, Trauma, History*, "temporal continuity is radically disrupted by trauma," so strictly demarcating the prewar, wartime, and postwar moments was yet another way for Americans to deny or alleviate traumatic symptoms.[61]

Very early texts portray characters suffering from symptoms that we now associate with post-traumatic stress disorder (commonly, PTSD). Physicians specifically began to treat war-related mental health issues in the nineteenth century, and the term "shell shock" was used both medically and popularly around the First World War. But treatment of battle neurosis in combat changed dramatically during World War II. According to Penny Coleman:

> As quickly trained psychiatric recruits were rushed to the front, the evacuation rate for psychiatric casualties fell dramatically. The recruits were instructed to emphasize cheerleading over therapy and cautioned never to mention 'war neurosis.' Instead, they were to talk about a man's responsibility to his comrades and his country, and to offer firm reassurances that with a little rest he would soon be ready and willing to rejoin his unit. These new guidelines reflected the newly accepted idea that, given adequate stress, a trauma response was inevitable and universal. . . . That observation marked one of the central paradigm shifts of World War II military psychology.[62]

After exhibiting signs of neurosis, a soldier would be removed from the front briefly, offered beer, cigarettes, entertainments, prayer, and, especially, sleep. He would be back in battle in a matter of days or even hours. This new anti-evacuation policy shows a great deal of faith in "morale" to simply keep a man going. Coleman also emphasizes a critical revision of ideas about battlefield neurosis: men with pre-existing mental health issues were no more likely than "sane" men to experience it because it was a natural response to battle. These two shifts in military psychology formed a template for thinking on the postwar veteran mind: any man, and perhaps all men, could suffer from some form of war neurosis and needed infusions of distraction and indulgence to carry on.[63]

Few people outside of the medical profession or the military understand what causes PTSD in war veterans. Laypeople rather casually link the disorder to a veteran's extended wartime anxiety and fear for his life and safety. This veteran with PTSD (or, before that, battle neurosis or fatigue) is figured as hiding from grenades and shrinking from gunfire, and the most common portrayal of the shell-shocked veteran includes his shaking and maybe calling out in fear at loud noises. This is not inaccurate, but it is only a slice of what PTSD includes and what tends to trigger it. Many psychiatrists argue that most cases—and certainly the most severe cases—of PTSD occur in men who have killed. It is not fear of losing one's life or limb, but a fear of one's capabilities and guilt over one's actions that are most associated with the disorder.

Harvey Langholz argues that earlier psychologists and, especially, laypeople have avoided portraying a clear picture of PTSD in veterans, simply affixing the label: "It seems axiomatic that the survivor of war or tragedy deserves to be accorded a measure of sympathy, and perhaps a diagnosis of PTSD can be considered a clinical expression of that sympathy."[64] Perhaps for this reason, PTSD in veterans—toward whom we might feel guilt—is equated with PTSD in "victims" of other traumas, even when the evidence suggests that the symptoms differ according to the triggering incident. For example, as Hendon and Hass point out, "aggression—often explosive—is a common feature [of PTSD] with combat veterans. Unlike concentration camp survivors, for example, for whom such outbursts would be maladaptive, those who used aggression in combat continue to use it in peacetime" (14). MacNair further points out that PTSD symptomatology has been all but ignored in the study of "perpetrators" of violence in war situations, except in a very few cases in which those studied have committed "atrocities." This is so even though battlefield PTSD does share some symptoms with other forms of PTSD, particularly "acting out" sexually and substance abuse. Simply having killed in battle does not seem to warrant such study, possibly because it is so common.

Research by psychiatrists Haley and Shatan in the 1970s shows that clinicians struggle to listen to identified "perpetrators" in therapy; likely anticipating this response, veterans are more likely to remain silent on the events which precipitated their trauma than are members of other traumatized groups (13). These "strong silent types" of the Greatest Generation are not unique in concealing the source of their trauma: they may be as responsible as their treatment professionals and the culture at large for obscuring the realities of PTSD for veterans. More recently, some researchers and clinicians have made the special effort of separating perpetrators from sufferers who are exclusively "victims," recategorizing the condition as PITS (perpetration-induced traumatic stress); this shift is finally getting some veterans the care they need, treating the symptoms particular to battle-related PTSD, which are specifically silence, unpredictability, anger, and violence (25). William Chamberlain, a psychologist in the PTSD unit of the VA hospital discusses the particularities of PITS:

> My experience with PITS veterans indicates that they are very in touch with their anger. By being in touch with their anger, the temptation is

to think they would have little difficulty controlling or regulating their anger. But this is not the case. They are made anxious by getting in touch with their anger because they are afraid for themselves! They have little confidence they can manage intense angry states because they are uncertain of the consequences of their behavior. Their conclusion is that if their anger/rage becomes intense, they will kill someone. If you look a little deeper, they are terrified their rage will separate them from the rest of humanity.

Chamberlain acknowledges what many who study veterans find: "getting in touch" with their emotions may not be merely uncomfortable for them, but dangerous to everyone. Events like the My-Lai massacre and Abu Ghraib bring to light something far more frightening to the civilian than the idea of stalwart Americans shrinking from Nazi fire and returning home with a fear of loud noises. Among the many sacrifices that American servicemembers make, including their loss of time with family, their almost unimaginable discomfort, and their risk of life and limb, they risk their souls, their morals, and their belief in the value of life itself. While we certainly should not then assume that soldiers come back "bad"—clearly most do not—we should accept that they took that risk, along with many others, when they went to war. They took the chance that they would be forever "separated from humanity," once exposed to profound moral injury.

The spectrum of symptoms, a denial of its causes, and the ubiquity of service in the World War II generation together obscured the prevalence of PTSD in the postwar American male population. As Coleman notes: "World War II is not associated with combat-related stress in the popular imagination. While images of World War I shell shock and Vietnam flashbacks both have a place in public memory, World War II is remembered as the 'good war' whose soldiers defeated an unequivocal evil and returned with Gene Kelly optimism."[65] Childers, too, suggests that World War II is somehow outside of other conflicts in the discussion of trauma:

> more [served] than in all the other conflicts of the twentieth [and twenty-first] centuries combined, but . . . the tortured emotional legacy of the Vietnam War generated tremendous public interest in the plight of many veterans, but in ways that seemed to suggest that any problems [were] . . . somehow unique features of the Vietnam experience. Bad war, bad outcome, bad aftereffects. If veterans of the Second World War were invoked

at all, it was to draw a striking contrast: habitues of American Legion and VFW posts, they have fought 'the good war' and returned home to a grateful nation, happy, healthy, and respected.⁶⁶

Though many World War II veterans felt that they did not get enough understanding, gratitude, or respect for their service, it is safe to say that they were accorded substantially more than veterans of many other wars. Civilians' response to Vietnam veterans undoubtedly contributed to their alienation, and the sense that Americans are only barely aware of their service clearly impacts veterans of the Gulf Wars and the war in Afghanistan.

Spoken "gratitude" was only one manifestation of the differences in these wars: because so many men served in World War II and Korea, American culture was quite literally built around protecting citizens from the symptoms of PTSD. Waller put these concerns in stark terms. From education to housing, paperbacks to *Playboy*, the veteran was a man to be accommodated and treated with gloves on. Most film scholars argue that combat stories are critical to processing war: these stories are critical for soldiers and civilians. As Joanna Bourke and Jeanne Basinger have pointed out, combat literature and film seem never to die out, but to flourish again and again. Bourke notes that one-third of Hollywood films produced between 1942 and 1945 were war films, and audiences certainly packed in to see representations of World War II ranging from the harrowing *Guadalcanal Diary* (Lewis Seller, 1943) to the feel-good *Hollywood Canteen* (Delmer Daves, 1944). 1946 was the high watermark for American cinema-going. When veterans returned, they went to movies alone and with each other, their families, and their sweethearts in record numbers.⁶⁷ This trend reversed almost immediately.

Of course, if we are to account for the booms in American war movies, we must also account for the slumps. One such slump was, perhaps counterintuitively, from 1946 through 1956, the years immediately following World War II and during American engagement in Korea. Some major war films were produced in those years—notably during a detectable mini-spike in 1949, which included *Home of the Brave* (Mark Robson), *Twelve O'Clock High* (Henry King), *Sands of Iwo Jima* (Allan Dwan), and *Battleground* (William Wellman)—but, as a matter of proportion, the decade is not even comparable to the 1980s, a rare period in which the United States was not explicitly involved in a war.

Of course, as Philip Beidler points out, many of the literary texts about World War II were turned into Hollywood films, but not until the late 1950s.[68] If war films are made to help us cope with war, what does this postwar decline in war films tell us?

Hollywood in the late 1940s and 1950s quite effectively portrays the repression-expression conundrum so dominant in mainstream culture at the time. Though Hollywood studios made fewer war films, they made Westerns and continued to make the wartime-trendy crime films we now refer to as film noir. Both genres dramatized the conflicts between a man's violent past and his domestic present, his relationships with women and children versus his relationships with other men, and, in these ways, both genres obliquely but sensitively treated the costs of killing and postwar integration. By briefly favoring these genres over combat films, filmmakers allowed audiences to process war trauma—specifically the trauma of killing—without restaging the particular horrors of war. Some films in these genres made their protagonists' service prominent—*The Blue Dahlia* (George Marshall, 1946), *Act of Violence* (Fred Zinneman, 1949), *Bad Day at Black Rock* (John Sturges, 1955)—but these are rare. More often, a war past is barely if ever mentioned at all. In this way, these disguised war films had more latitude for their conclusions and so could validate Americans' fears about veterans. In these films, some men were not heroes: they could be and stay bad.

By the 1950s, two types of men emerge in Hollywood film: "the man who does" (the expressive man) and "the man who doesn't" (the repressed man). Particularly prominent in film noir and Westerns, these types are emblematic of postwar masculinity because they share the same urges, the same impulses toward violence and hypersexuality, but only one of the two acts on these impulses. These types allow filmmakers to explore the erotic potential of veteran identity, but also to optimistically posit free will for men, despite past transgressions and present compulsions. War films, of course, require both heroism and the acting out of violence, so replacing them with other genres opened up other narrative and character possibilities still attuned to postwar themes, and both portrayed and embodied the repression-expression conundrum.

Literature dealt with similar complexities, but some of the most famous works of the period concluded in ways that were remarkably similar to each other and certainly less stark than many of the Westerns and noirs. William Whyte complained of 1950s literature that "the vision of life presented in popular fare has been one in which conflict has slowly been giving way to adjustment" and this novel of resignation was common. Recently, scholars have rushed to point out that the 1950s were not just *The Man in the Gray Flannel Suit* but were also the period that produced texts of rebellion like Jack Kerouac's *On the Road*. They are right, of course. And the protagonists of both novels are veterans struggling with their return from the war. Both Sal Paradise and Tom Rath deal with urges to flee their lives, anxieties about their pasts and sexualities, and confusion over whether their places were in stable family units. Both Sal and Tom take the middle-class domestic life in the end. Both *The Man in the Gray Flannel Suit* and *On the Road* are, in the end, novels of resignation.

Novels of resignation were only one type among many that flourished in the postwar era. While many important literary works emerged, there is a legitimate argument that the literary mode appropriate to the post–World War I "lost generation" texts was no longer appropriate to telling the World War II or Korean War stories. Many tried immediately after they served. Some examples—Norman Mailer's *The Naked and the Dead*, Irvin Shaw's *The Young Lions*, James Salter's *The Hunters*, and Herman Wouk's *The Caine Mutiny*—succeeded beautifully. But much of the best-known and canonized fiction explicitly and entirely about World War II and Korea emerged in the 1960s: Joseph Heller's *Catch-22*, James Jones's *The Thin Red Line*, Thomas Pynchon's *Gravity's Rainbow*, and Kurt Vonnegut's *Slaughterhouse Five*.

Beidler further argues that the importance of the Lost Generation to war literature inhibited World War II novelists: "World War II writers by any definition as literary intellectuals would thus have to assimilate the liberal critique of war already mounted by their direct generational forebears," so these writers "eschew[ed] the radical modernist experimentalisms of their immediate predecessors although with frequent assimilation of modernist ironies," so that they could "reassume the more traditional function of the novelist as a popular realist."[69] Bernard F. Dick counters that, when it comes to fiction about World War II and Korea, the delayed output may simply be about the fact that "it is hard to say how many years must elapse between an event and its fictional recreation."[70] After all, by the time many novels about World War II would have been finished, another group of men was off to war: if an anti-war slant is a "literary categorical imperative" after the post-Great War novelists, it may have felt inappropriate to both writers and publishers to flood the market with at least partially anti-war novels while others were serving in a war, particularly one that many thought unnecessary in comparison to World War II. Whatever the cause, works set in postwar America or before the war dominated highbrow literature during the 1950s.

The fact that relatively few great World War II novels emerged in the fifteen years after the war does not mean that the war was absent from postwar fiction, nor that postwar literature was inherently inferior to fiction between the wars. Because so many men served, many major postwar writers were veterans, and this appeared in ways explicit and subtle in their work. In addition to Wilson and Kerouac's novels, Saul Bellow's *The Dangling Man*, *The Victim*, and *The Adventures of Augie March*; Ralph Ellison's "Flying Home" and *Invisible Man*; Allen Ginsberg's "Howl"; and J. D. Salinger's *Nine Stories* were among the many works of the 1950s in which veteran authors grappled with the existential discomfort of postwar life. In all of these works, men descend into self-destructive and even sometimes murderous chaos, interrupted only by sentimental nostalgia for love, family, and community, which they often realize was not quite what they wanted it to be.

Of course, a remarkable number of men who were turned away by the armed forces or ineligible to serve were able to spend the war stateside honing their craft. These included James Baldwin, Ray Bradbury, William Burroughs, Truman Capote, Chester Himes, Arthur Miller, Philip Roth, John Updike, and Tennessee Williams; for many of these men, as for major women writers like Lorraine Hansbury, Mary McCarthy, Flannery O'Connor, and Dorothy West, the fact that they were not in the armed forces did not lead them to omit the war from their work. Some of their works, like O'Connor's *Wise Blood* and Miller's *All My Sons*, are about the rage, alienation, confusion, and dislocation of World War II veterans. Beyond those examples, issues of veteran reintegration appeared beneath most major works of the late 1940s and 1950s.

What lay beneath much postwar "literary" fiction defined postwar paperbacks. For a very brief period after the war—less than a decade—crime paperback fiction was not simply bloody, but this blood was on the hands of veterans seeking vengeance. Just as in the years after World War I, this bloody pulp fiction was phenomenally popular, but, unlike the "hardboiled" pulp of the 1920s–30s, post–World War II pulp emphasized the corruption of the individual man rather than the society in which he was forced to live and work. One of these novels' key questions was whether one was born or made a psychopath. In the novels of writers including the bestselling Mickey Spillane, the veteran's vengeance was clearly plotted: his combat comrade was killed, so he killed the killer. Other writers, like Dorothy Hughes and Tennessee Williams, sketched male protagonists so psychically deranged by war that their rage simply exploded against the women around them: they abused, raped, and murdered out of revenge against those who were never called upon to serve and who, they imagined, profited from their service. In all of these writers' work, men who have served together share an unbreakable bond, a bond forged in violence that begets violence. Women's (often willful) ignorance of men's experiences nearly justifies the violence against them. Few women make it through these novels and plays unscathed.

This particular form of sexism is mostly absent from *Playboy* magazine, which came several years later. I do not argue that the magazine was not sexist—it was—but that its aim was to facilitate a more peaceful reintegration than that which appeared in the paperbacks. *Playboy* is perhaps the cultural product of the period that most effectively adopted the repression-expression conundrum. As inspired by the work of Freud and Kinsey (or at least the popular notions of them) as by wartime periodicals and pin-ups, Hugh Hefner realized there was a market for the safe expression of sexuality and, indeed, for manipulating an "unhealthy" wartime sexuality into a safer postwar model. Hefner and his staff scrubbed the magazine of explicit war material, but insightfully integrated less explicit aspects of war experience. What's more, *Playboy* perpetually called attention to the repression-expression conundrum, which other mainstream products typically treated more subtly. In this way, the magazine and its ilk essentially created (or at least perfected) a brand of marketable male heterosexuality that soon dominated popular culture.

If *Playboy* sought to neutralize male sexuality, admitting the repression-expression conundrum as a way of exploiting it, then 1950s sitcoms did the same thing with violence, but with an appeal to a much broader audience. The 1950s sitcom has become nearly synonymous with the 1950s itself. This conflation is not unreasonable: the domestic sitcom is ideally placed to enact the intra-family dramas that dominate memories of the period, especially for the generation of children at the time. Men, women, and children, it was imagined, watched television together. Treatment of men's violence and sexuality, then, had to be modulated to feel both real and relatively unthreatening to all parties. Lucille Ball and Desi Arnaz created the template for the sitcoms that followed, which differed in important ways from earlier radio and capitalized on their star personas in order to suggest analogies between their family and the families of viewers. In the ensuing years, the shows that are most often referenced, including *Father Knows Best*, *The Donna Reed Show*, and *Leave It to Beaver*, took cues from *I Love Lucy* to establish an atmosphere of family tension.

This book treats postwar reintegration in different ways because the texts under discussion are themselves very different. Their difference lies in their media and genres as much as in any features of narrative content; that is to say, their contents are enabled by their medium. Repatriating men trained to kill is not simple, but fortunately popular culture is not either. Many types of popular culture worked in service of this effort, but the incredible variety of media and genres in the period led to incredible variety in approaches, and these media allowed different ranges, degrees, and combinations of masculinities, in expression and repression. I hope to make it clear that the study of "culture" requires an understanding that no texts are saying exactly the same thing, and that no text is even saying something similar in the same way. Nevertheless, I link hundreds of texts via masculinity—a category that is initially defined by the prevalence of wartime service, but not dependent upon it.

TURNING TOWARD REINTEGRATION

Historians, including Andrew J. Huebner and Mark D. Van Ells, have meticulously documented and insightfully interpreted the homecoming of American veterans after World War II and the ways in which American culture reflected the "warrior image" to use Huebner's term. In fact, both Huebner and Van Ells see Waller and Wechter's ideas as formative and reflective of attitudes toward veterans in the transition out of World War II. This book in no way disputes their arguments but emphasizes instead the less overt invocations and representations of the servicemember, the veteran, and the related anxiety, and the ways in which the trappings of the war or history in the military fall away, while similar anxieties remain. Each chapter delves into media, genres, and texts which, in different ways and at different times, take as a given or effectively de-emphasize the fact that the men they represent are veterans—some to the point that their service is omitted altogether.

Over the course of the 1950s, postwar Americans' concerns about veterans became less explicit in popular texts, mandated to what theorist Eviatar Zerubavel calls "active disattention" in which "ignoring something, in other words, is often a result of more than simply failing to notice it."[71] Past any celebration of their service or Allied victories, "veterans" had to become "men."

Much canonical scholarship on the postwar period has emphasized atomic anxiety in the war's aftermath and the attendant anti-Communist fervor of the 1950s. To suggest that Americans' major concern was the apocalyptic possibility of a generation of men lashing out is not to suggest that they were not simultaneously concerned about the Bomb, anti-communism, or conformity. Contrarily, Morris Dickstein argues in *Leopards in the Temple,* responding to Elaine Tyler May's canonical *Homeward Bound: American Families in the Cold War Era,* that "'containment' *is* a metaphor, a questionable analogy between personal and international security."[72] Questionable or not, this metaphor has opened the door to a remarkable strain of cultural history.[73] For most Americans though, these anxieties occupied different psychic spheres. Americans' concerns about the War on Terror in the twenty-first century do not resemble the concerns of the servicemembers in Afghanistan and Iraq or their families in most ways. However frightening, the Bomb remained an abstraction to many Americans; the man next door, the man upstairs, the man in your bed, and the man within were not.

Harry Truman dropped the Bomb because doing so would end the war, but he admitted—and Americans knew—that the Allies had another option: Americans could simply keep fighting and would win, just later and with countless more Allied casualties. But after the incredible savagery in Okinawa and Iwo Jima, he felt compelled to get American troops out of harm's way. In other words, American men at their most savage could have won the war. American men, in numbers, were equal to the Bomb. And millions of these men were coming home. The "atomic age" and its variants in popular 1950s discourse may have been partly about the Bomb, and partly euphemisms for the period during and after (if there was an after) veteran reintegration. The dropping of the Bomb was simply the continuation and completion of a military mission rather than a separate event. It was a substitute for—not a trumping of—American soldiers.

Anti-communism, too, was an undeniably important element of the national conversation, but, though many Americans of renown paid the price for leftism, average Americans primarily read about it in the news. Of course, anti-communism is also the reason for American participation in the wars in Korea and Vietnam, which were tragic debacles and shifted the idea of warfare from a nationally satisfying unified effort to a futile and misguided exercise. Anxiety about conformity is quite often linked and reduced to anti-communism. The other-directed organization man in the gray flannel suit who disappears into corporate lockstep was decried frequently and from many corners at the time yet is now conceived as a symbol of the period.

Another sort of guilt grounds this discussion and, in fact, further explains other readings of the period: A generation of men were taught to kill, and then they came back, and then the country had to live with them, and it was terrifying. A generation of men were taught to kill, and then they came back, and then they had to live with themselves, and it was terrifying. Americans' national indebtedness to these veterans—an indebtedness narrated by people in power and ordinary folks from the earliest days of the war—superseded an extended and forthright acknowledgment of these fears, and it is difficult to write scholarship about the unspoken, especially if it has been unspoken for decades and the spoken around it has hardened into history. Waller argued in advance that this guilt scared civilians away from acknowledging the true danger of veterans: "Apparently our national psychology reacts sharply to the emotional spree of a war: we feel guilty and ashamed and disillusioned, we feel so guilty toward the veterans that we do not permit ourselves to think about them" (303). Of course, one of the conflicts was that many civilians believed that seeming ungrateful or not reverent enough toward veterans would set off exactly the behavior that they wished to prevent. So, while these discussions happened—especially right *before* most veterans were back home—they had to happen primarily through fiction and, even in fiction, in cloaked terms. Even in more recent popular accounts—*Saving Private Ryan* (Steven Spielberg, 1998), *Band of Brothers* (HBO, 2001), *The Pacific* (HBO, 2010), and Ken Burns's *The War* (PBS, 2007)—the issue of reintegration is treated exceedingly carefully.

This book offers alternative and complementary readings and suggests that readers consider the following questions. What if the ostensible preoccupation with the Bomb masked a more pernicious and personal anxiety about the returned serviceman's potential to "explode"? What if the cultural push and pull over conformity and collectivity, the publication of texts like William Whyte's *The Organization Man* (1956) and David Riesman's *The Lonely Crowd* (1950), was not just related to a peaking anti-communism, but rooted in the knowledge that American men had demonstrated a remarkable capacity for coordinated and collective violence on a global scale? Further, what if anti-communism was partly motivated by an abiding sense that a nation, collectively and efficiently dispatched, had enormous capacity for destruction? What if Americans' burgeoning paranoia, skepticism, and conspiracy theory were not just responses to the Bomb or the fear of communists in their midst, but also to a wariness of men whose "minds could not be known"? What if families fled to the suburbs to escape the dense proximity to other veterans whose very nearness could provoke a wartime ethos of violence? What if the consumerism and mass entertainment of the postwar era—the booming of men's magazines and the paperback market, the advent of television, but also the unabashed consumption of goods—were experienced partly as a Roosevelt-inspired cultural quarantine of "comfort" and the violence and sexuality therein as a form of mild inoculation? Finally, what if the particular variety of sexism prevalent in the postwar era was not a response to women's workforce participation but was, ultimately, experienced as justifiably compensatory and part of a gender complementarity that the war required?

In fact, scholarly "revisionist" treatments of the 1950s have often ignored or diminished veteran reintegration, obscuring the issue further beneath layers of readings of the period, though this is changing. Now, the 1950s is no longer the halcyon white past, but a decade of civil unrest, sexual license, and artistic rebellion. For the last several decades, the bulk of scholarship on the postwar era which lies outside of "nuclear criticism" calls itself "revisionist" and attempts to "destabilize" or "complicate" general ideas or myths about the period. This shift in emphasis was long overdue, and the authors of these works have developed crucial new readings of the period from perspectives once ignored, paying particular attention to the ways in which women and men of color, white women, conservatives, liberals, leftists, religious minorities, sexual minorities, and the poor and working class constructed their identities against a dominant white centrist heterosexual, patriarchal Protestant "ideal." Scholarship in this mode typically denies that there was conformity, insisting instead that the "nostalgic" "white middle-class suburban nuclear family" is a concept which does not account for a great deal of what was happening at the time, and this is so: no concept ever does or can entirely account for an era. In the words of one revisionist historian of American women, "in the years following World War II, many women were not white, middle-class, married, and suburban."[74] Many were not; the majority were. Marriage rates were at record highs, the middle class was larger than it had ever been, more Americans lived in suburbs than in cities, and the very category of whiteness was expanding with the assimilation of white ethnics. In fact, the *homogeny* and the feeling of consensus—not the diversity—may have created the conditions for the rise of collective bargaining, civil rights struggles, women's liberation, and gay rights movements of the 1950s–70s. A sense of consensus and homogeneity is certainly not synonymous with contentment, particularly when one feels excluded.

If World War II created a collective American masculinity, the Korean War solidified it. Because another nearly two million men served in Korea mere years after the end of World War II, Americans could continue to be concerned about the new veteran returning home. Just as importantly, war became a legitimate rite of passage for American men. As such, ideas about raising male children came under the expectation that they would themselves become soldiers and sailors.[75] Of course, this assumption was mostly wrong: very few of these boys would have any military experience whatsoever.

In fact, gradually, actual military experience became unimportant to defining this collective masculinity. A lot of the most frightening, least flattering ideas about "the veteran" were displaced onto "the man," thereby associating military service with heroism, but masculinity with aggression and sexual profligacy. Our troops are heroes; our men are promiscuous at best, sadists at worst. Through popular culture, Americans attained discursive mastery over war and lost control of masculinity.

In Arthur Schlesinger's postwar classic *The Vital Center*, he voices the central, overriding principle of postwar American unity. Though Schlesinger is the clear-eyed realist against the "doughboy optimists" he pillories, his iconoclastic hope for the nation is palpable: "The totalitarians view the toleration of conflict as our central weakness. So it may appear in this age of anxiety. But we know it to be basically our central strength."[76] Yet Schlesinger fails to realize the manner by which Americans turn conflict into strength. He argues against a "soft and shallow concept of human nature," which makes its adherents avoid examining the "aggressive and sinister impulses" (40). Indeed, this "soft shallow[ness]" in popular culture is precisely what enabled the average postwar American to deal with the sinister.

Conflicted we were—standing at the junction of repression and expression—and a strong and multifarious popular culture emerged.

PROLOGUE

BEFORE WE PICK UP WHERE WE LEFT OFF

The postwar period is defined by the repression-expression conundrum in which both full openness and complete silence are imagined to be dangerous. A sample of letters written during the war offer some of the earliest glimpses of this conundrum. Clearly, the examples that follow cannot and do not represent more than a fraction of all correspondence, but offer opportunities for reading some servicemembers' negotiations of wartime communication. Importantly, the locus of the repression-expression conundrum is uncertain: at times, the writers are responsible for rendering it, but also the very fact of military censorship forced a feeling that much was being held back. For many families and couples, communication was more consistent and more intimate than ever before—many letters from GIs and from their home front correspondents claim that the two are closer than ever as a result of letter-writing—but censorship, both official and unofficial, simultaneously compromised this newfound intimacy. Servicemen needed their lovers and families more than ever in their absence, and their relationships with them became anchored by both secrecy and desperation as the gulf between their experiences widened and homecoming approached.

Historians have repeatedly struggled with the meaning of letters as documents. Jeremy Popkin offers an overview of such preferences and controversies: "When historians do distinguish between autobiographies and other personal documents, they often tend to prefer letters and diaries, on the assumption that they are more reliable evidence of what their authors were thinking at the time of the events than are texts written later, and also because they seem more spontaneous and less governed by rules of genre or propriety. Neither assumption is necessarily justified." Jurgen Kuczynski, a historian-memoirist who also wrote a theoretical work on autobiography, argued against privileging the perspective found in letters and diaries over the retrospective view. Hindsight may allow a clearer view of what was really important about past experiences than the author had at the time, and in any event, such documents "are hastily written products of an author who, in comparison to the autobiographer, was a not yet developed or very different person, in any case another person." Letters and diaries are subject to their own generic rules and never constitute a pure, unstructured account of their authors' thoughts and actions; diaries "can only be relatively autonomous from the culture they inhabit," as the literary scholar Felicity Nussbaum has written.[1]

Paul Fussell critiques the use of letters for understanding war in particular: "One reason soldiers' and sailors' letters home are so little to be relied upon by the historian of emotion and attitude is that they are composed largely to sustain the morale of the folks at home, to hint as little as possible at the real, worrisome circumstance of the writer."[2] Yet, the very things that make war letters unreliable as historical documents of the war itself make them valuable as literary and cultural artifacts.

THE REPRESSION-EXPRESSION CONUNDRUM AS THE WAR BEGINS

Well before they set foot on the battlefield, servicemen communicated the different world they were experiencing and what they were preparing to face. Syd Stringer tells his wife about the discussions the men had as they got ready to leave for battle: "We did a lot of thinking that morning. There was a peculiar sensation that all this wasn't new—that our ancestors somewhere had experienced the same tightening around the stomach. Perhaps the feeling was inherited from our animal forebears. Were we not about to engage in the birthright of beasts?—Soon we were to live, eat, hate, fight like the beasts of yesteryear. Man hadn't changed much. Sure, we had tanks, carbines, mortars, planes—They were only aids to man's ativism."[3] Stringer sees himself and those around him as essentially animals and war as their "birthright," even an inevitable consequence of men's very existence.

Morton Elevitch's letter from boot camp offers a very different perspective, but with many of the same implications for the postwar era. Unlike Stringer, Elevitch sees himself and his comrades as learning how to be what they are not rather than indulging in shared primal instincts:

> This week they are teaching us to kill. Now you probably looked away and shuttered. Well, mom, I don't like the idea, either, but we all know it's for our own good. The most strenuous work we do takes place as we stand in one place—bayonet drill. We lunge about in definite movements and are required to growl, grimace, and look at each other with hate. Five hundred of us dance about, screaming, shouting, and snarling.
>
> A rifle seems to weigh a ton more with a bayonet on. Our arms feel as if they're going to drop off as the Lt. holds us in one position and talks! Our bayonets have sheaths on them so that no one has his head cut off. They teach us how to withdraw our bayonets in a certain manner, too, because steel sticks to warm flesh. (This sounds awful bloodthirsty, but everyone keeps serious minded about it.)
>
> We are learning jiu jitsu holds—and to put it bluntly—plain dirty fighting. This will be invaluable in case anyone ever tries to pick on me. Maybe I shouldn't put this in—in fact I know I shouldn't—but it is going on so—Our instructors emphasize that we should be quick or be dead—always try to kill a man—break his arm first—then clip him under the nose—throat, neck, or kidneys to kill him. . . .
>
> They even teach us how to scientifically stomp on a man. I've left out many gory details. . . .
>
> S'long,
>
> Mort[4]

Mort's letter overflows with self-consciousness, but also suggests that he lacks a certain control over what he shares. He imagines his reader—his mother on the home front—literally turning away from the text when he admits he is being trained to kill. Of course, Americans on the home front were well aware that such training was imperative, but Mort believes that it ought not to be discussed openly. And yet, the letter enacts an emotional process, a confusing overture for intimacy. First, he thinks that "maybe" he should hold back the details of his training, then becomes certain that he should, then feels the process of sharing his experience overwhelming—"it is going on so"—he cannot help himself he so wishes to be understood. He wants his mother to understand what he is experiencing, so he rushes headlong into what he feels he should not say. But he also wants her to know that she cannot possibly understand his experience in full: "I've left out many gory details."

Servicemen's letters quite often denote this paradox: they want their loved ones to understand them and their experiences, but they do not want to inflict upon them the trauma that they are undergoing. What they choose to share and how they choose to share these things varies enormously from man to man and from situation to situation. Some are more up front about this paradox than others. Richard King consciously decides to breach the barrier of home front protection when writing home:

> Maybe you will think this is cruel, but I want you to know what it was like.
> Nearly all the Americans were killed and lots of them were my friends. When they ran out of ammo, they used axes and their fists. Both Americans and Japs had axes buried in their chests, in their stomachs.
> You asked how I got the Jap saber. On June 8th, we were cleaning out caves, I was first scout on patrol, and moving down a valley of vines and coral. My second scout yelled to duck, and I turned around as I ducked. A Jap officer had the saber just ready to chop my head off. I knocked it out of his hands and bayoneted him. That's the story. Look at the nicks on the blade where my bayonet hit.[5]

King is willing to be "cruel." He does not suggest, as Mort does, that his sharing is out of his control. He has chosen this "cruelty" because he feels that he cannot return home unless his family knows him as he really is and realizes what he has been through. For King, this is not simply about telling the tale. He asks his readers to actually see an artifact of this experience and look at it closely to imagine its part in his experience, to touch, in a physical sense, this moment of his kill. First, however, King tells of others' kills and not his own. He sketches the carnage and the savagery of hand-to-hand combat. In order to tell his parents about his own kill, he must frame it as an answer to their question. While he seems relatively comfortable with his decision to share the things he has seen, to deal with the particular cruelty of exposing them to their own son's killing, he must say: "You asked for it." This pose of reticence appears repeatedly in the letters. The men struggle to respond to women who consistently tell them not to change due to their wartime experiences. For example, Marjorie Elizabeth Griffith writes her fiancé: "I so often think of the Army, 'hope' and pray you will not be changed by association with a lot of men who indulge in coarseness to different degrees." Helen Stringer, on the other hand, attempts to understand that her husband is "different" in the war context, but comforts herself with the idea that this is situational and simply the way that he appears to the other side: "I have a hard time trying to imagine you as the enemy, but of course you are, in Germany" (258).

While most men send less gruesome souvenirs like coins, insignias, and jewelry, some like King send killer's trophies home. Whereas King seems to vacillate between pride in his actions and reticence about sharing them, others seem to have internalized the values of war such that they seem only to have pride. As Robert "Guy" Easterbrook writes: "P.S. In my next letter I'll send a piece of shirt. It has blood on it—but don't wash it. Just put it away in my room." (314). In this moment, Guy shows that he is proud of his kill and, in fact, wants to remember it. Yet, he imagines his family completely unable to comprehend the meaning of the shirt—they would, in fact, want to scrub away some of its significance. Guy believes that home front Americans launder their sons' actions by instinct. They must be explicitly told to retain the bloody character of the war.

Charles "Bub" Steinus Young, serving in the European theater, offers another confusing picture of civilians at home. He wants them to know that he fought his instincts for the effort, but also to make it clear that peace is his underlying nature, however damaged by his service.

> Just after we passed over that village I saw an 88mm flak battery consisting of 4 guns. They were pointed at us. Four Germans or Romanians were handling shells over the revetments and I opened fire on them. Killed all four of them and blew up something in the battery.... I must have killed 30 or 40 men in the 2 batteries. There was a woman standing by the 20mm and I killed her with a shot in the back. I felt sorry but she should have never been there.
>
> Then into town I go and on every house top and building there were guns. I fired constantly and killing and wrecking as we go....
>
> Dad if you get a chance go to Caldwell and see Mr. H. H. Womble and tell him that his son is pretty positively alive and either a prisoner of war or a guerilla warrior now in Yugoslavia....

If I ever have to go on another mission like that I think I will balk.

Tell everyone including my two sisters I send my very best of love to all. And to you Mom and Dad if I don't come back from this war you can say I was a fighting fool. But I'm coming back.

Well, that's a little story of my life away from home. I broke off all marriage ideas so you don't have to worry about that.

I'll close now.

Love to you all.

Bub (203)

He believes that his parents will be proud of him for being a "fighting fool," so he is not afraid to admit that he will "balk" if a similar situation appears again. He feels terrible about having killed a civilian woman, but he also makes the point that it was not his fault; it is just how it is in his "life away from home." The description he gives of this life away from home he follows with the suggestion that he can never reintegrate; he is unmarriageable.

Young's discomfort with killing is not universal. In men's letters to their *fathers*, they often present a very different attitude toward their kills. As Bill Madden writes his father of Iwo Jima:

I got my first Nip on the second bank. He raised up to throw another grenade & I shot him in the neck with an armor piercing shell. You can imagine what was left of him!

Do you remember me telling you about "Best" winning the "Silver Star" overseas before? This time I saw him charge a Jap pill-box alone while they threw grenades at him, keep on going when shrapnel from one hit him in the mouth and jaw, shoot one, & kill the other two by beating them over the head with his rifle butt when it failed to fire. He did it so fast they couldn't even use their bayonets on him. (298–99)

Also writing to his father, Robert "Bobby" Black indicates he is a "changed man" in his relationships with women as part of his service:

The men in the Naval Service have a reputation that is practically a tradition. Namely, as individuals, they are the sweet, innocent sons of ordinary American families. Once they get together in uniform, though, they are as tough and efficient a fighting machine as they are a suave, smooth functioning team when it comes to the women. If you need a personal example to confirm the above statement I've cracked and been cracked over the head with beer bottles in the toughest and most notorious dance halls and bars of the West Coast and the Orient. Secondly, I've a girlfriend in every port you have marked on the map I sent home as well as in 'Frisco, Oakland, San Jose, and Mt. Vernon, but I'm still Mom's little Bobby. (282)

Black's letter is particularly telling: it is men's camaraderie that makes them different. Alone, they are civilians, but together they are "tough and efficient" as both fighters and lovers. Furthermore, it is the presence of women that individuates him—he is "Mom's little Bobby" when he is not part of a masculine collective.

Edgar "Shep" Shepherd also links antisocial behavior to the close bonds between men. Writing after he is injured, he tells of his friend's saving him:

Moving along the narrow trail, we ran into a jap patrol, and Russ instead of getting away, chose to die fighting to save my life. He dropped me to the ground and stood with a knife in his hand and the three japs charged him with bayonets. With the cool art of a true Marine he used certain tricks (we had often practiced together) to kill the first two and the third one stabbed him in the back with a bayonet. He fell and the jap ran. . . . I'm in training again and in perfect condition. I swear by God to avenge the death of the best pal I ever had before I'm another year older.
Sincerely, Shep (198)

Shepherd's life was saved, but he was also inspired by his friend's use of "tricks" that they shared. Shepherd longs to tap into that collective battle knowledge in order to avenge Russ's death, but also to experience an intimacy with his dead friend through this experience.

HOW TO WRITE THE WAR LETTER

As the war progressed, many servicemen found it increasingly difficult to write. The things that they experienced were difficult to discuss and often simply prohibited. As Mock put it, writing from the Pacific (likely after the Battle of Iwo Jima): "There strictly isn't anything to write about around here. The things that take up most of our time are those things of which we can't write."[6] Indeed, when their letters are aligned to their stations at the time, many men emerged from the bloodiest battles to write loved ones about having been "busy" or some other version of the term. This word—"busy"—comes up again and again as a proxy for combat.[7] Sometimes their loved ones would glean their meaning through reading the papers and watching newsreels, but not until long after the fact. Other times, they would simply never know the meaning of "busy" to men whose words were so heavily censored.

Military censorship also had another complication: home front readers could not, of course, determine what was self-censored and battlefield writers could not always predict what would be censored, so their self-censorship may have exceeded its necessity. Furthermore, the process of military censorship—passages marked out or, even more strikingly, cut out—acted as a physical symbol of their thwarted communication. Masuda writes to his wife that he hopes his letter comes to her in "not too cut up a form" but that "it's often difficult to distinguish between what we consider conversation and that which is information."[8] Because the servicemen were not entirely sure what would make it through the censors, their relationships were out of their control, managed—like so much else—by the military.

In the earlier days of the war, many seem less bothered by censorship, believing that their loved ones will intuit that which they are unable to write. Smith, days before the Bataan Death March, wrote to his wife: "I could write a lot of nonsense and a lot of foolishness but I know you will read between the lines and see more in spirit than what I write."[9] Masuda defends censorship for protecting him but is strangely playful with it as well, saying, "We're doing stuff and things which I can't write any gory details about, but we're occupied most of the time"—whether the "stuff and things" are indeed gory is obscured (20–21).

Servicemen certainly dislike the fact that they have to censor themselves and be censored, and their female correspondents also chafe at these restrictions, wanting further glimpses of the war and more intimacy with their loved ones. Mock seems to be responding to his correspondent's complaints that he is being oblique: "They tell me what I can and can't tell you so I follow the rules. After all, it's for a purpose. It's of military importance.... I want to take care of myself and get back home. See what I mean. It's important or they wouldn't spend all that time going over the mail. After all, it's a big job and our officers don't have that much time to waste and if they did they would much rather spend it doing other things." Other reasons for censorship seem less transparent. Many women in particular seem to struggle with the fact that their men are not as erotic or romantic in their letters as they were able to be at boot camp. Mock further responds: "Honey, if my letters aren't as romantic as you would like it's not my fault. The censor asked that we leave as much out as possible. This is a romantic place—if you were with me it would be—so I'd like to write some romantic letters—but those are the rules. Boy, could I tear into one of your pies right now. My mouth drools as I think of it." This equation between the home front and its baked goods, mentioned in the introduction, here takes a distinctly sexual tone; the reader is expected to "read between the lines" as Smith indicated his wife could.

Sometimes the writers expose an inability to "read between the lines," as the correspondence between Stringer and his wife makes plain. Syd to Helen: "I am in a whirl from your letters. I am also confused. I think I know what you mean—and then I don't" (228). Helen to Syd: "Incidentally your letter this morning still stabs me. How could I have left room between my words to inspire your misunderstanding" (234). Though the writers often express great faith that they are able to truly communicate, even in censored and abbreviated forms, they occasionally admit these interpretive struggles.

A subtler form of censorship runs through the correspondence: the particular manner in which each writer discusses the war is subject to correction by their readers and by their own hands. For example, Masuda tells his wife that her writing about the war must change in future letters, approximating further his war talk with his buddies: "Don't speak so seriously of war—it's not as bad as all that. Over here, we treat it lightly, but know its brutalities. Our sense of humor is always there even though the clouds of war are black and threatening. That is the one big way to morale. Once you let it get you down, you're not much good. In fact, from outward appearances, it seems hard to believe that there is a conflict going on from the horseplay and joking of the men" (42). The heavier the censorship, the more servicemen relied on the trappings of morale culture for connections to home. A movie, for example, could provide a link between the disparate worlds of battle and home front. Sometimes this works, but other times men seem angry at what they get to see, how they get to see it, and the extent to which depictions of war ring false. Many times, home front women try to talk about movies or books or magazines with their men, only to get disappointing responses, reinforcing the notion that civilians "just don't get it." As Masuda explains to his wife:

With the night getting colder, the wind blowing dust in our faces, and us sitting on the gravelly ground, you can imagine that it can be quite a detraction from the enjoyment of a film such as *Madame Curie*—it must have been a good film in the theatre—to us out there, well, less than half were there at the end. Then, of course, the artillery had to start booming right behind us periodically, as if the sound system wasn't bad enough. Walter Pidgeon mouthing like a bullfrog and Greer Garson barely audible to our straining ears. Quite a disappointment, but the good intentions were there. Somehow, it all seemed queer to sit there watching a movie while just a few miles forward men killed and were being killed. (60)

Mock complains often of Hollywood inaccuracy: "In *Time* Sept. 11 there was a good letter from a soldier overseas in the Letters section entitled 'G.I.s v. Hollywood' which we had a good laugh over. It tells how ridiculous the GI considers the war hero as depicted in the Hollywood versions of war. Last night we saw a movie—'Two Man Sub' and it was terrible. It seems that every other picture is a Hollywood version of the war." Other times though, soldiers and their partners can share a critique of a film. While some couples, like the Stringers, discuss these things at length, often servicemen just offer a brief assessment ("Saw 'Miracle of Morgan's Creek' night before last and I agree with you. It didn't knock me out"). Most importantly, discussing films, shows, and magazines means having something to write about outside of the suffering of war and the immensity of the distance between the correspondents.

SEX AND THE LONELY SOLDIER

Lacking the sexual connection they once had—or at least experiencing its ultimate strain—letter writers deal with their sexual longings and jealousies in several different ways.

Sometimes jealousy is coded and careful. Syd Stringer scolds his wife about her drinking, clearly feeling that too much alcohol could lead her into sexual indiscretion: "You rascal you—two drinks are your limit. You said so. Remember we agreed to that. Beyond two drinks is a delightful privilege reserved to us alone please" (182). Days later, he tries to bribe her to keep her drinking under control: "By the way I have never told you that I am carrying in my foot-locker a bottle of Armegnac Cognac which I got in Cannes. I am saving it for the express purpose of having it as our first drink together. Then you shall have more than two drinks! That is if we have time for any drinks at all!" (184). Stringer asserts control over his wife's sexuality: he tries to keep *her* in control of her own actions in his place.

Some couples are rather passive-aggressive in ensuring their partner's fidelity, writing as though willing it to be true. As Charles Lewis writes his wife, Garnetta:

> Thank God that we are able to communicate with each other. Just think there are many soldiers overseas that haven't heard from their wives in many months and I can just about imagine how they feel.
>
> Even amidst all of the misery and longing that I am now living in, I have an awful lot to be thankful for. I have a good wife who is tried and true and above all one who loves me faithfully. I know that because you have proved it to be. As lonesome as I am without you and as much as I would like to be with you it still brings me an immeasurable amount of happiness to know that you are patiently waiting for me.[10]

As a Black soldier, Lewis would have been far more constrained than the other letter writers in his own opportunities for infidelity; that inequity certainly could have impacted his sense of security.

Other times, letter writers are blatant in discussing the dangers of infidelity. A recurring theme emerges: the writer, uniquely, resists temptations to infidelity while those around him or her indulge. In a typical such example, Maxine Meyers writes to her husband:

> No one is left except the middle-aged, the 4-Fs, and the very old. I have failed to see any men who, in my opinion, could be classified as 'attractive.' But the women, so it seems, have gone 'nuts' and 'gush' over anything that can be identified as a man. Not all the women have gone nuts, but the majority of them have, at least around these parts. . . . As for yours truly, all men are just fellow workers or shipyard wolves that I want no part of, and my attitude towards them reflect the way that I feel.[11]

Women are "nuts" who would be interested in the men around her. It's not just that Meyers is in control, but that she need not hold back exactly because of these men's general undesirability. Restraint alone, these writers might have feared, is not convincing. Men often write similar things, as Mock (a white Marine) does:

> Let me tell you, my dear, that you are wasting time over wasting time (damn, I didn't know this record was cracked!) worrying over the white women on this rock. The only ones are nurses (officers), if you get what I mean. It's difficult for anyone under a captain to even speak to them. . . . If I didn't play [piano] for some of the dances, I would hardly average seeing one white woman per month and she would probably flash by in a jeep or something. You can save that Lil Abner groan for future operations. I haven't seen over three native women since I've been here. Everyone in the states has the idea that there is a beautiful native girl sans clothing dancing in the hula under each and every palm tree in the Pacific and it ain't so, believe me. Hollywood has given a false atmosphere to these islands. No, I haven't run into Tarzan or Dorothy Lamour.

Mock assures his wife that he cannot help but stay faithful to her, scarce as women are in his vicinity. His own self-control may not be enough for Rosemary, but his circumstances may be reassuring.

On rare occasions, a letter writer admits to infidelity. John David Hench's wife writes to him she has been unfaithful during his training, but still wants to be with him. Though we do not have his wife's letter, we have this:

> The reason behind my hurt, however, cannot be disregarded. I find it comes from being or at least trying to be an officer in the United States Marine Corps. I am no longer an individual. My ego, which has always been large, is now part of the Espirit de Corps that make the corps the fightenist bunch of men in the world. A Marine is more honest, more truthful, more military in his bearing than any other type of man. He is forced to be all Marine by those under him and unless those under him respect and admire his judgement, ability and character, those above him will soon lose faith. To be a good Marine is to be more than a man, and to be, as I want to be, the best Marine is to draw more outside of myself and make me more than I am now. I am fighting every weak impulse, every soft tendency in my body to gain for myself the respect and approval of other Marines. This is hard. I work long hours, fly long hours, and study

long hours to be all that I dream you, staying behind me, hope I am. The forgoing gives you some background as to why I was so dreadfully hurt by what you told me. Now, a failure of will or character to me, regardless of reason, is so much graver an offense than ever before, primarily because if I ever failed in one of those respects, I'd have to quit. . . .

 I started formation today. How I hate it. It keeps you keyed up fit to kill.[12]

Hench makes several critical points to his unfaithful wife. First of all, she is unpatriotic for cheating on him while he is serving. Moreso, she may well not be good enough for him when he returns, given the discipline that he is developing and the weakness that she has shown. Finally, of course, he ends by telling her that, as much as he hates it, he is "keyed up fit to kill," a terrifying end to a letter of wavering forgiveness.

 Simply by following up this wavering forgiveness with a reminder that he is trained to kill, Hench creates a sense that unfaithful women are endangered. Mock puts this in the boldest terms, encouraging his wife to stay faithful and to avoid flirtation with other men for her own safety, not from him specifically, but from men in general as he has seen them debased by desire:

Last night I felt very low so I started reading your letters, but instead of absorbing the sweetness and love from each one, I was in a critical, jealous, and evil minded mood, so I imagined—you might say—between the lines. If you mentioned going someplace and you didn't mention with whom you had gone, the devil, in controlling my mind, said, "Aha! She didn't say that because she went with someone she didn't want you to know about." I can honestly say that it's the first time I've given it a thought since I've been overseas and I don't like it. Makes me want to go over the hill and get drunk or something. I've always had so much faith in you that I felt that to display the jealousy I've always had for you was useless. But I find I can't control my feelings as I used to with all the blood—men, women, and children—that I've seen spilled in this war. I honestly believe that I could kill any man who so much as touched your hand and never bat an eye now—I find that all living means to me is you. That's the way it has to be—no sharing of you with anyone. I know how you used to play a man for a sucker to satisfy some little whim, but the war has changed a lot of men—I've seen our own boys [commit sexual assault]. They were the average clean cut American youth—probably many of them had never had a woman before. I've seen fellows here shot and killed by guards as they tried to go over the fence at night to spend a little time with a prostitute. I've seen them wade a sewer ditch filled with the dirtiest sewage for the same reason. Would you say they're cracked up on the subject of sex. I hope they get it out of their systems before they return to the States. These are the boys who have been living in these beautiful romantic South Pacific islands where the only women they see are a few nurses who were there for no reason except to keep up the morale of the officers.

Here the gov't has taken over geisha houses for the troops. During liberty hours all you have to do is stand in line and pay the fee. Enlisted men have one house with a line several blocks long. The better houses are saved for officers. . . .

No darling, I haven't been in a geisha house. I've been a total abstainer and will remain so—don't worry.

Though this letter seems very candid, it was censored. Parts were cut out. Mock tells his wife what he has seen—rape, murder, men risking their lives for sex—and that it has changed men and changed him. First of all, his jealousy is heightened, and he believes it is justly so. Because of his service—something he is surviving only for her—their monogamy is imperative. Though he has trusted in her before, he also would not "bat an eye" at murdering a man of whom he was jealous now that he has seen such blood spilled. He "cannot control [his] feeling as [he] used to." Second of all, he fears that most men cannot handle their sexual urges responsibly, without disease or violence. For a woman with a wandering eye, such a letter was designed to share with her what he had seen and to keep her in check through both sympathy and fear.

COMING HOME

All the letter writers anticipate their reunions after the war. Many of the writers look forward to "picking up where we left off," but they occasionally acknowledge that things have changed and that this process of reintegration may take time. From the earliest letters, coming home is a key subject. As

Dom Bart writes after obliquely discussing D-Day, "Let's forget about the past for awhile and talk about today."[13] Masuda tells his wife early on that he intends to detach from her emotionally and that he feels uncomfortable putting his feelings into words: "I think you know what I mean and understand my subjugating my feelings for you—for to allow it to occupy my thoughts is to undermine my morale. I think time will help me out a great deal in this respect, but don't think that I don't love you nor miss you as much as ever—let's say the passage of time will help dull the sharp edge of loneliness for you" (19). As the war progresses, he betrays this distance, telling his wife that he is simply not up to attempting to truly communicate with her: "A lot of things happened that I could tell you but maybe I'll let that wait until I get back home," and "I'm sorry darling, but I'm in no frame of mind to do much talking tonight. I know you'll forgive me for this . . ." and

> Sorry that I didn't write you yesterday as I'd planned, but there are so many distractions among which are 1) we are quite busy what with one thing after another 2) its so hot that one doesn't feel like writing in the day 3) movies and band concerts at night are a distraction, it being after midnight when we come back 4) the days are so long that time is deceiving and first thing you know, it's time to go to sleep. I think that's enough of alibis; quite a mess of 'em but you know that I'm only procrastinating anyway.

Masuda does not claim that the war is unspeakable, just that it is unspeakable at the time. Days later, Masuda apologizes for sharing what he has withheld, telling her of his first day on the battlefield: "Now, you see we can never forget that first day when we received the baptism by fire. There were other days, terrible days, to follow but I won't go into that now. I got rather carried away in this relating, so you'll excuse it" (233). The pressure to share or withhold becomes more and more intense as the war comes to an end, as both men and women anticipate sharing their wartime experiences with each other. Stringer writes: "I have been thinking of what you wrote about our need to have a few days to ourselves if I do come home. I am heartily in favor. After getting acquainted with my brood again, we should plan on taking off. I want a place isolated enough so that we can be ourselves, where we can take moonlight swims, where we can walk and talk. I want a place with a fireplace where we can chip away the memory of these months when we sit in front of it in complete solitude." Though many letters still idealize the future, others begin to acknowledge the difficult reintegration to come. Early in his service, Masuda tells his wife that, when he returns, "Everyday will be like a Valentine's Day," but he later fears trying to relate to her (160, 220). At the announcement of the war, Lewis writes Garnetta that he is "happy," but "I've been a nervous wreck ever since I heard it because I know that means that it won't be long before I'll be coming home to you and I'm so excited and filled with anxiety and can you blame me?"

Others substitute the struggles of other men for their own, explaining that they have not "cracked up," but simultaneously suggesting their own precarious emotional state. Mock writes:

> I started this letter but I was interrupted—one of those things. One of my good buddies was sitting there writing. I noticed nothing unusual. I turned and looked at him and spoke to him. I noticed he had tears in his eyes. When he tried to talk, he broke out in sobs. Laid his head down in his arms and cried like a baby. You probably say, well that's odd, a big, husky man suddenly doing that. All the injuries of the war aren't physical. He said, "Oh Lewis, I don't know what to do." I took him for a walk, let him talk and tried to ease his mind. We walked and talked for several hours. Mostly family problems. He gradually came around and felt better so we hit the sack. Many fellows aren't affected injured to a point where it can be noticed, mentally I mean. You return to camp and then something happens—maybe it's bad news from home as in this case. The guy could stand it and cope with it usually, but it seems that a mental reserve has been depleted to a degree that his nervous system can't fluctuate to handle it. It makes my heart ache to see these things happen. Lots of these are just kids between 18 to 21. It's sad. So much the horrors of war.

However, mere weeks before he returns, Mock acknowledges his own emotional vulnerability when he writes that "when it's over I'll be ready for a straitjacket. . . . I'll be happy when I can lie with my head in your lap and forget this whole bad dream while listening to your soft voice. That's what I dream about darling. That's what I'm holding out for. Just to be with you." Mock sets up a pressure to forget rather than to communicate, as the war ends.

Ultimately, Mock and other servicemen could not simply "forget this whole bad dream." When Mock returned to the United States, he disappeared for weeks. Rosemary's father eventually hired a private investigator, who tracked him to a bar in San Francisco and brought him home to begin his life with his family. The pressures to communicate the past and the pressures to forget it were nearly too much for some of the men who returned. They and the women who loved them would rely on popular culture to manage the gulf between them.

ONE

"IT WAS EASY"

Postwar Paperbacks and the Veteran Killer

It was 1948. Mickey Spillane's critically maligned *I, the Jury* was a phenomenal paperback success, selling millions of copies beyond anyone's predictions and resurrecting the postwar paperback market. Hollywood heavyweight Humphrey Bogart started his own Santana Productions to much fanfare and immediately purchased the rights to *In a Lonely Place*, the new work by crime novelist Dorothy B. Hughes, hiring Nicholas Ray to direct. Tennessee Williams's *A Streetcar Named Desire* won the Pulitzer Prize. These three texts, *I, the Jury*; *In a Lonely Place*; and *A Streetcar Named Desire*—all written and set in 1946 and published in 1947—were like an enormous number of others at the time in that the men they featured were World War II veterans. All three also entered into a marketplace ready for precisely what they were selling.

Clearly, the publishers marketing these three texts had no trouble spotting some of their confluences. The cover art alone suggests that the "seediness" of the works was something that publishers wished to highlight: all three covers feature beautiful young white women and dangerous-looking men, seemingly ready to harm them. Of course, this was not an unusual sight. Over the course of the war, this cover template became relatively commonplace. Bold graphics, like the single centered black falcon on a yellow background for *The Maltese Falcon*'s 1944 edition, were falling away in favor of these more salacious depictions as paperbacks came to dominate the market. In his work on Black pulp, Kinohi Nishikawa defines his trend as "sleaze": "mid-twentieth century print commodities (pulps and pinup magazines) whose aim was to circulate fantasies of putting women in their place. Readers of sleaze felt they were victims in a world given over to feminization, or to the idea that masculine self-possession was being squelched by the demands of social conformity and domestic life. Sleaze rebuffed that trend, assuring readers that men were still on top and that, despite many challenges to it, the male ego remained intact."[1] Chester Himes's *If He Hollers Let Him Go*, discussed in the Introduction, is a good case study of this transition in pulp images, though it also makes plain some of the views of white women which were absent from the covers of these other works, though readily available in the texts. In its first edition—a hardcover—the jacket was, like *The Maltese Falcon*, yellow, but only marked with text: the title in red lettering. In paperback, the novel's multiple covers featured highly sexualized, blonde white women though, in these cases, these women are the menacing ones, not the ones in danger. The Ace Books cover shows the woman wearing a skintight red dress in an alley, as a Black man in the foreground looks anxiously over his shoulder. The Signet edition shows a common image of a woman holding her shirt loosely closed. In this case though, she points threateningly at a fully-clothed fearful-looking Black man.

The similarities of these covers to the covers of *I, the Jury*; *In a Lonely Place*; and *A Streetcar Named Desire* are as telling as their differences. White women are the ultimate helpless victims and *also* the ultimate scheming villains in many of the paperbacks of the 1940s: blackmailers, pedophiles, liars, manipulators, and murderers. More dangerous to Black men than to white men in real life, white women in these texts can be as vicious as the white men with whom they share book covers. To some veterans in these texts, these white women are the picture of privilege: they did not have to serve.

To some extent, each text was selling something different, and literary history has emphasized those differences: *Streetcar* most often seen as a work of high art (even to those who dislike it), *I, the Jury* is the most degraded of macho pulp fiction (even to those who like it), and *In a Lonely Place* beautifully illustrates the feminist potential of crime fiction in the period (and everyone seems to like it).[2] This chapter will not dispute these distinctions, but will treat the important confluences, connecting them as a constellation representing remarkably similar notions of veteran masculinity in a single year. This version of masculinity, ubiquitous in 1946, would haunt the coming decade, repeating with degrees of variation. The surrounding conditions of this masculinity—how those around the men inhabiting it responded to it and denied it—also reappear. Furthermore, these three texts coalesce into an active countertext: the year that *The Best Years of Our Lives* won the Oscar for Best Picture is also the year that *I, the Jury; A Streetcar Named Desire;* and *In a Lonely Place* were composed.³ The three texts in this chapter foreground different issues related to veteran readjustment, including the contradictions of postwar heterosexual relationships, the primacy of bonds between men who served together, and the very definition of "normality" among veterans, in addition to the ever-present anxiety that the urges expressed during the war would not be tamped down in its aftermath.

The fact that these texts differed in quality, style, and reception did not prevent their sitting beside each other on the shelf, however controversial this seeming equation. Paperbacks did not constitute a "genre" unto themselves, but their very proximity and tangible, handheld similarities created a surrounding market, and the blending behind this market was controversial. As Evan Brier points out, contemporary critics like Cecil Hemley saw two concurrent problems with paperbacks: "First, they degraded what used to be high culture by placing quality books right next to low-quality fare. . . . [I]n Hemley's view, paperback vendors degrade Shakespeare by selling him alongside Mickey Spillane. . . . For Hemley, the second, more pertinent problem with paperbacks is that they encourage the production of lowbrow genre fare."

Indeed, *I, the Jury*'s runaway success provoked an explosion of "pulp" crime fiction, which continues to dominate the paperback market today. It is certainly also possible that readers devalued Williams and Hughes, reading their work as carelessly as they may have read Spillane's. On the other hand, for *Streetcar* in particular, paperback publication made the work more accessible, since only a fraction of potential American readers could see *Streetcar* produced in New Haven or New York. Famous as it was and is, until the screen version in 1952, most Americans knew *Streetcar* by hearsay (as in reviews) or paperback (which likely inspired much of the hearsay). Also, given the play's content, the paperback may well have allowed *Streetcar* to appeal to audiences who would have been turned off at the idea of reading drama.

Hughes may have benefited from the paperback sales as well: the image on the cover likely overshadowed her gender to potential male readers. Readers may not even have noticed the book's author, indistinguishable as the novel seemed from others on the shelf. Whether diminished or elevated by paperback publication, all three writers profited financially from paperback sales, which was important for each of them at the time.

Paperbacks flourished during the war for many reasons, but Avon, Pocket Books, and other houses' marketing of these texts as patriotic—"BOOKS ARE WEAPONS!" they read—may have played a role. Those on the home front were encouraged to buy them for service members and, eventually, companies like Penguin even changed the size of the novels to fit into standard military pockets. As in camp shows, magazines, and other entertainments, paperbacks were offered as an "escape from the war" (25).

It was not a given, then, that paperbacks would be a success in the postwar period, since men no longer had the war from which to escape (at least not literally). In fact, Ashby and others point out that the paperback market, in full flower since its advent in the late 1930s, had begun to wilt by the mid-1940s. Ashby and O'Brien both attribute this decline to the fact that, "veterans were busy rebuilding their lives" and therefore had less time for paperback fiction. *I, the Jury*'s success certainly undermines this thesis; its millions of copies sold suggest instead that the earlier texts themselves, rather than the paperback as a form, were unsuitable for the period. Sutherland traces these shifts to Spillane, Hughes, and Williams-style work, claiming: "Crime fiction in the mid-1940s [had to become] even harder-boiled than it had been in trend-setting *Black Mask* days. The depths of human depravity revealed by the liberation of Germany and the ruthlessness of the War in the Pacific were reflected in the genre."[4] American paperback fiction—just like magazines, film, and other popular art and entertainment—had to adapt in order to attract veterans. Who better to originate this adaptation than a new pulp crime writer, a combat veteran himself?

THE VETERAN DIASPORA AND THE MAKING OF A MARKET

Mickey Spillane, a comic book writer whose credits included *Captain America, Captain Marvel,* and *Plastic Man,* enlisted in the United States Army Air

Forces on December 8, 1941. He was a combat pilot and later an Army flight instructor. Upon his return from the service, Spillane determined that the comic book business was in a slump, and he resolved to write a novel in order to pay for the new house that he and his wife wanted to purchase (presumably to "rebuild their lives"). He completed that novel, *I, the Jury*, in nineteen days, and sold it to E. P. Dutton. Dutton, a publisher responsible for a number of relatively highbrow original novels, chose to print Spillane's debut merely for profits. Dutton's Editor in Chief, Nicholas Wreden, said simply, "It isn't in the best of taste but it will sell." Clearly, Wreden had high hopes for *I, the Jury*, but he passed it to Signet Paperbacks in 1948 after being disappointed by the initial sales numbers. Released in January of 1948 with a scandalous image on the cover—a beautiful blonde undresses as a man points a gun at her—the Signet paperback made New American Library and Spillane very rich and forever changed the landscape of American publishing. What Wreden failed to understand was that the cost and feel of the paperback, and its accordant potential to evoke war nostalgia, quite possibly enriched the novel's content. A novel largely about veteran reintegration—and this is not a hyperbolic description of *I, the Jury*—could simply sell better in the physical format of the wartime "escape."

His commercial aspirations were never in doubt, but nor were Spillane's inspirations or target audience. He told Michael Barson: "When I started the Mike Hammer thing, everybody was fresh out of the war. I knew what people wanted. They didn't want wishy washy heroes. Guys out there, they had seen violence, real violence. You've got a pretty horny bunch during the war too. A little more sex in the story wasn't going to bother them."[5] Spillane's philosophy of literature could hardly be put more baldly. Not only did readers want real violence and "a little more sex," but this taste had been triggered by the war—in other words, there was good reason for paperbacks, in cover and content, to become more salacious than prewar and wartime varieties. This is not the common notion that all lowbrow audiences crave salacious material, but a specific audience for whom salacious material is of *particular* interest, and an audience divided not by class or income, but by "taste" developed out of real, shared experience: after all, "*everybody* was fresh out of the war" (emphasis mine).

Even its plot indicates the extent to which *I, the Jury* is a postwar novel written for veterans (and, perhaps, those interested in the veteran psyche): Hammer finds his friend Jack Williams murdered:

> In there was my best friend laying on the floor dead. The body. Now I could call it that.
>
> Yesterday it was Jack Williams, the guy that shared the same mud bed with me through two years of warfare in the stinking slime of the jungle. Jack, the guy who said he'd give his right arm for a friend and did when he stopped a bastard of a Jap from slitting me in two. He caught the bayonet in the biceps and they amputated his arm.
>
> Pat didn't say a word. He let me uncover the body and feel the cold face. For the first time in my life I felt like crying.[6]

He promises that he'll torture and kill the culprit, later adding that that promise to do so is, to him, "sacred." Mike further suggests that the war prepared him for this case: "Someday I'll trigger the bastard that shot Jack. In my time I've done it plenty of times. No sentiment. That went out with the first. After the war I've been almost anxious to get some of the rats that make up the section of humanity that prey on people" (14). The rest of the novel concerns Hammer's fevered quest for vengeance, a vengeance to which he trusts no one else. No one else, Hammer believes, can properly avenge Jack because no one else feels for him as Hammer does. Hammer can kill with "no sentiment," since he cultivated this emotional posture during the war, but he is also capable of cold-blooded murder partly because of the *depth of his sentiment* toward the war and his comrade.

Ultimately, Hammer determines that his own fiancée, Charlotte Manning, is Jack's murderer, and he takes painful pleasure in killing her in the novel's final chapter. That Charlotte is responsible for Jack's death is not, of course, new to pulp crime fiction. Hard-boiled protagonists often find that the women with whom they are involved are the killers they seek, whether by their own hand or through others. The extremity of Hammer's erotic pleasure in killing the woman he loves and to whom he has committed his life is, however, shocking. Just as there are innumerable ways to incorporate graphic sex and violence into a paperback—we will see those in these three texts—there are many ways of narrating the plot of *I, the Jury*. In one version, a man looks for love and finds it impossible. In another, a man avenges the death of his war buddy. The fact that these two issues and narratives are entirely intertwined—the protagonist's fiancée is the one who murdered his war buddy in cold blood—reveals the degree to which these figures were in tension in this and the other texts I treat here, but also in American culture more broadly.

In the years immediately after World War II, there was much anxiety over what readjustment would look like. One aspect of this tension was the proximity of veterans to each other, the importance of their relationships with each other, and the simultaneous importance of building stable marriages and comfortable homes for developing families.[7] Certainly, men who had survived the war together could not be expected to simply forget about each other, and VFW and American Legion halls popped up in greater numbers to serve the swelling population of GIs (though this was not without controversy). Yet, the GI Bill looked, in some ways, like a blueprint for disconnecting veterans from their prewar and wartime lives, the creation of a veteran diaspora. Zero-interest, no-down-payment home loans facilitated a mass migration out of urban centers and into the suburbs, which had once been the province of the wealthy, making the home possibly both more attractive (bigger, quieter, prettier) and more isolated. Suburbanization was not, as many assume, an entirely white phenomenon, though some scholars suggest that suburbanization, especially in the American West, may have facilitated the growth of the conservative right.[8] Like any major migration in American history, this move to the suburbs did not happen overnight. Nevertheless, the fact that the government invested in that move indicates that it was not only encouraged but prioritized. Furthermore, the urban space made coupling easier, and by the time children arrived, the movement to suburbia was in full swing. Also, while the upward mobility signified by suburban living was no doubt part of the appeal for veterans and their families, the very design, style, and sensibility of the ranch-style suburban home seems fitting for the "neurotic" veteran: quiet, spread out, far from intruders, and assumed to be a place where a man need not fear for his family's safety.

Typically, scholars read the specifically gendered implications of the suburban house in one of two ways. First, the design, scope, and location of this house offered homemakers a space of mastery, accomplishment, and experimentation. Contrarily, scholars argue that the suburban house created a "container" for women, in which their power and sexuality in particular was kept out of the public sphere. Rather than undercut them, I simply add a third reading: the suburban house created a space for the enactment of troubled gender roles within a relationship, which diminished the influence of outside factors as much as possible. Given that many disturbances were figured outside the home, this impulse to protect the home via isolation is quite sensible. Men were, in this way, kept not only from each other, but also from the day-to-day demands of urban living.

The unprecedented number and accessibility of small business loans also encouraged movement out of urban centers and into these newer developments in which small businesses could flourish. Though VFWs and Legions spread, men living in suburbs were less able to access them and were certainly able to access them less regularly. Furthermore, this movement of the family outside of the city meant a more distinct separation of spheres, leaving the domestic a safe space supervised by an accommodating woman, safe and warm away from the working world of men. The rise of shopping centers, for example, kept wives closer to home, farther away from urban centers.[9] When men came home, then, they were in a safe space: here they were more protected from the stresses of work and the memories of war. War nostalgia was threatening, privileging the wrong actions and the wrong relationships. In the late 1940s, war-oriented film was dominated not by combat films or service comedies, but by films about some form of postwar maladjustment, though most veterans recuperated in time for a happy ending with the help of a loving partner. Though victory in the war was a good thing, the experience of war was not to be remembered positively. Again, the cultural emphasis was on *moving on*.

It is no surprise, then, that three works written the year after the war and published two years after would portray the danger of investing in relationships between veterans, but would also caution women against interfering in them. In *A Streetcar Named Desire* and *I, the Jury*, women attempt to get between war buddies and are violently punished. In *In a Lonely Place*, a woman seems to separate the men successfully, but she is in no way the model housewife nor the novel's heroine. In that novel, women are in the way and simply cannot be "gotten around"; violence is the only answer here too.

Unlike some later women characters, women in these three texts do not have strictly stable, wholesome motives. Like the women on the covers of *If He Hollers*, they are violent in their manipulations of the men around them. Men who may wish to "move on" right away, growing healthy families and lives in the immediate postwar period, are sometimes thwarted by the women who make their many demands. While they say that they are, *Streetcar*'s Stella and Blanche, *I, the Jury*'s Charlotte, and *In a Lonely Place*'s Laurel and Sylvia don't seem compelled by urges for safe suburban family life. These women are mercenary, motivated by money or lust provoked by violence. Men do not simply enjoy women's sexual admiration in the manner portrayed by most popular texts before and after this period. The fact that women are turned on by violence, consciously or subconsciously, is consistently a problem for the men in these works. Dix, for example, is disgusted as the women around him get sexually excited by news of the Los Angeles serial killer (which is, of course, Dix himself); Mitch's jealousy and confusion at Stanley's savage sex appeal is palpable throughout the play; Mike Hammer's brutishness lands him in bed with wanton women whose interest he dismisses, avoids, takes advantage of, and demonizes. How can these men "move on" when their violent tendencies provoke women's interest, but heterosexual love is the only lasting container for these very tendencies?

THE IMPOSSIBLE LOVE OF A GOOD WOMAN: THE EARLY WORK OF MICKEY SPILLANE

I, the Jury's Mike and Charlotte—he the detective avenging his war buddy's murderer, she the as yet unknown murderer—have their "first date" in Central Park. She is pushing a baby carriage, sitting for a friend's child. The opening conversation is on their desire for children: Charlotte claims to love kids and wants six. Mike wants them too but is concerned about having enough income to support that many. Charlotte immediately reminds Mike that she is a "working girl," by which she means a successful practicing psychiatrist, and so the two of them could earn enough money for a big family. Within seconds, bullets come their way, and Mike lies on top of Charlotte to shield her (84). Without the prior conversation, Mike's action might seem typically chivalrous—he would unthinkingly take a bullet for a woman. After that conversation, in which family happiness is established as a financially collaborative effort, this moment is reminiscent of Jack's heroic effort to protect Mike, risking his life for his comrade, losing his arm in the process. Mike does not merely want a woman: he wants a partner.

Famously, Mike avoids having sex with Charlotte (though he has few qualms about sleeping with other women in the novel), preserving her presumed virginity for their awaited wedding night. Mike is firm in this decision, though she is (sometimes painfully) desirable, and though she pleads with him, having been turned on by his violence in defending her: when two men leer at her in a bar, Mike "put [his] hands on each side of their heads and brought them together with a clunk like a couple of gourds. . . . The two guys fell off their stools and hit the deck like wet rags" (120). "My protector," she swoons, and when they get home, she reminds him that she is sexually available, even without a wedding.

It is tempting to read Mike's refusal to have sex with Charlotte as protective of her, a condescending preservation of her innocence, and a refusal to "use" her. Again, I do not dispute this reading, but add to it. Given that his violence and brutishness provoke sexual desire in nearly every woman he meets, his resistance could be to being "used" himself. He wants to be certain that Charlotte's feelings for him run deeper than sexual desire, as he repeatedly says his do for her. If he honors her lust for violence by yielding to sex with her, the marriage will only continue this pattern of violence, making his husband persona a mere replica of soldier Mike, playboy Mike, and street Mike. The marriage—not only the bride—must be "pure."

Seeing this "containment" of female sexual desire for men in this way offers texture to many other scholarly accounts of the "threat" of women's sexual agency. The association between sex and violence is clearly attributed to men's matrix of desire, but perhaps this matrix is influenced by a deeply conflicted view of their own desirability. Indeed, the virgin-whore dichotomy dovetails with this complicated vision of (particularly American) femininity: the virgin is an attractive life partner because she seems to lack desire, and desire is associated with a kind of bloodlust. The woman who is actively sexual flatters a man's sense of masculine power—so she may be an attractive sexual partner—but she is, in this way, flattering a man's "worst self" or "dark side." For this reason, she is a less desirable companion.

Gabriele Dietze briefly mentions that Spillane's view of women may have been inspired by the pin-ups he viewed during the war, but that he (and other veterans) returned to "encounter a generation of virginal women committed to marriage, domesticity, and childbearing."[10] Dietze is right to pick up on that tension, but Spillane's treatment of these issues is contradictory. Whether those women were indeed virgins, whether they were in fact as committed to marriage, domesticity, and childbearing as they appeared: these are questions in the Spillane books. Velda, Hammer's faithful assistant to whom he later becomes engaged, makes no secret of her desire to marry him, but she is also willing to surrender her virginity to a criminal in order to get important information on a case. Other women are less eager to marry: the Bellamy twins, for example, are uninterested in marriage because they are financially secure and get their sexual needs met elsewhere. Turned on by Mike's brutality, they and many other women in the novels offer themselves to him sexually without the expectation or even interest in love or commitment.

The notion that Mike must protect himself from the cravenness of women's sexual desire, its roots in his darkest behaviors, is related differently elsewhere. All cultural products are somewhat incoherent, but Spillane's fevered process of composition lends itself to further incoherence. Though he tells Michael Barson that his work is addressed to veterans—and this seems inarguably the case—he occasionally flips the script and seems to address someone else entirely. Take, for example, the opening of *My Gun Is Quick*, the second installment in the Mike Hammer series, published soon after *I, the Jury*:

> When you sit at home comfortably folded up in a chair beside a fire, have you ever thought what goes on outside there? Probably not. You pick up a book and read about things and stuff, getting a vicarious kick from people and events that never happened. You're doing it now, getting ready to fill in a normal life with the details of someone else's experiences. Fun, isn't it? You read about life on the outside thinking of how you'd like it to happen to you or at least how you'd like to watch it. Even the old Romans did it, spiced their life with action when they sat in the Coliseum and watched wild animals rip a bunch of humans apart, reveling in the sight of blood and terror. They screamed for joy and slapped each other on the back when murderous claws tore into the live flesh of slaves and cheered when the kill was made. Oh, it's great to watch, all right. Life through a keyhole. But day after day goes by and nothing like that ever happens to you so you think that it's all in books and not in reality at all and that's that. Still good reading though. Tomorrow night you'll find another book, forgetting what was in the last and live some more in your imagination. But remember this: there *are* things happening out there. . . . The razor-sharp claws aren't those of wild animals but man's can be just as sharp and twice as vicious. You have to be quick, and you have to be able, or you become one of the devoured, and if you can kill first, no matter how and no matter who, you can live and return to the comfortable chair and the comfortable fire. But you have to be quick. Or you'll be dead.[11]

Spillane was not himself a detective or a criminal; he was not among the likes of Hammett and Himes, writers who experienced the criminal underworld for themselves. He had a very specific and circumscribed experience of violence, and his experience ended with the war; he, like most men of his generation, came home to the "comfortable chair and the comfortable fire."

While the above passage seems to be in Hammer's voice (it is the first in the novel), it is not yet attributed to the character. And though Hammer addresses the reader from time to time, at no other point in the texts of the Hammer series does he have an extended soliloquy in which he expressly critiques and addresses his reader. The passage is sometimes illogical: is the reader enjoying "events that never happened" or "someone else's experiences"? In other words, were the events imagined through fiction, or were they real? The former phrase later seems to have been written with sarcasm, though that is never continued or explored.

Spillane and Hammer, criticized for taking pleasure in violence, scold the reader for doing the same, despite the fact that the Hammer novels seem perfectly designed to evoke that reaction. The second "you"—the "you" that is not the reader—*has* to kill. He does not crave the kill or relish the kill, but does it for his own survival. It should be noted that self-defense justifies many of Hammer's killings in the series, but not the most important one: his murder of Charlotte Manning, which ends *I, the Jury* and remains Spillane's most memorable scene. Charlotte's death is required, of course, by a comrade code developed out of the same necessity for survival as self-defense. In the logic of the battlefield, it *is* self-defense.

Spillane also fascinatingly juxtaposes public and private voyeurism. The group cheering at the Coliseum is followed immediately with "life through a keyhole," suggesting hidden spectatorship. A cultural celebration of violence either conditions or accompanies a private craving to see this violence played out. The political imperative of war perverts personal taste and preferred recreation.

The first "you" has not considered "what goes on outside," but the second "you" has experienced it and escaped it to "return to the comfortable chair and the comfortable fire" where the reading is taking place. Thus, Spillane awkwardly posits two readers: one infuriatingly naive and "comfortable," able simply to "forget" what was in the last novel, and another who has returned to "comfort" only as a result of having killed to survive. Perhaps two people sit in front of that fire, novels in hand: a veteran and his wife. Perhaps the violence against women which often defines Spillane's novels is a message: a misogyny rooted in resentment at the women who cheered as their men came home from battle.

Despite this opening, and though Hammer likes to claim that he hates women (and certainly Spillane's critics tend to agree), he does not seem to hate them in *My Gun Is Quick*. In two out of Spillane's first three novels, the victim of the major crime is a war buddy of Mike Hammer's, and Hammer's mission is to bring his friend's killer to justice. *My Gun Is Quick* is the exception. In *My Gun Is Quick*, Hammer meets Red, a young woman struggling with alcohol abuse, for a matter of minutes. Hammer encounters Red in a diner and, immediately charmed by her innocence—not by her sex appeal—he gives her money. When he hands over the cash, Hammer is moved and discomfited by the way she views him: "I don't ever want anybody to look at me the way she did then. A look like something belongs in church when you're praying or getting married or something" (158). Moments later, Red is killed. When his friend, policeman Pat Chambers, gives him the news, Mike feels automatically responsible: "Anytime I touch anything it gets killed!" (160).

As he did of his friend Jack in *I, the Jury*, Hammer has flashbacks to his time with Red, though in this case, they spent only moments together:

> That one word, MURDERED, kept jumping at me like it was alive. I was seeing Red standing there with the dimples in her cheeks, kissing her finger, and smiling a smile that was for me alone. Just a two-bit tramp who could have been a lady, and who was, for a few short minutes, a damn decent friend.
> And I'd jinxed her. (163)

Given their short and uncompromised acquaintance, Hammer's guilt in this scenario is inexplicable. On the surface, it is impossible to understand why Hammer would feel responsible for, nor even why he would be so personally troubled by, her murder. Hammer has watched many people—some apparently innocent of any crime—die over the course of these two novels. But he cannot shake the feeling that he contaminated her. Even as he begins to investigate the case, his flashbacks continue to disturb him: "I went home and hit the sack. I didn't sleep too well because the redhead would smile, kiss her finger, and put it on my cheek and wake me up" (173). Red's mistake, Mike has somehow determined, was in believing in him, believing in his capacity for good. Red knew Mike only as the man who offered her a moment of kindness in her time of need, and she looked at him with "a look like something belongs in church when you're praying or getting married," making of him in that moment a "good man." In his self-loathing, guilt, and defeatism, he "[doesn't] ever want anybody to look at me the way she did then."

Mike's affection for Red and his flashbacks to that moment rest on a conflation of prayer and marriage: both ought to be holy, rooted in the pure and the good. Even (maybe especially) after his fateful encounter with Charlotte, Mike believes that marriage must rest on this shared faith in the sacred. Mike realizes that the love of a good woman is his only chance for redemption, and his violence is actually provoked by missed opportunities for this redemption.

Red's moment of innocent love for Mike, his feeling of goodness in that moment, inspires him to crusade for vengeance against her killer, his mission in this novel similar to his purpose in *I, the Jury*. In both cases (and later in others), Mike is motivated by a sense of loyalty. Jopi Nyman, like many critics, argues that the "hard-boiled character is loyal to himself only," but Spillane's entire oeuvre features pathologically loyal protagonists.[12] Furthermore, contrary to being committed to "defend[ing] the ideal of the autonomous male," Spillane's protagonists are actively hostile to autonomy, finding it only by tragic default (4). Whether Hammer is a hard-boiled character is certainly arguable, though I will not make that argument here. Regardless, he is operating within a canon of hard-boiled detective fiction, examples of which illuminate his motives and actions, highlighting a particular element of tragedy.

Take, for example, Hammett's *The Maltese Falcon*, which is clearly an important precedent to *I, the Jury*. Detective Sam Spade turns over his lover, Brigid O'Shaunnessy, to the police upon finding out that she killed his partner. As he reveals his betrayal, he famously says to her: "I won't play the sap for you." The relationship between Hammer and Jack bears a fascinating correspondence to the one between Spade and his partner, Miles Archer. Sam Spade was the best-known private detective figure of the 1940s, appearing beyond the novel in radio plays throughout the 1930s and, of course, in the 1941 John Huston film starring Bogart. Spade, like Hammer, avenges the man in his life. However, Spade does so largely against his own will, feeling that he has no choice but to seek justice for Miles, despite the fact Spade was sexually involved with Miles's wife, Iva, and that he didn't much like him. Leonard Cassuto argues that Spade lives by a code that "emphasizes self-preservation and a nihilistic sense of duty that arises, as Sam Spade puts it in *The Maltese Falcon* (1930), because one is 'supposed to do something.'"[13]

Hammer's relationship to the man he avenges is entirely different. He kills Charlotte not just out of a sense of justice or of obligation to simply "do something," but out of a deep love for his comrade-in-arms. Hammer's love for Jack is clear throughout the novel, but the fact that he kills Charlotte slowly, taking pleasure in her painful death, suggests that Hammer's vengeance is very different from Spade's. Like Spade, he felt that he had no choice, but it was the strength of his emotions rather than an external code that forced him to kill her. Spade is blank-faced as he watches Brigid's arrest, but Hammer is literally thrilled watching the slow death of the only woman he has ever loved. His love for Williams is far greater than his love for Charlotte; for Spade, love is either entirely hidden, beside the point, or both simultaneously. Once Red looks at Hammer with such innocent love, his emotions drive his crusade for justice: whatever he may be "supposed to do," he cannot stop.

In addition to his affection for Red, Hammer befriends two other women in *My Gun Is Quick*. He bonds quickly with Nancy, and with Lola, an ex-Army nurse's aide afflicted with VD, who has been cast out as a result of her disease. As with Red, he needs only moments to connect to Lola specifically because of her innocence. Hammer is at peace as they "hug" and "nuzzle" and "laugh at foolish things," and he thinks, "She was the kind of a girl who could give you back something you thought you had lost" (273). But, importantly, her innocence is not a function of a lack of life experience: they are both trying to go back to being the people they were before the war. She is deliberately trying to turn good, to shed her shame about her past: "I'm trying so hard to be . . . nice. . . . I want to be worth a love that's returned" (286). Hammer cannot contain his empathy: "You can forget everything that has ever happened. I don't give a damn what went on this year or last. Who the hell am I to talk anyway? . . . You were always nice, Lola. I haven't known you long, but I bet you were always nice" (269). She tells him that she "still ha[s] a long way to go." Hammer feels exactly the same way. He cannot have faith in his own ability to be good, but he can in hers.

For Lola, he wants to be a better man, but he essentially begs her *not* to love him, saying, "you're made for a brand-new guy, somebody more than me. I'm trouble for everything I touch" (313). He does not want her to love him for his dark past. She puts her hand over his mouth and the two make love, in spite of the risk of infection: she too has been contaminated by the war, and she too wants a way out of it.

Even after sex, Hammer praises her for being his "kind of woman, the kind of woman you didn't have to speak to, for words weren't that necessary . . . honest and strong" (313). Hammer feels he has found a woman who understands him. He involves her in the case and treats her like a lover and a partner, calling her "chum" when she makes an important discovery (326). Of course, Hammer's fears are once again realized: she is killed because of her involvement with him and the investigation. He cannot be a "brand-new guy," as circumstances will never let him.

Though entitled *My Gun Is Quick*, Hammer's murders therein are not quick, nor reliant entirely on his gun. When the moment comes to kill Feeney, the first of the culprits, he says, "I didn't want my gun then. Just my hands," and proceeds first to strangle him and then he "took that head like it was a swollen rag and smashed and smashed and smashed" (334). Later, as the novel ends, he catches and kills Berin, the rich and connected head of a major prostitution ring responsible for Red, Nancy, and Lola's deaths. A burning timber falls across Berin's chest and Hammer leaves it there, even though he knows that failing to put it out means that he will likely die too. The fire spreads, and Hammer enjoys watching as Berin himself begins to burn. Finally, firefighters arrive and, just as their ladder connects with the window, Hammer puts Berin's own gun in his face as time passes, "Minutes. Seconds," and Hammer pulls the trigger (343–44). Though unexpectedly saved by the firefighters, Hammer is willing to put his life on the line for women like Red and Lola; more than that, rather than simply shooting Berin, he chooses a long, slow, painful death for himself. as recompense for his contamination of their innocent lives. In his way, he feels as guilty as Berin for their suffering and deaths.

Mike's guilt is also unjustified by his actions in these novels, if his take on them is reliable. He kills only the guilty, and his pleasure in killing them is always accompanied by his lengthy reiteration of their sadistic crimes. He justifies his crimes and their particulars even as he commits them. If he only kills for good reasons, why is Mike certain that he is a bad guy? A 1952 profile on Spillane in *Life* magazine noted that, while he directly kills only killers, "In the five Hammer cases 48 people have been killed, and there is reason to believe that if Mike had kept out of the way, 34 of them—all innocent of the original crime—would have survived."[14] Perhaps Hammer is indeed a sort of contaminant, and this feeling is amplified by the sense that he has contaminated Red and Lola, who are not just innocent of crimes, but who believe him innocent as well. These women are rare: they do not love him for his violence, and his violence does not turn them on sexually. They let him be a good man. His desire to die in the fire at the end of *My Gun Is Quick* is an appropriate conclusion given the opening of the novel, a rebuke to women and others fascinated and aroused by violence.

Women throughout late-1940s texts, but specifically Spillane's, Hughes's, and Williams's female characters, are deeply compromised on the issue of their men's violence. Many women urge their men to be careful not to get hurt, but seem to care very little about their hurting others; they simply want their men to come back. Moreover, the women often enjoy hearing of their exploits and are attracted to their physical prowess and even their violence. As Dennis Porter puts it, "for the private eye as for the Indian scout, the hunter, the cowboy, and the soldier, the final test of self-worth and of the quality of an individual's manhood occurs in violent action."[15] It is important to note that this evaluation of quality extends beyond the "self"; the violent "quality of an individual's manhood" is rewarded both by women and by the nation.

NORMAL AS YOU OR ME: THE SEXUAL PSYCHOPATH OF *IN A LONELY PLACE*

Violence against women is, of course, not specific to the postwar period, but combat veterans' disproportionate perpetration of domestic violence is well-documented. In an era in which so many men had served, it stands to reason that, whether domestic violence had, in fact, increased, paranoia about its prevalence was warranted. By the 1950s, this domestic violence was frequently figured literally: sitcoms, for example, show men beating their wives and children. However, this violence against women was simultaneously specified and pathologized, leading to a frenzy over the "sexual psychopath." Whiting points out that the 1950s offered a particularly fertile moment for considering the figure of the "sexual psychopath"; in the wake of the sex crime panics and with the meteoric rise to popularity of psychoanalytic discourse, an intersection of social, political, and intellectual forces formed the backdrop for the transformation I am describing.[16] What amounted to a new species of monster, the sexual psychopath, had emerged on the US landscape.

Like Whiting, Estelle Freedman sees the sexual psychopath as particular to the period. In her history of "sex crime panics," she points to several moments in American history during which concern over "sexual psychopaths" was at a height.[17] In 1949–55, she argues, this panic was enabled by complementary trends: "The postwar years, however, provided a climate conducive to the reemergence of the male sexual psychopath as a target of social concern. The war had greatly increased the authority of psychiatrists, who had been drafted to screen recruits and to diagnose military offenders. Postwar psychiatric and social welfare literature stressed the adjustment problems of returning servicemen, some of whom, it was feared, might 'snap' into sociopathic states" (96). As a social scientist, Freedman can see through her research what literary scholars (including Whiting) have not: these adjustment problems are clearly associated with the rise in sex panic. Freedman further argues that the fear of the sexual psychopath, which other scholars in many disciplines have claimed was encouraged in order to curb female sexuality, was definitively about policing *men's* actions: the hiatus in sex crime panic during the early 1940s suggests that its central concern was men, not women. The legitimization of male aggression during World War II and the shift of national attention toward external enemies combined to reduce the focus on violent sexual crimes. Although arrest rates remained high during the war, both newspaper and magazine coverage of sex crimes tapered off markedly, and only one state—Vermont—enacted a psychopath law.

In other words, when some form of aggression was necessary, laws about sex crime and specifically about the so-called sexual psychopath were loosened or left alone, and the popular press ignored these stories. Freedman's research suggests that the public and experts both viewed sex crime as about violence rather than sexual desire, a perspective on rape that second wave feminists justifiably and tellingly felt it necessary to resurrect (96).

However, Freedman is careful to point out that there was a counterperspective to what Whiting describes as the "new Monster" of the sexual psychopath. She notes that while, in other eras of sex crime panic, sexual psychopaths were strictly isolated as a category, this was less true in the discourse around sex crime in the 1950s, even as sexual psychopath legislation mushroomed: "Critics of the psychopath laws increasingly suggested that, in the words of one state report, 'aggression is a normal component of the sexual impulse in all males'" (102). Freedman reads both the critiques and the legislation as part of an emerging and shifting idea about male sexuality in the postwar era: "The response to the sexual psychopath was not, then, a movement to protect female purity; its central concern was male sexuality and the fear that without the guardianship of women, either men's most beastlike, violent sexual desires might run amok, or men might turn their sexual energies away from women entirely" (103). These shifts were partly related to the concurrent shift away from sex as a strictly procreative act and, interestingly, also related to an increasing sense that women and even children had sexual agency of a kind: "The discussion of the sexual psychopath influenced the redefinition of rape as not only a male psychological aberration, but also an act in which both women and children contributed to their own victimization" (100). That women could be and were attracted to men with sexually psychopathic tendencies, "egging them on" as it were, is not much of a leap, but it was a position with which many writers of fiction experimented.

The sexual psychopath was a common figure in psychoanalytic and criminal justice literature of the period, but also in fiction. Whiting productively juxtaposes two novels—*The Killer Inside Me* and *I, the Jury*—to explore the valences of this trend. Jim Thompson's *The Killer Inside Me* (1951) is a key example, and it is the pulp crime novel of the era that has received by far the most attention from literary critics. Considering it alongside *In a Lonely Place* is equally effective.

Thompson's Lou Ford had an initial motive for his crimes, though that motive's relation to the crimes themselves was often twisted. Lou was raped as a child by his widowed father's housekeeper (with whom his father was engaged in an extended affair). He has repressed the memory throughout much of his adult life, but experiences flashbacks (triggered by erotic photographs of his father and his rapist) midway through the novel, explaining his seeming socio-pathology to himself and to the reader. His shocking acts against women—beating seemingly innocent women into "stew meat," anally raping his own loving girlfriend without any apparent provocation, and brutally murdering a sex worker—are thus explained through his response to traumas (his rape and the loss of his mother), with the sort of pseudo-Freudian implications common to 1950s texts. Lou is out of step with his time and his culture in many ways: for one thing, he is not only not a veteran but he sneers at other men's service. In particular, he pokes fun at Hendricks, a local politician who caught shrapnel in his buttocks during World War II, and suggests that his election and overall importance in the town is only because he has "metal in his ass." Lou recommends that Hendricks use an x-ray of his ass as a campaign flag.

Lou is, therefore, a fascinating foil to Hughes's serial killer and sexual psychopath, Dix Steele. Dix is defined by his service, and we are meant to believe that, whatever his faults—he appears to have been rather lazy, snobby, envious, and selfish before the war—he is a killer specifically because of it. Furthermore, whereas Lou is deeply, profoundly different from other folks, a killer since his victimization as a young child, Dix is simply a shade more "noir" than normal.

This insistence that the serial killer is "different" from other people—whether he is born different or has experienced things that differ from what "most of us" have experienced—has profound political implications when correlated with the fact that so many men of the generation I treat here experienced battle. Simpson and Tithecott argue that the "construction of the serial killer in narrative representation as part of a growing cultural tendency to reject intellectual critique of one's own cultural values as contributing factors to violence. . . . The popularity of the serial killer in fictional narrative, then, is a symptom of a larger cultural denial of responsibility in the production of violence. If nature (or God or destiny) intends one to be a serial killer, and this nature is perceived as unknowable and uncontrollable, as so many of these narratives imply, what is the point of trying to do better as a society?"[8] In terms of this subject, what is the point in trying to avoid war? What is the purpose of offering broad mental health services for veterans, including medication, personal, family, and marriage therapy? What is the purpose of acknowledging widespread cultural anxiety over so many men?

Dix is a serial killer and rapist of women. *In a Lonely Place* is set in Los Angeles, just after the war, and Dix has recently arrived in the area. He is now near Brub, his closest friend in the war and a longtime Angeleno. Brub is now married to Sylvia (to whom he was engaged during the war) and is an accomplished police detective. As it happens, he is assigned to find the killer stalking LA, the killer who is, of course, his best friend. His inability to see his best friend as a killer relates very directly to issues of normality: Can a man be normal after a war? If he can, what does it take? If he cannot, why can't he see that? Whereas Lou is distinct, clearly *different* from the people around him, one of the fundamental paradoxes of *In a Lonely Place* is that the two men in the forefront—Dix and Brub—have an inordinate amount in common, though one is the killer and the other the man who is hunting the killer down.

Lou and Dix both perform normality or "pass" as normal people, while signaling repeatedly to the reader that this is a performance. What's more, both men enjoy the performance and seek out opportunities to indulge it. Lou famously collects homespun clichés and integrates them into his conversations for his own amusement; his denigration of others' use of language is an inside joke with himself. Dix's pleasure in his own performance is often specific to his crimes: he sees playing at normality as a risky pleasure, not self-protection. At other times, he seems not even to doubt his own normality, seeing himself as essentially on a continuum with other men. While Lou sees others as idiots for being unlike him, Dix sees stupidity in others' inability to see their likeness to him.

Having taken one of his victims, pretty young Mildred Atkinson, out to dinner before killing her, he looked back on that evening: "Certain gambles were legitimate. Like appearing in a lighted place with Mildred. Gambling on the muddled memory of waitresses and countermen who served hundreds of average-looking men and women every day, every night. Risks were spice. Stunt flying. As long as you used them like spice, sparingly; like stunts, planning them with precision, carrying them out boldly" (43). Unlike Lou, Dix does not "break character." Lou will acknowledge his own psychopathy in moments in which he thinks he would be served by it, particularly in threatening others. Dix does not. Dix also marvels at the inability of others to conceive of the very normality of his crimes: "Cary Jepson was a clod. . . . The obvious reach of his imagination was, 'He's insane, of course.' It would never occur to him than any reason other than insanity could make a man a killer. That's what all the dolts around town would be parroting: *he's insane of course he's insane of course*. It took imagination to think of a man, sane as you or I, who killed" (232). Again, whatever Dix's prewar faults, the novel insists that the war kindled an urge for thrills that only rape and murder could satisfy in the postwar world. One of many things that make the above passage so fascinating is its last line: "a man, sane as you or *I*, who killed" (emphasis mine). He may be the only one who knows it, but Dix is a serial killer. As if to illustrate his point, he invokes not only the reader's sanity ("as sane as you") but also, bizarrely, his own. Frequently in the novel, characters formulate their notion of "sanity" through these comparisons, Brub included. When Dix says this, "as sane as you or I," he has already heard it from others. Brub uses this comparison earlier in the novel, describing the killer to Dix as "a maniac walking the streets, looking just as normal as you or me" (32).

Dix and Brub, though intimate war buddies, do not share precisely the same perspective on the war. Their dialogue traces these differences directly to two circumstances: their relationships with women and their comfort in their class positions. Dix went to war a bachelor and came back to the United

States the same way (having had a meaningful relationship in the meantime with a woman who became his first victim). Brub was already involved with Sylvia when he enlisted and he returned to marry her. When the two men discuss their motivations to enlist, Brub touches upon that difference, saying: "Why do you think I fought the war? To get back to Sylvia" (10). His comment is knee-jerk and common to ex-GIs: it as though he never really let himself think about his motives for enlisting.

Brub then makes fun of Dix, saying that he only served in order to meet girls abroad, but Dix is serious, saying that he, by contrast, has "thought about it frequently": "Why did I or anyone else fight in the war? Because we had to isn't good enough. I didn't have to when I enlisted. I think it was because it was the thing to do. And the Air Corps was the thing to do. All of us in college were nuts about flying. I was a sophomore at Princeton when things were starting. I didn't want to be left out of any excitement." Dix's explanation is disturbing and suggests that he sees a deeper sickness in his own generation: he and they would rather kill than be left out of the excitement, or at least that's the way the situation looks in hindsight. Brub responds, "It was the thing to do or that was the rationalization. We're a casual generation, Dix, we don't want anyone to know we bleed if we're pricked" (210–11).

While the conversation begins with Brub's nod to Sylvia, it ends with Brub's implication that men of their generation are not emotionally forthcoming, that they are not just hiding something, but "rationalizing" their decisions; here, Brub is perhaps admitting the shallowness of his earlier comment. Also, though, Brub suggests that, however frequently his friend has thought it over, Dix too is rationalizing his wartime decisions, hiding his own motives and feelings. Brub defines their "generation"—clearly comprised primarily of veterans—as what he calls "casual," by which he seems to mean wrapped up in denial and secrecy.

In *In a Lonely Place*, the very notion of normality is complicated—perhaps even obliterated—by the omnipresence of the war. As we have seen elsewhere, the man who manages to have a successful, "normal" life after the war is the one who compartmentalizes it, almost attempting to pretend that it didn't happen. Hughes makes a point of showing that Dix thinks about the war, whereas Brub seems to try not to, but one passage in particular shows the depth of this disconnection between the normal and the veteran.

In one of their many conversations about the murders, Dix clarifies Brub's point about the killer's normal appearance: "'Like you and me,' Dix dared, 'an ordinary man'" (155). Dix often provokes monologues about the killer's normal appearance, but Brub's reaction here is strange: "'Yeah. An ordinary man. With the nerve of a jet pilot.'" Of course, though he does not mention it here, he and Dix ("you and me") were combat pilots themselves, with nerve to risk their lives to end others. Elsewhere in the text, this idea that the killer is "like you and me" is repeated, but this particular passage suggests something specific. In addition to the many issues surrounding a killer's normality that I discuss above, here, Brub quite unthinkingly places the war experience that he and Dix share—"the nerve" that was required of the pilot—outside of normality or the "ordinary," while conflating his own and his friend's identities in the same sentence. Brub is not only unaware that his friend is a killer, he is in denial about his own similarity to the killer. He is, in fact, so unaware that he betrays this similarity without skipping a beat. Brub's lack of self-awareness, it seems, makes it difficult for him to track down the killer. He cannot see that the killer is his best friend and war buddy because he refuses to honestly see himself as the man who once had "the nerve of a jet pilot." Or, on the contrary, Brub does see himself as having had the nerve of a jet pilot but is desperate to believe that that nerve was conditional: he and Dix, unlike the killer he imagines, have moved on.

Dix sees Brub differently. Whereas Brub cannot or will not see the jet pilot in himself anymore, when Dix sees him again for the first time after the war, he describes: "Brub hadn't changed . . . he rolled like a sailor when he walked. Or like a fighter. A good fighter. That was Brub. . . . He knew exactly what Brub saw [when he looked at Dix], as if Brub were a mirror he was standing before" (11). Just as Brub believes that Dix has changed because he has, Dix believes that Brub hasn't changed because he hasn't. Each sees the other's postwar adjustment in terms of his own, but also believes that other sees him the way he sees the other, as his mirror image.

Hughes amplifies the sense of Brub's denial and similarity to Dix and the killer at other points through her free indirect style, allowing Dix to seem both to speak and to be observed. Just the fact that Brub is seeking a serial killer makes his mental landscape similar to the killer's own. In order to pursue the killer, Brub has to think carefully about the crimes and crave the killer's capture, knowing that this will likely lead to the killer's execution. In this respect, Brub's detective mission is not unlike his mission in wartime: he captures/kills the killer before he can kill again. Dix examines the room at a party he attends with Brub and Sylvia: "Nice people, healthy and wealthy.

Normal as you and me. Normal as Sylvia when she didn't have the megrims. But you didn't know what was beneath beach-tanned faces and simple expensive clothes. You didn't ever know about thoughts. They were so easily hidden. You didn't have to give away what you were thinking. No one exchanging pleasantries with Brub would know that the man's mind was raw with murder" (34). Of course, Dix is right: Brub is thinking much about murder in order to catch the murderer. Here though, Dix suggests that Brub is himself a sick man, hiding his own violent mental landscape beneath his appearance of perfect health. While Dix does not remark on his friend's denial in the "nerve of a jet pilot" example, here he/Hughes must acknowledge everyone's ignorance. Furthermore, he invokes the "normal as you and me": Brub, in this scenario, may be the sicker of the two. His "beach-tanned face" is like Dix's: as Hughes/Dix describes himself, "his face covered his mind" (37).

If Brub and Dix are "ordinary" and "normal," so too is Brub's colleague, Detective Jack Lochner. When Dix meets him, he is described: "His clothes were a little too big for him, as if he'd lost weight worrying. His face was lined. He looked just like an ordinary man" (85). Though Brub, Dix, and the killer appear physically healthy—that is one of the many ways in which we can identify them as "normal" and "ordinary"—here, through Hughes's free indirect narration, she shows that Dix sees this worry, too, as "ordinary." Though Dix and his friend do not betray this worry in their bodies, he assumes that it is ordinary to be so disturbed.

Lochner generally occupies a middle ground between Dix's intense self-identification as a veteran and Brub's strange denial. In a long monologue in which he explains his desire to track down the killer, he says:

> "I don't like killing. I saw too much of it, same as you did. I hated it then, the callous way we'd sit around and map out our plans to kill people. People who didn't want to die any more than we wanted to die. And how we'd come back afterwards and talk it over, check over how many we'd got that night. As if we'd been killing ants, not men." His eyes were intense. "I hate killers. I want the world to be a good place, a safe place. For me and my wife and my friends, and my kids when I have them. I guess that's why I'm a policeman. To help make one little corner of the world a safer place." (92)

Lochner partially explains his choice to be a cop in terms similar to Brub's (and many other men's) explaining his wartime service: it was for others.

However, Lochner connects the violence of the war to his choices in its aftermath and implies that it is compensatory. He "hate[s] killers" because he was a killer. Having killed, he wants to rid the world of killing in order to preserve and protect the people for whom he killed. His career is, in one respect, an argument against the notion that "a killer has to kill," but it is simultaneously an acknowledgment that the "killer [who] has to kill" may exist and must be stopped.

Dix is (tellingly) interested in the killer's motive and asks Brub about it frequently. At one point, Brub replies: "'It all comes back to one focal point, the man is a killer, he has to kill. As an actor has to act.' 'And he can't stop?' Dix murmured. 'He can't stop,' Brub said flatly" (83). In addition to its implications—if he is correct, Brub too "can't stop"—Hughes uses this conversation to reinvest in Dix's strange insistence on his own "normality": "A murderer has to murder. Dix wanted to laugh. They knew so little, with all their science and intuition" (90). The novel is about Dix's compulsion to kill, but he refuses to identify himself as "different."

Brub's relationship with Sylvia is at the root of his denial: his marriage offers him a veneer—even a real feeling—of normality. That Brub's contemplation of violence finds a socially acceptable outlet in his police work is not simply a professional but a personal containment strategy. Brub, in financially supporting Sylvia, is forced to find a form of violent activity that is adequately profitable. Dix is offended by work and relies primarily on his uncle's largesse, meanwhile pretending to write a novel. When he meets Laurel Gray, he hopes to live partly off her alimony (which should not diminish the depth of his love for her). Dix resents the fact that, having returned from war, he is expected to take on the trappings of normality, which include a paying profession.

Dix may, indeed, be writing a novel of sorts. Though he scarcely types a word, he finds an outlet in his crimes. Fascinatingly, he sees his writing as part of what makes him typical of his generation, but also as part of what makes him distinct. When he talks about his work, he acknowledges: "Like ninety-three and one-half per cent of the ex-armed forces, I'm writing a book. . . . Unlike ninety-two and one-half percent I'm not writing a book on the war. Or even my autobiography. Just trying to do a novel" (12–13). Here, Dix contradicts Brub's contention that the men of their generation "don't want anyone to know we bleed if we're pricked," instead arguing that men's emotional lives are siphoned off, their feelings and memories expressed, but outside of their day-to-day lives. Of course, this is the way in which Dix handles his own memories and the emotions these memories evoke, but, in his case, these "coping" methods operate otherwise: he replays his trauma on the bodies of women. Dix cannot even admit to writing a memoir, but claims to be writing a novel; in this generic twist, he is able to distance himself from the origins of his own violence (one might say inspiration). Some men—these memoirists—are caught up in the past. Dix is merely writing a crime novel, which can read (ironically) as *moving on.*

Sylvia—like the vast majority of women in postwar fiction, film, and television—either does not understand or pretends not to understand the gravity of veterans' experiences. Dix often plays into this image in order to deflect any connection between war behavior and criminality. His clothes become a bizarre symbol of the war's benignity and the fact that the clothes Dix and Brub wore before the war no longer fit them is repeated several times by several characters in seemingly unrelated situations. The fact that they both gained weight during their service—given that they were barely twenty years old when they went, this development seems fairly predictable—is a touchstone, licensing Sylvia to laugh and say things like, "They fed you gentlemen altogether too well" (26). Sylvia sees the clothes as symbolically benign, but the reader extends the metaphor: the life that these men led before the war no longer "fits." What they "fed on" during the conflict has made that mundane life uncomfortable and, for Dix explicitly, too small.

Dix's sense that postwar life is too small waxes and wanes throughout the novel. Desperate for Laurel's love, achingly nostalgic for the happiness he found with his wartime girlfriend Brucie, Dix spends hours meditating on the beauty of true love and his yearning for it. Christopher Breu, in his article on *In a Lonely Place,* points out that, while Hughes frequently disrupts the reader's identification with Dix, she always re-establishes it by casting Dix "within the generic trappings of the lovesick romantic hero: we follow along with him as the world can't seem to match the intensity of his love."[19] In fact, both Dix and Hammer long for the security of home and hearth, and they love desperately. Both men want wives and real intimacy. They want to understand and be understood. They envy, respect, and are sometimes comforted by the couples they know who have achieved this. Dix sometimes wants to be near the Nicolais couple, just to be "warmed by their safeness" (28). But other times Dix's jealousy is overwhelming. When he first arrives at the Nicolais' home, he is enraged that Sylvia is there, intruding on his relationship with Brub (8). Later, even though Sylvia is flirtatious with and sexually attracted to him, he envies what the Nicolais have and even Brub's obliviousness to his wife's interest in other men. At times, he feels guilty for interfering in their marriage, for drawing loyalty and interest toward him, but he also sees them as deluded: "happiness was made of quicksilver, it ran out of your hand like quicksilver.... To hell with happiness. More important was excitement and power and the hot stir of lust. Those made you forget. They made happiness a pink marshmallow" (20). He wants a love big enough to make him forget what he has gone through, and a love short of that may not be worth having. Fittingly, in Brub's moment of sympathy for the killer, being alone is what seems most painful: "I honestly don't think he ever does escape. He has to live with himself. He's caught there in that lonely place" (80). Being alone with one's urges is the real danger.

IN THE COURSE OF A NORMAL RELATIONSHIP: THE MEANING OF MARRIAGE IN *A STREETCAR NAMED DESIRE*

Dix and Hammer share the desire for real, companionate, domestic love with Mitch, the secondary male character of *Streetcar*. While Stanley's bombast and rage are similar to Hammer's, Mitch's "good guy" is tellingly similar as well. *A Streetcar Named Desire* follows the arrival and intrusion of the eccentric and aging Blanche DuBois into the lives of her sister, Stella, and Stella's husband, Stanley Kowalski. Blanche is emotionally disturbed and, as the play unfolds, the characters and the audience become privy to her history: having revealed his sexual liaisons with other men, Blanche's husband, Allan, committed suicide (and Blanche feels responsible, having shamed him). After this trauma, Blanche began to engage in sex (likely, but not necessarily or exclusively, for money) with American GIs waiting at the port to serve abroad. When the war is over, she seeks sexual succor elsewhere: she seduces a high school student under her charge and is dismissed from her post as an English teacher at a private school. Having lost the family's estate (Belle Reve) through her irresponsible behavior, she is forced to live at the Kowalski's'. While there, Blanche becomes romantically involved with Mitch, Stanley's more retiring best friend and war buddy. Passive-aggressively abusive of her sister, perpetually deceptive, and an intolerable nuisance to her brother-in-law, Blanche is unwilling or unable to leave until she is taken away to a mental institution after Stanley rapes her.

Almost as soon as we meet Mitch, we are made aware of his desire to marry (scene 3). He is afraid to be alone, especially because his friends are all married and his mother is dying. Seeing Stanley's dependence on Stella (and he sees such dependence among his other friends as well), he does not wish to avoid it, but to accept this dependence. Furthermore, he defends the Kowalskis' turbulent marriage, recognizing it as the only way by which Stanley and Stella can negotiate postwar intimacy. When Blanche is terrified by the intensity of their fights, Mitch offers his perspective: "There's nothing to be afraid of. They're crazy about each other. . . . It's a shame that this had to happen when you just got here. But don't take it serious." Love, for Mitch, is enough: he and those around him feel there is no alternative.

Stella later describes and explains the fight similarly. She tells Blanche that, "it wasn't anywhere as serious as you seem to take it. In the first place, when men are drinking and playing poker anything can happen. It's always a powder-keg" (scene 4). When Blanche remains aghast, Stella goes on, "No, it isn't all right for anybody to make such a terrible row, but—people do sometimes." And finally she admits to her sister that she sometimes finds Stanley's violence "thrill[ing]." Stella's progression in the scene represents her overall approach to her marriage: she accepts what she must accept ("anything can happen . . . it isn't all right . . . but—people do sometimes") and she allows herself even to find it attractive. Stella has eroticized the very difficulty of her marriage.

Mitch identifies the complexity of both lust and intimacy between veterans and their female partners in his own relationship with Blanche. While he defends the disconcerting manner in which Stanley and Stella relate, he also polices gender boundaries in other ways. However, Stanley sometimes joins him. Both men, for example, are concerned about Stella and Blanche's proximity to their poker games.

The landscape of Mitch's desires and aims, then, does not run parallel to, but intersects with Stanley's. However unlikely this appears through most of the play, Mitch too is motivated by masculine pride, entitlement, and sexual compulsion. Blanche piques his interest through flattery and through her self-presentation as an "exotic" and highly sensual woman. Enraged as Mitch is at her past sexual transgressions, his desire for her was partly rooted in his intuiting of her sexual experience. While Blanche has lied, cheated, and stolen, she garners our sympathy in the last scene she shares with Mitch not only because of the physical threat she is under, but also because Mitch's hidden rage and entitlement have risen to the surface. His performance matches hers: they both actively seek and want a happy married life, but neither of them can handle the emotional intimacy required for it. It is not overstating the case to say that the war experience of each has had a part in making this intimacy intolerable. Mitch cannot handle Blanche's prostitution to and affairs with soldiers, nor her many sexual transgressions; Blanche is more clearly readable as Mitch's victim.

Mitch, for his part, almost demands to be sexually desired in the manner of Stanley, and Blanche tries to comply. Blanche is aware enough of the connection between masculine pride and a man's sense of his own intimidating qualities, so she flatters Mitch by telling him how "imposing" he is and he responds by asking her to punch him in the stomach. She responds with her hand to her chest: "Gracious! . . . Oh my goodness me. It's awe inspiring," satisfying Mitch's need to offset his "sensitive" "nice guy" persona with physical prowess. Mitch wants to have it both ways. He wants to be the sensitive man, loved for being good unlike Stanley. Yet, he cannot stifle his desire to be desired, and he sees the ways that Stanley and Steve's brutality evoke passion in the women around them, Blanche included.

Stella, unlike Blanche, accepts the intensity and importance of Stanley's bond with Mitch. As Larry Blades points out, the bond between the men is off-handedly set up by their shared service; their relationship need not be explained but by this shorthand.[20] Blanche's inability to understand this shorthand—the implication that the bond between Stanley and Mitch is paramount—leads to her feelings of betrayal and confusion. Of course, Stanley tells Mitch about Blanche's "checkered" sexual past with other soldiers since, after all, they "were in the same outfit together" (scene 7). Blanche is a fool to be surprised, but this "foolish" attitude toward the war is continuous with Blanche's perpetual denial of everything around her.

For example, Stella tells Blanche that Stanley was a Master Sergeant in the Engineer Corps, but Blanche insists that he must have been an officer. Blanche simply cannot recognize the appeal of Stanley's violence and she must elevate him to officer status. As Blades astutely puts it, "It probably makes Stella's marriage more acceptable [for Blanche] to see it as the result of an attraction to the glamour of 'an officer' rather than as the sexually charged and Dionysian relationship it actually is" (12). Blanche asks whether Stanley was in decorated uniform when Stella met him and Stella replies, "I assure you I wasn't just blinded by all the brass" (scene 6). Stella is attracted to what's beneath the decoration.

Though attracted to Stanley herself, Blanche fights this feeling and urges her sister to do the same: "some kind of people some tenderer feelings have had some little beginning! That we have got to make grow! And cling to, and hold as our flag! In this dark march toward whatever it is we are approaching . . . don't—don't hang back with the brutes!" (scene 4). Earlier in this scene, Blanche attributes Stanley's violence to an inherent unevolved primitivism, denying its potential roots in the war. Not long after, she suggests to Stanley and Stella that Stanley's behavior is rooted in his astrological sign: he is clearly, she assumes, an Aries. In fact, Stella tells her, he is a Capricorn, an astrological sign associated with temperance. Again, Blanche is unable to incorporate his war history into the narrative of his aggression. If she were to do so, she would have to acknowledge that Mitch might share these traits.

Blanche continually tries to "save" the men she meets, including Allan and Mitch, but she has neither the compassion nor the stamina to see it through. As Blanche describes her relationship with Allan: "He came to me for help . . . He was in the quicksands and clutching at me . . . [After Blanche finds out about Allan's homosexual affair] we pretended that nothing had been discovered . . . A few moments later a shot . . . It was because—on the dance floor—unable to stop myself—I'd suddenly said—'I saw! I know! You disgust me . . .'" (scene 6). Though Blanche "pretends," embellishes, and deceives throughout the play, when it comes to love, Blanche is incapable of "pretending that nothing" had happened, in the manner than Stella does to preserve her marriage. Even though Blanche herself believes that pretending would have been a kindness toward Allan, she is unable to maintain this pretense. Stella's path of resignation is the one which leads to heterosexual companionship. Stella's resignation is the "realism" that Blanche famously says that she doesn't want.

Blanche's is a cautionary tale: women must change their behavior to accommodate the changes in men. Her desire for younger men, in particular, is traceable to her disinterest in and unwillingness to change her notion of gender roles for postwar men whose wartime experiences have remade masculinity in a more disturbing image. This desire for younger men goes past her relationship with her seventeen-year-old student. Sexually aroused by Stanley and disappointed by Mitch, she attempts to seduce an adolescent paperboy at one point during the play.

Williams sets Stanley and Mitch's service in the Battle of Salerno, one of the most vicious battles in the European theater of the Second World War. While Salerno has faded behind other renowned battles in the decades since, it was prominent in the popular imagination in 1946, when Williams composed the play. September 14, 1943 was the climax of the battle, and the Allies declared victory the following day. Three years later, on September 15, 1946, Stanley rapes Blanche. As he begins the assault, Stanley says to her: "We've had this date with each other from the beginning." While perhaps a seemingly minor detail, Williams made a point of the date: the rape occurred on Blanche's birthday, which she points out falls on this date, a date known to many audiences for its anniversary significance. Given the emphasis on the date, Williams's use of September 15 warrants notice. Blanche expects Stanley to privilege their family connection—or, specifically, his love for Stella—over his relationship with Mitch, a relationship forged most deeply on this very date. (And, of course, she expects Mitch to privilege his love for her over any information Stanley gives him about her past.)

Again, while Blanche seems to be Stanley's most immediate and direct victim, Stella is the character for whom his actions will have the most day-to-day, hour-by-hour significance, presumably for the rest of their lives. Throughout the play, Stanley is obsessed with the idea of the "Napoleonic code," as it indicates that Blanche's irresponsible loss of Belle Reve is a transgression against his own finances, entitling him to investigate her decisions and to demand recourse. According to Stanley, this code says that, "whatever belongs to my wife is also mine—and vice versa" (scene 2). Stanley never indicates that he has ownership of anything to share with Stella. However, his war liabilities—his anger, alcohol abuse, and rape of Blanche—may in fact be the things included under "vice versa."

Part of what Stella accepts is the raucous macho atmosphere of her own home. Living in the urban space as she does, Stella must allow the poker games in her living room. She must allow her bond with Stanley to be rather particular: they relate primarily sexually. Her sexual satisfaction is, of course, related to her attraction to Stanley's brutish presence.

Williams, however, suggests not only that Mitch shares Stanley's more aggressive feelings, but also that Stanley, in fact, shares Mitch's more domestic, softer side. Clearly, Stanley and Stella relate to each other mostly via raw and powerful sexual attraction, but there is more to it. The famous "Stella!" scene portrays Stanley seized by another kind of longing, the longing for a homely, domestic, safe love. While we understand that Stanley and Stella make up through sex, this sex act is motivated by the profound vulnerability of both characters and their desire to put everything aside in order to create a family. The drama of this scene—perhaps the reason it resonated then and now—is partly rooted in a feeling of utter romantic desperation, as Stanley essentially begs Stella to save him. The drama for Stella is her compulsion to do that for him, a compulsion partly sexual, but also born out of a deep-seated resignation: this is what it means to love a man like Stanley or, perhaps, to love a man at all.

Stanley, more than any other character in the play, comes close to a safe domestic happy ending. We assume that he goes on to think that his loving wife believes his lie (that he did not rape her sister) and enjoys his newborn daughter. His home accommodates his dishonesty about and concealment of his past; he is loved anyway. Stella is expected and chooses to live with the knowledge of his crime, protecting herself and her child through denying this knowledge. This is her lot in life.

Blanche, however sympathetic at times, is undeniably dishonest, careless, and self-involved. Even if Mitch were to remain unaware of Blanche's deceptions until after their wedding, the potential for his happiness with her is compromised from the beginning. His rage is personal, but it also operates socially: Mitch's fastidious performance of normality—one in which he may have, to some extent, believed—entitles him to love and marriage. Unlike Stanley and other men, Mitch has consistently resisted his desires, privileging a stable future in a companionate relationship. Blanche's behavior deprives him of what he has earned.

In short, according to Eunice, Stanley, Stella, and Mitch, the chaotic relationship between the Kowalskis is "normal." Part of the tragedy of Blanche DuBois is that she cannot accept a "normal" relationship: she doesn't want postwar marital "reality." While few would argue that Williams is offering a blueprint for marriage, the ending certainly communicates that women must tolerate extreme violence in their male partners if they wish to have them at all. Blanche, of course, cannot tolerate Mitch's violence (nor her ex-husband, Allan's, irrepressible homosexual desire), so she is essentially driven mad with unfulfilled desire. Whereas Stella is turned on by Stanley's brutishness and indulges the relationship for this sexual frisson, this is not enough for Blanche.

ONWARD: ADAPTING SPILLANE, HUGHES, AND WILLIAMS TO THE 1950s

I, the Jury; In a Lonely Place; and *Streetcar* all suggest that notions of normality must be rethought for the postwar era. As I discuss throughout this book, assumptions about and methods for managing men's capacity for violence changed gradually over the following decade, such that these raw portrayals of the mid-to-late 1940s receded behind more mixed and hopeful perspectives of postwar readjustment. By the early 1950s, *In a Lonely Place, Streetcar,* and the Hammer series were all reworked in ways that suited these shifts. Among the several differences between the screen adaptation of *Streetcar* and the original play, two are most important. The screenplay omits Stanley's line, "We've had this date with each other from the beginning," a moment which emphasizes the connection between the Battle of Salerno and Blanche's rape, positioning her assault as inevitable. Though the film does show his military decorations, it downplays Stanley's combat experiences.

Even more significantly, censor Joe Breen demanded that Stanley be punished for the rape, so Stella leaves him at the close of the film, taking their child with her. In the play, of course, Stella stays with Stanley, accepting or ignoring his brutality. While this version revokes Stanley's semi-happy ending, its conclusion acknowledges that his behavior is "abnormal" or, at least, unacceptable for Stella. Ostensibly, Stella can find a better man or may in fact be better off without a man at all. Perhaps Stanley himself can become a better man if he accepts his penance. Certainly, both Stanley and Mitch must contemplate their losses.

In a Lonely Place undergoes a similarly significant transformation: in Edmund North and Andrew Solt's screenplay, Dix is not the killer. He *seems* like a killer because he frequently overreacts in rage, but he is actually just a threatening man. Whereas the novel's Dix looked normal, but wasn't (or at least his normality falls on the farthest end of a very wide spectrum), Bogart's Dix looks abnormal, but essentially isn't. Dix does not end up marrying his girlfriend Laurel; he flies into a rage when he detects that she plans to leave him but stops short of harming her. However, potentially, both can find true love one day. Of course, in the film, true love is possible. Unlike in the novel in which Sylvia's love for Brub is suspect, Jeff Donnell's simple Sylvia seems truly devoted to Frank Lovejoy's Brub, and their home life seems basically ideal, though not glamorous as in the novel. Importantly, though, there is one scene in which Dix's presence seems to complicate the relationship between Brub and his wife. Reenacting the Atkinson murder after dinner at the Nicolais' house, Brub mock-chokes Sylvia and does so a bit too realistically for comfort. When Dix leaves, Sylvia is anxious about Dix, and she praises Brub for being different from him, for being "attractive and average."

This formulation is fascinating, given the book's emphasis on Dix's ladykiller persona, but also because of the novel's preoccupation with normality, ordinariness, and averageness. In the novel, the fact that Dix is a bit dangerous and is physically very attractive leads to flirtation with Sylvia and other women. Dix's sex appeal is actually a (marginal) threat to the Nicolais' relationship. The film conflates attractiveness and averageness (here figured as "safety" and "niceness"), which means there is nothing about Dix worth imitating. Peter Biskind reads the film as a conservative paean to normality: Brub and Sylvia are "average" which is what Dix should aspire to, and this line, among others, supports this perspective.[21]

Spillane's Hammer goes on to become a sicker and sicker sadist in the future novels, each of which ends with a drawn-out murder scene, like the one in *I, the Jury*. Quite possibly in response to the emergence of the James Bond novels and other spy paperbacks, the Hammer series becomes more narratively complex and broader in scope, involving international mystery and politics, and Hammer himself experiences more torture and trauma. But, also as the Hammer series progresses, Spillane begins to develop an argument for Hammer's sadism: Mike is by nature a vulnerable man, but his violence was enabled and trained by the war, and his relationship with Charlotte—the thwarted possibility for "normal" happiness—drove him into a life of violence over which he is, in some sense, powerless. "Normality" was taken away from him and his life is now ruled by his conviction that he was robbed: he maims and kills to deal with the trauma of Charlotte's betrayal as well as his war experiences.

The fact that Spillane's work becomes increasingly violent in the 1950s seems counter to the film adaptations of the other works, but Spillane's novels were concurrently adapted for the screen: *I, the Jury* appeared in 1953 and an adaptation of *Kiss Me Deadly* (Robert Aldrich) in 1955. *My Gun Is Quick* (Phil Victor and George White) was not adapted until 1957, and screenwriters Richard Powell and Richard Collins made radical changes. Nancy (Whitney Blake) is murdered by the novel's villains, but she is the key villain in the screen version, which omits the deadly fire, ending instead with Hammer (Robert Bray) handing Nancy over to the police, a move completely out of his vigilante character. The film is less violent, of course, but it is also no longer about Hammer's self-loathing, guilt, and shame.

The final scene of *I, the Jury* was different in the film, but only barely. The chilling final moment in Spillane's novel remains intact, as Hammer articulates a culture's deepest fear. Hammer (Biff Elliott), trained and desensitized by the war, enraged by the death of his beloved brother-in-arms, looks at Charlotte (Peggie Castle) as he shoots her. She looks at up at him in pain ("the pain preceding death") holding her gunshot wound, and asks him "How c-could you?" Hammer "had only a moment before talking to a corpse but I got it in. 'It was easy,' I said" (147).

TWO

"DO WE BECOME WHAT WE DO?"

—

Glenn Ford and Van Heflin in Hollywood

Pulp novels show an unmistakable starkness of right and wrong, and a black-and-white, fatalistic perspective on men's relationships with each other and with women. Men, particularly veterans, cannot help but slip into violence: any relationship with any party will likely provoke it and, once it begins, it will surely finish with rape, murder, or both. These men scarcely attempt to avoid criminal actions or cruelty, and the women around them find those uncontrollable urges appealing, even if they lead to their own victimization. These texts offer an image of postwar white masculinity as an unfixable problem, and an unstoppable menace. To a large extent, this uncomplicated, singular portrayal of unmoored, dangerous masculinity is a product of the years immediately after the war: it is not unchallenged in the years that follow.

In the late 1940s and 1950s, Hollywood was responding to economic and political shifts, including the 1948 antitrust ruling against Paramount Pictures.[1] Because casting and casting direction were entirely different in the twilight of the studio system, the careers of second-tier actors were not just accumulations of directors' perceptions and agent–studio machinations, as is often the case among Hollywood-made actors in the years that follow.[2] Coincidence, long-term studio contracts, and availability informed—often even determined—the roles an actor was able to play. Because the studios maintained a hold on many players even into the 1950s, it was difficult for actors to gain the independence to fully participate in selecting their own roles, managing their own publicity, controlling their own schedules, and, therefore, crafting their own personas. However, the late 1940s and early 1950s were a time in which the very notion of the "actor" changed. Some of these changes took place from a labor perspective, as actors advanced their own agency and sought to establish autonomy. Other changes took place as the public began to take the actor's craft seriously and to view him as a professional and as an artist.

Hollywood actors in the 1940s and 1950s, inspired by the earlier activism of technicians and writers, engaged in strikes and took on the studios in court, seeking improved working conditions, but also limitations on the control that the studios had over their long-term careers.[3] Olivia de Havilland, best-known for her Oscar-nominated turn as Melanie Hamilton Wilkes in *Gone with the Wind* (Victor Fleming, 1939), famously sued Warner Bros., her home studio, for nearly a decade. Wishing to avoid typecasting, de Havilland eschewed scripts in which she would have played a weak ingenue. Backed by the increasingly powerful Screen Actors Guild (SAG), she won her court case, inaugurating the De Havilland Law, which declared that studios could not hold actors under contract for a day over seven years. The ruling diminished the power of the studios, but, just as importantly, it implied that film actors were artists. Furthermore, not only were actors artists to the extent that they could *play* a role, but their *choosing* of a role actually became an element of their creative self-expression. Following this triumph, SAG mounted a campaign against typecasting in 1950. SAG President Ronald Reagan and other union spokespeople argued that "an actor who is established in the public mind as the portrayer of one particular role [should not be prevented] from being given the opportunity to display his acting talents in other types of roles."[4]

Again, an actor's choices of roles, not just inside of roles, are critical to his work as an artist. The De Havilland Law and the SAG protests, along with the shifts in acting training and approaches, contributed to the growing appraisal of actors as artists, rather than the tools of a director, producer, studio, or all three. Not only were those in the industry being forced to see actors differently, but actors asserted themselves as professionals, as laborers, in the public eye.

Some actors became primarily or partially defined by their portrayals of men at war. Two such actors were James Edwards and Van Johnson, though their biographies and performance styles differed. Importantly, Edwards served as first lieutenant of the US Army during World War II, while Johnson was designated 4-F after a disfiguring car accident, which left him with a metal plate in his head.

Johnson's status provided him many wartime opportunities to play servicemen, which some GIs resented, especially as he became nearly emblematic of them (especially aviators).[5] Referring to his whirlwind of servicemen roles, he joked, "I didn't know which branch of the service I was in!"[6] His box office popularity peaked immediately following the war: film exhibitors ranked Johnson second and third in popularity in 1945 and 1946, respectively. Johnson ultimately appeared in some of the finest combat films of the wartime and postwar period, including *A Guy Named Joe* (Victor Fleming, 1943), *Thirty Seconds Over Tokyo* (Mervyn LeRoy, 1944), *Command Decision* (Sam Wood, 1949), *Battleground* (William Wellman, 1949), *Go for Broke!* (Robert Pirosh, 1951), and *The Caine Mutiny* (Edward Dmytryk, 1954), as well as many lesser-known combat films, and played servicemen in several films not set in combat. Though many of the films offered complex portrayals of combat distress and he played characters experiencing regret and injury, Johnson was known for his image of "innocence" that homefront girls found "comforting," and critics praised for "heart and simplicity."[7] Because Johnson cut his teeth as a dancer and social club entertainer, with no formal theatrical training, he was well-positioned to play these roles.

James Edwards, on the other hand, earned a master's degree in Theater at Northwestern University on the GI Bill and went on to develop a serious acting pedigree, becoming affiliated early on with Langston Hughes and Helen Spaulding's Skyloft Players. Returning seriously injured from his Army service and struggling with anxiety about his injuries, Edwards pursued acting in place of his doctor's suggestion to undergo therapy. In his own words, "If I hadn't been in the Army, I guess I never would have become an actor."

Though he was recognized by critics in smaller parts right away, his stage portrayal of Army officer Brett Charles in *Deep Are the Roots* allowed him to shift into leading man parts on both stage and screen. Edwards understudied to imminent actor Gordon Heath in Elia Kazan's production and understudied to Henry Scott in Chicago, but became the breakout star when the play came to Los Angeles. Having served honorably and been treated well during his service in Europe, Brett is rightly appalled by the racism he faces in the American South upon his return. The play does not diminish the extreme prejudice to which African American servicemen were subjected; though Brett is only implicated in petty theft, his relationship with a white woman makes him a target for lynching when in jail for such a minor crime.

Playwrights Arnaud d'Usseau and James Gow represented the dangerous conditions for African Americans in the postwar South, even anticipating the Moore's Ford lynching of 1946, in which George W. and Mae Murray Dorsey, and Roger and Dorothy Malcom were shot and killed by four white men in Georgia. World War II veteran George W. Dorsey had only been back in the US for eight months after five years serving in the Pacific when he was murdered. Only months prior, the confrontations later referred to as the "Columbia Race Riots" took place in Tennessee.[8] The events were instigated by Billy Fleming, a white man, who threatened Gladys Stephenson, mother of Black Navy veteran (and trained boxer) James Stephenson. James Stephenson fought back. A white mob gathered at the scene and Stephenson was later arrested for attempted murder and threatened with lynching. After a horrific night in which armed white men invaded the Black business district, shooting randomly, and Black men armed themselves and shot at streetlamps to protect their community and property, state highway patrolmen entered the neighborhood, shooting and looting, conducting warrantless searches, illegally confiscating hundreds of weapons owned by Black citizens, and arresting 100 Black men for various (often trumped-up) charges. Two days later, white policemen killed two Black inmates and injured another in an armed confrontation that took place during an interrogation. Though this ended the violence in Columbia, the threats to and harassment of African Americans did not end there, nor did it end immediately following the many related court cases: Black and white men were tried, but only Lloyd Kennedy—a Black resident of Columbia—served time. These two events are only the most extreme examples of the widespread terror Black Southerners experienced in the postwar years. D'Usseau and Gow articulate a parallel message in their authors note: the play is about the "cruel and irrational things that prejudice leads people to do."[9] Brett is fundamentally good, but the white characters around him prove duplicitous at best, terrorists at worse.

Working with this script no doubt prepared Edwards for the role of his career as Private Peter Moss in *Home of the Brave* (Robson, 1949). Crucially though, Edwards learned the differences between stage and screen performances, saying that his colleague Robert Ryan pointed out these nuances: "On the stage, you express emotion more or less with complete freedom; on the stage, mostly with the eyes with very little facial contortions." It is safe to say that Edwards is among the masters of this style of screen acting in the postwar era and his performance in *Home of the Brave* is arguably the best example.

In *Home of the Brave*, Moss joins a unit of white men in the Pacific for what seems like a suicide mission. It turns out that his former best friend, Finch (Lloyd Bridges), serves in this white unit. The two have become estranged due to Moss's assumption that, deep down, Finch is like the other racist white men around him. These racist white men include Corporal TJ (Steve Brodie) who provokes and insults Moss from the moment he joins the group, even giving his own imitation of a subservient Black man to Moss's horror. Ultimately, Finch dies in Moss's arms and Moss goes into business with another of his "band of brothers," Mingo (Frank Lovejoy). The film's framing device is Moss's psychiatric treatment for paralysis—he is unable to walk for reasons the doctor assumes are psychosomatic. Indeed, his illness is linked in part to Finch's death, but revealed to be about much more: Moss is paralyzed by the feeling that he is "different" and frustration and sadness that he has submitted to racism throughout his life. In the film's most memorable moment, the doctor prompts Moss's psychological breakthrough by screaming a racial slur at him. Shaken, Moss resolves never to let racial prejudice hold him back again. His paralysis is healed. As Pamala Deane documents, not everyone found the film convincing, but Edwards's performance stands out. Viewers of other postwar cinema cannot help but notice Edwards's particular vulnerability: Moss's eyes fill with tears several times in response to the racist attitudes aimed at him, not just at the death of his war buddy and longtime friend. In Donald Bogle's words, he is the "postwar good sensitive Black man."[10] He is not "the strong and silent type" by any means, but he is far from the Method actor pursuing suffering. In fact, Edwards and his colleagues Sidney Poitier and Harry Belafonte were well-served by and impeccable practitioners of this acting style. The style itself offered Black men in 1940s Hollywood an alternative to what Bogle calls "The Entertainers" and "The Problem People."

Like Johnson, Edwards would go on to embody the GI, playing servicemen in many significant war films, including *The Steel Helmet* (Samuel Fuller, 1951), *Bright Victory* (Robson, 1951), *Battle Hymn* (Sirk, 1957), *Men in War*

(Anthony Mann, 1957), *Pork Chop Hill* (Lewis Milestone, 1959), *Blood and Steel* (Bernard L. Kowalski, 1959), and a bit part in *The Caine Mutiny* with Johnson. Also like Johnson, he would play men outside the service, but be defined by his military roles.

The state of Hollywood film in the postwar period accommodated—even demanded—a greater variety of images than either the war films or the pulp paperback examples might suggest. As marriages and families were built both on screen and in the "real world," the meanings for masculinity became more various and some of its prospects more cautiously optimistic. Though the issues in Hollywood film did not entirely change, the possibilities for their portrayal were expanded, which allowed for the rise of everyman actors like Van Heflin and Glenn Ford, even as Bogart and Brando offered their stylish and memorable performances. Heflin and Ford were in many more films than Brando and a wider variety of performances than Bogart and, therefore, show other sides of masculinity in postwar Hollywood. By virtue of their professional approaches and veteran identities, Heflin and Ford were able to portray an array of masculinities, including versions of the "everyman," whose relationships with both men and women, beliefs and feelings about family and sexuality, and susceptibility to violence varied but drew on each actor's prior roles. Heflin and Ford play many variations on the two "types" of men that I discuss in the introduction: the "man who does" express sexuality and violence and the "man who doesn't." Not simply "good guys" and "bad guys," both harbored the same urges, but struggled with and controlled them differently. The "man who doesn't" represents a faith in both free will and the inherent goodness of man to protect women and children, whereas the "man who does" reveals a terror that free will and goodness were only delusions. This chapter argues that Heflin and Ford represent a gamut of masculinities which are nonetheless caught up in similar themes, not that either consistently played a single "type," nor that Hollywood offered a coherent masculinity or message. Heflin and Ford are by no means the only men whose performances can stand up to such readings, but their careers overall offer a clarity which should shed light on the rest of postwar Hollywood. In the rest of this chapter, I will read many films briefly rather than single films closely, touching on multiple genres and collaborations in order to illustrate the cumulative impact of each actor's catalogue and to address the parameters of the postwar white masculinities that Heflin and Ford embodied, closing with their performances together in *3:10 to Yuma* (Delmer Daves, 1957).

MORE THAN A METHOD: ACTORS' TENSION VERSUS REPRESSION

Most scholarship on film acting focuses mostly, or even exclusively, on Method actors and their training. The Method not only defined a mode of training, it eventually became the mark of seriousness and boldness that went beyond the specific techniques that these actors used. Our understanding of film acting and actors since the 1950s is so heavily invested in the notion of the Method (and other Method-influenced immersive techniques) that, on this, film historians and audiences are typically in accord. "Heroic" actors are almost always in thrall to some aspect—however revised—of Strasberg's, Adler's, or (the original) Stanislavski's principles. In Graham McCann's study of Method actors Montgomery Clift, Marlon Brando, and James Dean, he credits them with "[seeking] out roles that led to suffering."[11] R. Barton Palmer adds that their embrace of these roles "challeng[ed] conventional notions of what constituted entertainment" and that the films in which these actors appeared were superior to most cinematic efforts of the 1950s: "[most other] Hollywood films of the decade did not indulge in such powerful, disturbing anatomies of the self."[12]

It is safe to say that these approaches have taken hold to a large extent, even outside of Method-identified actors, studios, productions, and training programs, such that actors who refuse these techniques—and even directors who avoid their direct invocations—are often taken less seriously as artists. But this perception of appropriate study for actors is anachronistic. In the 1940s, when Heflin and Ford emerged, this expectation was less common, and the reputations of these men as "expert"—Oscar- and BAFTA-winning Heflin in particular—were not compromised by their non-Method approach. As with their near-absence in the tabloids, Ford and Heflin's (at least partial) refusal of the Method has likely played a role in their seemingly premature disappearance from treatments of postwar cinema.

The fact that they did not vow allegiance to the Method does not mean that Heflin and Ford's performances were shallow. On the contrary, that may have been what playing characters of their generation demanded. It is also possible that, like their characters, their own wartime experiences made Method-style approaches dangerous for them on a personal level as well. Heflin and Ford ought to be studied alongside Method icons like Brando and Dean because their performance styles and acting philosophies show a minute, but significant, generational rift: the "narcissistic" Strasbergian Method was the very opposite of what the veteran generation wanted to pursue or, perhaps, was capable of. Leo Braudy, one of the only scholars ever to touch upon Ford's acting, makes a passing, but stunningly clear distinction between the two styles in his discussion of "Actors and Objects," contrasting "Kazan-Brando tension" with "Fritz Lang-Glenn Ford repression."[13] Because Method-oriented discussions of acting have become customary, Braudy's use of the word "repression" seems like damning criticism. "True acting" is supposed to be the opposite of repression. Yet even this privileging of Method technique restricts our ability to view the films of the 1940s and 1950s with clarity. What Naremore calls the "introspective, neurotic style" that characterized Method performances by men was counter to the very demands of day-to-day postwar masculinity and would have been, therefore, unrealistic and possibly even false for Generation GI.[14] Women were scared of men and men were scared of themselves. Wallowing in the deep recesses of the soul was not a way to inhabit many of the characters these men portrayed. In fact, these men played characters who were often working to *avoid* being in touch with these deep recesses. The closer they got to plumbing their depths, the closer the characters got to being punished for it. While Dean's Rebel, Joe Stark, could sob to his father in an effort to heal their relationship, that depth of emotion was a risk that Ford's David Bannion or Heflin's Peter Denver took only at their peril. When they let themselves slip, they ended up like Ford in *The Big Heat* (Fritz Lang, 1953): surrounded by dead bodies. Only when they didn't could they, like *Shane*'s Joe Starrett, find any hope for peace and stability, those twin demands of postwar American men.

THE TWO BODIES OF THE ACTOR

Understanding an actor's training and approach is only one element of understanding his performances. As with actors who were more unequivocally stars, Heflin and Ford's very physical presences evoked a plethora of associations. Though this would vary according to the viewer's viewing history, we might say that Heflin and Ford—like all established actors—carried in their faces, voices, and bodies an incredible backlog of characters, each of which might emerge or wane within a new performance. As such, it is never just their performances themselves—their approach, physicality, or vocal qualities—but also the very words they speak and the texts that they inhabit, the other actors with whom they interact, and their diegetic relations with them—which carry through their careers and are evoked by their simply being on-screen.

Richard Maltby, in his book *Hollywood*, claims that the star has "two bodies": one of which is the form consumed across various films, and the other the single character belonging to the single film.[15] Maltby's dialectic is useful because, unlike most notions within star studies, it offers a picture of the star that is not integrated and, as such, not a stable "product." The existence of the second body, the body of the single character, gives the performers we study the chance to be viewed as actors, rather than complexes of material accumulated outside the performances (in the manner of most star studies). However, the first body continues to be incredibly alluring and tremendously illuminating for cultural historians, even when that body belongs to someone only peripherally a star.

By the time Ford and Heflin met as Ben Wade and Dan Evans, respectively, they were dragging a great deal of character baggage behind them. Though *3:10 to Yuma* has already been the subject of scholarship—however occasional and glancing—these treatments have suffered from the oversight so common to textual readings of film: the extratextual resonance of this baggage. The deeply unsettling, strangely familiar quality of *3:10 to Yuma* is partially rooted in the element that these treatments ignore.

A major hurdle for studying actors who are not strictly stars is that there is relatively little to go on in determining how audiences actually viewed them. Despite this limitation, it seems important to speculate: why were these actors cast as frequently and prominently as they were, even without legions of swooning women and envious men? Though their service had downsides, the fact that these men had served in World War II, in my opinion, can hardly be exaggerated.

Like many successful actors in the early 1940s who served in World War II, they found themselves in far less demand upon their return. Most never expected that their service would compromise their careers, but "[in] 1945 some of the Hollywood players would begin to realize their vulnerability. Returning veterans were seeking to replace the wartime leading men, and usually even the biggest names like [Clark] Gable were having difficulty re-establishing themselves."[16] This displacement exacerbated the insecurities many already felt about the impact of their service on their acting abilities. As James Stewart put it, "When you've been away for four and a half years, you know, maybe you forget how to act. Maybe the whole thing's gone."[17] Stewart, like Ford, Heflin, and many others, only improved after the war, but it took time for them to get their second chances.

Though their status as veterans would seem to make them attractive choices for soldier parts during the war movie boom, they found it difficult to compete with those actors who had attained or maintained passionate followings on the home front during the conflict. Established actors who were classified 4-F (or sometimes I-H)—including Gregory Peck, Gary Cooper, Ray Milland, and others—were offered more and better parts. Some men with 4-F status—like Johnson—managed to *start* enormously successful movie careers in the absence of other talent to fill key roles. Ironically, some of the actors who most famously played servicemen in the postwar period—including Johnson, Peck, Sinatra, John Wayne, Dana Andrews, and Montgomery Clift—were those determined unfit to fight. But, after a brief period of underuse just after the war, both Heflin and Ford managed to overcome this setback.

A bit younger and greener than Heflin, Ford had fewer bone fides and contacts to exploit when he was discharged from the Marines. Though he was well reviewed as a Jewish teenager fleeing Nazi persecution (and falling in love in the meantime) in *So Ends Our Night* (John Cromwell, 1941) and mostly held his own with more seasoned actors in *Texas* (George Marshall, 1941), his inexperience was glaring, and he was, for the most part, still an unknown quantity. Ford had the extreme good fortune of catching Cohn's eye just when the Columbia mogul was desperately seeking an appropriate co-star for Rita Hayworth, his prized creation and a wartime favorite of servicemen.[18] Ford was quickly dropped into a brooding, romantic, but complicated lead opposite Hayworth in *Gilda*, in which he proved himself a far more sophisticated actor after the war than he had been before it. The film propelled him to prominence inside Columbia, just as the studio began its ascent from a minor to a relative major after the Paramount decision. Ford was also in a relatively unique contract position as the Paramount decision fell, since MGM and Columbia negotiated a sharing agreement over him after his success in *Gilda*. MGM maintained major status, but Columbia boomed after the Paramount decision, making Ford's (now more negotiable) contract apparently more valuable.[19] However, even Ford was anxious to escape the limitations of a studio contract. James Mason spoke of Ford "counting the days until he is free of his contract with Columbia," but said the studio planned to "sweat the last ounce out of him before he is out of their clutches."[20]

Meanwhile, Heflin complained bitterly to the press about being ignored after his return from Europe with the Ninth Air Force; he made no secret of his desire to get out of his contract with MGM in order to seek more frequent and more interesting roles. He had reason to be bitter. After a brief, canceled contract with RKO and some time back on the New York stage, he was signed to MGM and placed in mostly simple, thankless roles until (and after) *Johnny Eager* (LeRoy, 1942). His knockout performance as poetry-quoting, alcoholic Jeff Harnett, desperately in love with Robert Taylor's "Johnny," earned MGM their only Oscar in 1943. He then starred in two back-to-back "B" crime pictures, *Kid Glove Killer* (Zinneman, 1942) and *Grand Central Murder* (S. Sylvan Simon, 1942), and was cast as President Andrew Johnson in *Tennessee Johnson* (William Dieterle, 1943), MGM's expensive and most notorious disaster of the 1940s. Priding himself on his loyalty to his employer, he was angry at MGM's non-reciprocity.[21] He was relieved when Mayer loaned him out to Paramount for *The Strange Love of Martha Ivers* (Lewis Milestone, 1946) with Barbara Stanwyck, through which he was able to resurrect his career: he received unfailingly rave reviews and the film itself was a success.[22] MGM immediately saw his value and began to cast him in some of their largest-scale, highest-budget productions of the late 1940s, including *Till the Clouds Roll By* (Richard Whorf, 1947), *The Three Musketeers* (George Sidney, 1948), *Madame Bovary* (Vincente Minelli, 1949), and *Green Dolphin Street* (Victor Saville, 1947). MGM also lent him out to Warner Bros. for *Possessed* (Curtis Bernhardt, 1947) and Universal for *Tap Roots* (George Marshall, 1948) during that time. But, as his MGM contract ran out, it was clear that he had very few remaining chances to be a leading man.

From a star studies angle, the sometimes weakness of their careers might disqualify Heflin and Ford from close study, but the impacts that these men made as performers share similarities with even the era's biggest icons. Since star studies has given us the opportunity to look at the associations that each star brought to each part, we can apply this methodology to seemingly lesser actors. Also, the fact that Heflin and Ford were able to play more and more variety of roles than the biggest stars of their day gave them each a wider swath of affiliations between "types," characters, and genres in their performance histories. By the time Heflin and Ford met in *3:10 to Yuma*, each brought over a decade of associations and roles of greater and lesser renown, including roles neither would have chosen, even roles their agents and directors would not have chosen for them. Even economic necessity was not behind many of these choices, but chance certainly was.

Many GIs had great affection for actors—mostly singers and comedians, though Bogart was an exception—who performed in USO and Canteen environments, but it is not difficult to understand why men who spent years in combat, or otherwise separated from their families and distant from their homes, might resent actors who meanwhile managed to collect enormous paychecks, golf in Beverly Hills, lunch at the Brown Derby, and inspire the fantasies of home front women. Certainly this resentment would not end on VJ Day. Though audiences—including men, of course—turned out in force for many films starring 4-F men and others who had not served, including war films, Heflin and Ford, with their fairly average looks and seemingly average wartime experiences, might have been seen as "men's men," and were unquestionably viewed differently from the day's "matinee idols." Cohan writes about "the standard version of hegemonic masculinity that all American men were supposed to have shared"—the transition from war service to marriage and fatherhood—and these actors were ideal for the roles that forwarded this "version" of "hegemonic masculinity" in ways that many other Hollywood players simply were not.[23]

MEN TOGETHER ACROSS THE 1940s: FROM *JOHNNY EAGER* TO *GILDA*, FROM *TEXAS* TO *THE MAN FROM COLORADO*

As chapter 1 explores, men's relationships with each other were suspect in the postwar era: these bonds could evoke dangerous impulses in both men, and it was unlikely that either could submerge these impulses and be good, stable men. Examining Heflin and Ford's roles over the course of the 1940s shows that alternative narratives exist and that on-screen relationships between men changed during this period. First of all, homosexual relations were rethought after the war. Further, some films even offered the possibility that the "man who doesn't" could retain his "goodness" in spite of his dangerous intimacies with the "man who does," which anticipate *Shane* and *3:10 to Yuma* in the 1950s.

In addition to being veterans, Heflin and Ford share another fascinating similarity: each had an early, defining role as a man romantically or sexually involved with another man. Heflin's Oscar-winning performance and Ford's breakout role were neither as heterosexuals. Spaced four years apart, the differences between these roles are indicative of the changed views of homosexual relations from before and after the war. Released just over a month after the bombing of Pearl Harbor, and filmed beforehand, Mervyn LeRoy's *Johnny Eager* offered a truly miserable picture of an apparently gay man.[24] Heflin's Jeff Hartnett is desperately in unrequited love with Taylor's Johnny Eager, a butch, criminal ladies' man, involved with no less than Lana Turner (not to mention Patricia Dane and Glenda Farrell). There is no indication that Jeff has ever had a sexual relationship with Johnny, but Jeff's desire for Johnny is intense and crippling. A sensitive, erudite young man, Jeff becomes inescapably involved in the criminal underworld through his connection to Johnny, which he admits to seeing as brutal and beneath him. Drunk and self-critical through the duration of the film, he explains his need for more and more alcohol: "Every now and then, I have to look in a mirror." He loathes himself for what his desire for Johnny has wrought. Jeff is finally reduced to utter solitude, after sobbing and cradling Johnny, dead of a gunshot wound, in his arms. Since he has devoted his life to Johnny's service, it is difficult to imagine a future for Jeff. This tearful, theatrical, yet surprisingly subtle performance certainly warranted Heflin's Oscar for Best Supporting Actor. When he accepted the award, in uniform, from presenter Gary Cooper, he had few to thank: LeRoy, MGM and Louis B. Mayer, the New York Theater "for training me," and the United States Army.

After he returned from World War II, Ford was cast as Johnny Farrell in Charles Vidor's *Gilda*. Quite unlike Heflin's Jeff, who pathetically clings to Johnny Eager, the film's protagonist and title role, Ford's Johnny is the key character in *Gilda*, offering voiceover as well as the anchoring performance. Almost immediately, Johnny meets Ballin Mundson (George Macready), an older dandy in possession of a distinctly phallic cane, over which the two exchange a sort of sadomasochistic tête-à-tête. Johnny's flirtations with Mundson are pragmatic: he offers to show "how faithful and obedient I can be for a nice salary," and promises Mundson that there will be no women in his life. This intention, however honest, is undermined by Mundson's surprising marriage to the irresistible Gilda (Hayworth), with whom Johnny has previously been and will soon be involved. Johnny's shock at Mundson's marriage is only barely coded.[25] Both Mundson and Gilda are aware that Johnny has been with both men and women; Mundson asks Johnny simply to put that in his past and out of his mind and Gilda makes no distinction by gender in her jealousies. After Mundson's violent death, Johnny and Gilda run off together, in a complicated happily-ever-after.

Heflin's homosexual-before-the-war is a man with specific attractions, desires, and love for another man: his sexuality is the opposite of fluid. He is disgusted by the women who make advances toward him and only has eyes for Johnny Eager. Jeff does not want to be a criminal, but his undying love for Johnny forces him to live that life. Ford's bisexual-after-the-war does not appear to feel love for anyone of either gender. He is sexually pragmatic with Mundson and overpoweringly attracted to Gilda. And, though Johnny is jealous of Gilda's relationship with Mundson, he is most jealous that he has lost his exclusive hold on both. Indeed, he is angry at Gilda for her power over him and his power over Mundson. It is fitting that Gilda is played by Hayworth, a favorite wartime pinup. Like untold number of men at war, Johnny is willing to have sex with Mundson while away from home in Argentina, even though his most intense sexual desire is for Gilda/Hayworth. What's more, Ford's Johnny is the narrator and the viewer surrogate; his liaisons with the same sex do not disqualify him from being the masculine protagonist. Jeff, on the other hand, is relegated to a depressing supporting role.

The relationships that Jeff and Johnny Eager and Johnny Farrell and Mundson share are not unique in 1940s Hollywood, by any means, though such relationships were rare.[26] Far more common were the friendships between men that I detail in the introduction and chapter 1, in which men manage to coax each other—implicitly or explicitly—into violence. Yet, Heflin and Ford (with a series of directors, writers, producers, and other collaborators) most often created different relationships between men, relationships which proved that, though male camaraderie was always somewhat dangerous, acting out was not necessarily inevitable.

The friendship between Ford's Colonel Owen Devereaux and William Holden's Captain Del Stewart in *The Man from Colorado* (Henry Levin, 1948) offers a powerful counterweight to typical war buddy portrayals. The film is among the most explicit portrayals of post-traumatic stress disorder in twentieth-century Hollywood, at least as it elicits violence, rather than strictly depression, fear, or "shellshock." Devereaux does not *want* to want to kill, but he craves it. The film opens with a Union massacre of Confederate troops at the end of the Civil War. Overcome by bloodlust, Devereaux commands his unit to trap and annihilate over 100 Confederate soldiers, even though the Colonel (and he alone) saw them raise a white flag. After this seeming triumph, Devereaux retreats to his quarters and records the event in his diary: "I killed 100 men today. I didn't want to. I couldn't help myself. What's wrong with me? I'm afraid—afraid I'm going crazy—No, it was the war, that's all. But the war's over—now. I can stop. I'm safe. God's helping me." Unsurprisingly, the end of the war does not bring an end to Devereaux's appetite for violence. When the men return to town, they are greeted as heroes and celebrated. They affably compete for the affections of one wholesome young Caroline (Ellen Drew) and are offered jobs defending justice and peace: Devereaux as the judge and Stewart as the marshal. Though Devereaux struggles with reintegrating, lashing out and even shooting people who insult him, Stewart seems virtually unaffected by the war. As Doc Merriam (Edgar Buchanan) says, "War affects different men in different ways. Time, that's what men need when they get back from a war. Time and people standing by that really care about them and believe in them." Unfortunately, Devereaux does not get the time that he needs to recover: he is expected to assume an even more demanding career with tremendous responsibility and authority the day after he returns from battle. The support that Stewart, Doc, and Caroline offer is not enough to make up for this abrupt reentry. Caroline chooses to marry him over Stewart, though Devereaux's insanity eventually drives her toward the other man, as her husband burns to death under a flaming house.

Columbia executives, producer Jules Schermer, and director Henry Levin quite blatantly used casting to reinforce the themes in *The Man from Colorado*, reminding viewers of *Texas*, in which Ford and Holden played some of their earliest roles, also with Edgar Buchanan as an older fellow named "Doc." In that film, Ford and Holden again play war buddies (this time Confederates) whose reactions to their shared moments of violence differ dramatically. Ford's character, Tod Ramsey, becomes an upstanding cattleman, seemingly recovered from the war (and the stagecoach robbery that the men witnessed and indirectly participated in), while Holden's Dan Thomas, under the influence of the shady Doc, becomes a criminal.

The reversal of roles between Ford and Holden that takes place in *The Man from Colorado* is spread by eight years, during which both men served in the war. Over the course of those years—but only after the war—Ford apparently acquired the potential for badness. The generic similarity between *Texas* and *The Man from Colorado*—Westerns set in the post–Civil War period, featuring men just out of armed service—shows the permeability between Westerns and war movies in the 1940s and 1950s. What Basinger calls a "curious affinity" between the genres, I would call full-fledged generic indeterminacy.[27] *The Man from Colorado* contains scenes of actual battle and Western shootouts. It also deals with veteran reintegration through Devereaux's post-traumatic stress and through a subplot in which soldiers return home to find their land seized. Three years later, in *The Redhead and the Cowboy* (Leslie Fenton, 1951), Ford's Gil Kyle tries to stay neutral during the Civil War but finds himself trapped between sides. Visually, and for the most part narratively, the film is a typical Western, but Fenton and screenwriter Jonathan Latimer, both decorated World War II veterans, make the film explicitly about the permeability between the Western and war genres. When a group of Confederate soldiers go outside their ranks to put a "posse" together to fight the Union, one objects: "They're going to make the war like a border incident." Alan Freed's Colonel Lamertine bemoans the Wild West nature of "modern" warfare (in the 1860s): "There was a time when war was the property of gentlemen on horseback who fought under a strict ethical code. Unfortunately, those days are over." These comments suggest that the overlap between the war film and the Western is not just about the fact that both explore a kind of violence, but that the violence on the battlefield and in the nineteenth century West are, in fact, the same. Neither is civilized, neither is entirely rule-bound, and neither can be perpetrated by "gentlemen." There are no Del Stewarts here.

Women's inconsistent and even wildly skewed expectations for men often define the violence and sexuality in Ford and Heflin's films. Eased from several unlikely ladies' man roles into relative impotency at the end of the 1940s, and thoroughly scrubbed of sexual power through his performance in *Shane*, Heflin is rendered essentially asexual for much of the 1950s. Contrarily, Ford's role as Johnny Farrell ushers in over a decade of (often perversely) eroticized, masculine characters of the sort that diminish Heflin's emasculated everymen, and draw the interest of all varieties of movie women. There are important exceptions to these characterizations, but their reach is undeniable and definitive of the paradox of postwar masculine sexuality. After being let back into the fold after the war, Heflin made three films in quick succession: *The Strange Love of Martha Ivers*, *Till the Cloud Rolls By*, and *Possessed*.

As Sam Masterson in *The Strange Love of Martha Ivers* and David Sutton in *Possessed*, Heflin showed himself capable of acting the ladies' man, seducing characters played by Stanwyck, Lizabeth Scott, and Joan Crawford. In both films, Heflin's character is a veteran with an excellent war record who seems unable or unwilling to assume the roles that the women around him expect him to. As Stephen Farber points out, "During the war years and immediately afterward, strong women flourished in American films, and were often presented as monsters and harpies"—so these noir films are among many films of other genres of the period to give women power, but, in these cases, their power extends to defining the film itself.[28] Stanwyck's Martha Ivers and Crawford's Louise Howell are the protagonists in their films and, in Louise's case, viewers are positioned to see the film's events entirely through her eyes. *Possessed* opens with Louise in a trance, roaming the streets of Los Angeles, murmuring "David." After she collapses in public, she is captured and brought to an institution for the mentally ill. Once she is institutionalized, the viewer inhabits her body, looking up at the doctor while being examined and hearing the music that the doctors claim is not real. The film's narrative is then explored strictly through Louise's flashbacks, so that we have nothing to trust but her memory to understand her murder of David (of which we are—like the amnesiac Louise—unaware until the very end). Louise's flashbacks show David as a callous, selfish cad, who rubs his many liaisons in her face and shows no passion or caring for anyone around him. When David returns from a business trip to the far North and tells her about being away from civilization, Louise says, "You sound like you were lonely," and David replies, "I was too busy to be lonely." He has been working to turn a parabola into a molder girder for defense purposes since he was in the Army and David's passion for his work is a source of constant frustration for Louise.

To Louise, David's interest in his work is a way of avoiding real closeness with her. Louise wants to be "inside his life," but he tells her, "Louise, we're all on the outside of people's lives looking in. You wouldn't like being on the inside of my life anyway. There's nothing there but a few mathematical equations and a lot of question marks," and on that, he abruptly ends the relationship. Trying to explain his disinterest in becoming more intimate with her, he says, "Blame it on the Army, blame it on the war, blame it on anything you like, but that's the way it is." David does not wish to marry Louise or to develop a better relationship with her and he does not see this lack of desire as a bad thing that he ought to change. He does not seem to "know himself," but he does not *want* to know himself or to be known. In the end, his impenetrability leads Louise to kill him and, to the viewer who has seen his carelessness and callousness toward her, it very nearly seems justified. Louise is pronounced "not responsible for her actions" by reason of insanity, and her doctors intend to keep her hospitalized for as long as it takes to restore her to a sound mind. Having experienced David through Louise's eyes, we know the true source of her insanity: her inability to bond with or to understand her highly interiorized lover drove her insane.

Martha, like Louise, feels that she can understand Sam if he will only let her get close to him and is, despite her deranged behavior, sympathetic. Because the two were involved in the death of her abusive aunt and guardian as children, she feels a deep bond with him, even though they have been separated from many years. In these intervening years, Sam not only built up "a war record few could equal," but also beat a murder rap, claiming it was self-defense. Martha is fascinated by the killings that Sam has done since they have been apart and, after he gets in a fight with a man at a bar, she asks, "You wanted to kill him, didn't you?" and she seems pleased that his answer was "Yes." After these discussions and an actual look at his war record, Martha determines that Sam would be a perfect accomplice in the murder of her husband. He is revolted by her suggestion and she begs him to care about her again, "I've dreamed of you coming back!" "Your whole life has been a dream," he says. Thinking herself in a superior position, she retorts, "You've killed. It says so in your record." Sam proudly corrects her, "I've never murdered." Martha kills herself, not Sam, who flees with Toni (Scott), telling her, "Don't look back, baby. Don't ever look back," advice in keeping with his veteran past.

Martha is not the only woman to think that the war has prepared a veteran for murder. Vicky Buckley (Gloria Grahame), the female lead in *Human Desire* (Fritz Lang, 1954) also believes that she has found an ideal accomplice for her husband's murder in Ford's Jeff Warren. Jeff has just returned from Korea and is resuming his work at the railroad. The first lines of the film are about his service record, which he admits is lackluster: when his coworkers ask if he won any medals, he jokes, "They ran out of them." When he meets his mentor's daughter, Ellen Simmons (Kathleen Case), who has a crush on him, she claims that she has "a million questions to ask" him about the war, but they are only about whether the Japanese women were beautiful.

Vicky's questions about the war are more profound and much darker. Alone with Jeff after making love, Vicky broaches the subject.

VICKY: Must be a strange feeling.
JEFF: What?
VICKY: To be surrounded by death. The way a soldier is during the war.
JEFF: You don't think about it after a while. You're usually so cold or hungry or sleepy that death comes as sort of an accident.
VICKY: Is it difficult to kill a man? I mean for a soldier.
JEFF: That's what they give you medals for. Why?
VICKY: I just wondered. Maybe because of what I saw on the train.
JEFF: No, it isn't difficult, Vicky. It's the easiest thing in the world.
VICKY: You make it sound so simple.

Jeff becomes uncomfortable and changes the topic, but the conversation clearly confirms Vicky's assumptions. The relationship between Jeff and Vicky is different from those between David and Louise and Sam and Martha because, though he is more forthcoming about his war experience, he says very little else in the film while Vicky talks anxiously and constantly. But like Louise and Martha, Vicky longs for her lover to show her love of an extreme sort, a love that she feels he can only prove violently.

VICKY: I guess it's only people like Carl who can kill for something they love.
JEFF: I'd have done anything for you.
VICKY: Except that.
JEFF: Yes, except that.
VICKY: You killed before.
JEFF: Before? In the war, huh? Well, I almost forgot. You thought I could do it because of that, huh? Well, there's a difference. In the war you fire into the darkness. Something moving on a ridge. Position, uniform, enemy. But a man coming home helpless, drunk, that takes a different kind of killing.
VICKY: Yes, and a different kind of a man.
JEFF: That's right. It takes somebody who doesn't think about anybody but himself. It takes somebody who has no conscience and no decency.

Vicky says what so many other female characters in postwar films only intimate: she is jealous, even sexually or romantically jealous, of the war itself. She wants to be worth killing for. Because he has killed before, in the war context, his love for her seems weak by comparison. Furthermore, because a "good man" will never kill outside of the war context, her desire for Jeff relies on his being bad; only a bad man can adequately prove his love for her.

Just as Louise's descent from frustration and desperation into outright madness frames the narrative of *Possessed* for its viewer, *Human Desire* portrays Vicky's desperation as understandable; despite her lies and violence, she is sympathetic. She feels trapped in an abusive marriage to Carl (Broderick Crawford), which causes her to latch onto Jeff and to provoke him. Jeff's protectiveness over Carl can partly be explained by casting history. Crawford's George Knowland saved Ford's Joe Hufford in *Convicted* and even explained his defense of the younger man through Hufford's service: "Do you want to know how I'd handle this case if I were on the other side of the fence? First, I'd object on any juror who didn't have a son in the service. Then, I'd drag out his war record. I'd spend two days on it. I'd take him from the day he entered boot camp to the day he got his decoration on Okinawa. Then, I'd pull in 50 character witnesses, from the old lady who knew him since he was born to his last commanding officer. *Then*, I'd start in on intent." Unlike *Human Desire*'s Vicky, Knowland views Hufford's service record as proof of his moral fortitude. It is possible, in fact, that Jeff made the wrong choice: the film ends ambiguously, with Vicky possibly dead at Carl's hands. Perhaps Jeff should have murdered him after all; perhaps the war ought to have prepared him to use violence to protect the woman he claimed to love.

CASE STUDIES IN COLLABORATION: FORD, HEFLIN, AND EVELYN KEYES

In the 1950s, Gloria Grahame and Glenn Ford were an unforgettable on-screen pairing, and their collaborations in *Human Desire* and *The Big Heat* (further discussion to come) yielded portrayals of masculinity asserted at a woman's expense. Heflin and Ford also shared a female co-star in the postwar era: actor Evelyn Keyes. Each actor's collaborations with Keyes offer a slightly different angle on what these postwar masculinities meant for women and, further, show the permeability amongst these masculine types and even the versatility of each actor's version of the postwar man. Whereas the female characters in the previous section are largely degraded and diminished by their love for or attraction to men, Keyes's characters have more nuanced measures of power, and varying degrees of desperation and alliance with the viewer, all of which call into question the stability of Heflin and Ford's masculine personas.

Ford and Keyes appeared together six times in the decade, including in two back-to-back features, the comedy *The Mating of Millie* (Levin, 1948) and the drama *Mr. Soft Touch* (Gordon Douglas and Levin, 1949). In *The Mating of Millie*, Millie (Keyes), the hard-charging career woman, desperately wants to adopt little orphan Tommy Bassett (Jimmy Hunt), whose father was killed in the war (for which he won the Congressional Medal of Honor) and whose mother dies suddenly in an accident. As a single woman, she is ineligible to adopt Tommy, but she and proud Army man (turned bus driver) Doug Andrews (Ford), whom she meets on her way to work, scheme to find a man to marry her or pose as her husband. The course does not run smooth, as Millie chafes at the notion of marriage and has no faith in men. As she puts it, "Most men act as if the principal reason for marriage is to have someone to cheat on." Millie resolves to marry for Tommy's sake, against her objections. Though Doug has gone on about the pleasures of bachelorhood throughout the film, the two unsurprisingly fall in love and Millie, Tommy, and Doug become a family.

The Mating of Millie's happy ending is a strange prelude to both Keyes's and Ford's very next project, in which Ford's Joe Miracle recalls his earlier Johnny Farrell: a disturbed sadist, but also a "Purple-Hearted hero of the United States Army." Joe's enemy, bespectacled journalist Henry "Early" Byrd (John Ireland), suggests that Joe enlisted to escape retribution for ratting out his fellow gangsters and that the Army is a safe haven for criminals. Joe meets social worker Jenny Jones (Keyes) and, in their first conversation, Jenny and Joe (seemingly like Millie and Doug) discuss their opinions about marriage. Then, Johnny explains that he beats his wife "because I love her," and tries to seduce Jenny by asking her, "Have you ever been beaten by someone you loved?" and implying that she is missing out if she has not. Though Jenny winces and fears Joe, she is also captivated by him, a masochistic impulse explained by her relationship with her abusive father, who beat her so violently that she lost hearing in her left ear. But, because of her victimization, Jenny tells Joe that they simply cannot be romantically involved. As in

The Mating of Millie and so many other films of the era, the seeming impossibility of their coupling actually justifies its occurrence: Jenny is the only one who can convince Joe that he has been wrong and that he can become right. The two finally get together after he uses his stolen money to rebuild Jenny's settlement house.

That Cohn and the rest of the Columbia executives could so easily flip Ford from nice-guy Doug to bad-boy Joe shows that, though there was truth to the accusations of typecasting that led to SAG's protests in 1950, studios were also willing to give some actors latitude. On the other hand, there is an everyman quality to both Doug and Joe, men who return from war success to find their possibilities limited and the jobs at which they had once excelled unsuitable. And, in the end, both become the men their girlfriends want them to be, embracing a respectable father role for children who are not their biological offspring. Despite their cynicism about men and marriage, Keyes's characters have a remarkable ability to inspire goodness in the men that they meet.

By 1951, Keyes's characters seem to have lost that power. After maneuvering out of her studio contract, Keyes took the role of Susan Gilvray in Horizon Pictures's *The Prowler* (Losey, 1951) opposite Van Heflin. Both actors' performances in *The Prowler* are among the best of their careers, partly enabled by the quality of the script (written by blacklisted screenwriter Dalton Trumbo), Losey's direction, and Arthur Miller's cinematography. Censor Joe Breen immediately rejected the first draft of the film's script, which led the writers, Losey, and assistant director Robert Aldrich to revise it so that Heflin's Webb Garwood and Susan believed themselves in true love, rather than intoxicating lust. Amazingly, this change allowed *The Prowler* to deal with both impotence and abortion, however briefly.

Susan is like Keyes's Jenny, but also like Stanwyck's Martha and Grahame's Vicky: she finds a man's seething violence magnetic. When she sees a prowler outside her home and calls the cops, Officer Garwood and his older partner Bud Crocker (John Maxwell) arrive to help her, but it is obvious right away that Garwood is intrigued, not concerned. He returns under the pretense of checking on her but attempts to rape her. She manages to break free and lock him out, but she lets him in when he returns to apologize and they have (consensual) sex.

One of the things that makes Heflin's Garwood remarkable is his strangeness. Despite his everyday looks and job, his interactions with others are awkward, he twitches, squirms, weeps, flies off the handle, and looks wide-eyed, he lapses into envious rants and self-justifying monologues, and, when alone, he pours over glossy muscle magazines in his tiny apartment, and performs calisthenics, with firing range papers on the walls. When confronted with his crime, the murder of Susan's husband, William (Emerson Treacy), he argues that it is actually an example of how normal he is: "So I'm no good. But I'm no worse than anybody else. You work in a store, you knock down on the cash register. You're the big boss, the income tax. The ward heeler, you sell votes. A lawyer, take bribes. I was a cop. I used a gun. . . . I'm not any different from those other guys." The fact that the gun is a method of violence seems not to distinguish it from any other unsavory path to riches.

The gun continues to be an important symbol for both Garwood and Susan. When she is reluctant to marry him because of his affection for weapons, he assures her that he has changed: "You remember that medal, that sharpshooter's medal I used to wear? And how much I used to like guns? Well, after what I've been through [killing William], it's like running some innocent kid down in the street—you never want to drive a car again. I couldn't bring myself to touch a gun again as long as I live." Her fears assuaged, she agrees to marry him, and the two move away to hide her pregnancy. On their honeymoon, Susan finds a gun hidden in Garwood's suitcase and realizes that her new husband is dangerous as ever. Her attraction to his violence has trapped her into the center of his crime spree, in which he plans to kill anyone who gets in their way, including the obstetrician who delivers their secret child. Susan manages to warn the doctor, and Garwood is killed fleeing the scene of his child's birth. When a man in the form of Heflin is deranged, he is not savable. Keyes's Susan is left alone with her newborn, in exact opposition to Millie and Jenny's fates. In short, the Ford repression of other films is absent here: he is flexible enough to become the family man, regardless of his starting point. Heflin's Garwood, by contrast, is trapped in a single identity.

KILLING THE WAR: *ACT OF VIOLENCE* AND *BLACKBOARD JUNGLE*

The Prowler is clearly more complex than *The Mating of Millie* and *Mr. Soft Touch*, but it also differs in the way it handles the war: it doesn't. As Hollywood moved from the 1940s to the 1950s, the war was mentioned less frequently and was a less explicit element of characterization and plot, but *Act of Violence* (Zinneman, 1948) and *Blackboard Jungle* engage the war directly. Heflin in the former and Ford in the latter play their last memorable veterans.

Act of Violence helped turned the page on Heflin's identity, perhaps because its dealings with the war were so forthright: a veteran's past quite literally comes back to haunt him and to terrorize his family. The film follows Enley and his wife (Janet Leigh) as Enley is stalked by Joe Parkson (Robert Ryan), with whom he served in Europe. Captured by the Nazis, Enley gave up the men under his command during their escape attempt, leaving some of them dead and Parkson injured. Parkson has been trying to track down and kill Enley ever since the war.

Act of Violence, like *The Strange Love of Martha Ivers* and *Human Desire,* portrays women's inability to understand their veteran lovers, but, for much of the film, there is a possibility that this can be overcome, when the two people are honest with each other and compassionate. In *Act of Violence,* Edith Enley does not imagine that her husband is capable of murder, until Parkson paints the brutal picture: "Did he tell you that I'm crippled because of him? Did he tell you about the men that are dead because of him? Did he tell you what happened to them before they died? Mike Garvey. He had a wife and a kid too, made a nuisance of himself showing everybody their picture. Afterward, somebody got his picture back. It was so covered with blood you couldn't tell what it was. The other men were moaning outside the wire all night long. I was lucky. They thought I was dead and left me there." The family picture covered with blood is a haunting symbol of what the war is doing to so many families, even after the war has been over for years, and this image clearly speaks to Edith's greatest fears. Edith does not initially believe Parkson's accusations, but, unlike many Hollywood husbands, Frank does not try to preserve her naivete. He tells her honestly, begging her to understand him, wishing her to know who he really is, what he has really done, and the context in which he learned his own capabilities: "Do I have to spell it out for you? Do I have to draw you a picture? I was an informer. It doesn't make any difference why I did it. I betrayed my men. They were dead. The Nazis even paid me a price. They gave me food and I ate it. I ate it. . . . They were dead and I was eating and maybe that's all I did it for: to save one man, me. There were six widows, there were ten men dead, and I couldn't stop eating." As in Parkson's monologue, the family—the six widows—play as large a role in the crime as the dead men themselves. It is impossible to tell for certain whether this and Parkson's recourses to family stability are specifically for Edith's benefit, but the anguish on both Enley and Parkson's faces suggests that the destruction of family is the biggest sin.

In marked contrast to most 1940s and 1950s movie wives, Edith never fails to try to understand Enley, even as his past seems darker and he presents it so starkly. Yet, when Frank gets drunk and ends up at the home of an older sex worker (Mary Astor), she tells him that his troubles cannot be that bad: "Is it love trouble or money trouble? Listen Frankie, I've seen 'em all, I've seen all the troubles in world, but they boil down to just those two: you're broke or you're lonely." He does not correct her, but her ignorance is astounding in the context of Enley's troubles.

Anne (Phyllis Thaxter), Parkson's girlfriend, tracks him down to the small-town motel where he waits for Enley. She is terrified that he will make himself a murderer and begs him to let go of his obsession and settle down with her for a life like the Enleys, complete with marriage, a baby, a stable job, and a suburban home. Though she desperately wishes that he would give up his pursuit and pulls out all the stops to get through to him, she also tries to understand his pain and the toll that his injury has taken on his body and mind. So, with the exception of Astor's Pat, *Act of Violence*'s women actively try to reintegrate their men into postwar American life rather than using them or playing dumb, and they see the promise of family stability as the ideal manner for achieving this goal.

While inebriated, Enley takes a hit out on Parkson, which he later tries to retract. As his anxiety mounts, Edith reaches out to him: "Ever since I first knew you, Frank, and up until yesterday I thought you the finest, most wonderful man in the world. Just that. Now I know that you're like everybody else. You have faults and weaknesses. If I hadn't been so young and silly, I would've known that all along and it wouldn't be such a shock finding it out now. That doesn't mean that I don't love you. Or that I don't want to be your wife. Because I do." Within several minutes, Enley has been mowed down by traffic, trying to prevent the murder that he commissioned. Parkson watches happily, saying with relief, "I didn't do it!" When someone in the crowd asks who will tell Edith of her husband's death, Parkson and Anne volunteer, and the film ends as they leave to do so, holding hands on the suburban street. Parkson and Anne will now be able to start a family; Edith and her infant will be forced to start postwar life over and without a head of household.

This ending is in keeping with the strange mundaneness of most of the film. When Parkson follows Enley, he goes to the lake where he is fishing, then to a business convention he's attending in a neighboring town, and, of course, to his suburban house on a nondescript suburban street. Enley does not live in a criminal underworld. He has done absolutely everything that he can to put his war experience in the past: marrying, becoming a father, building a business, and actively serving his community. Yet, from the moment the film opens—when he is introduced by a city government official as "a fellow veteran"—he cannot outrun it. What initially seems to be a boldly optimistic film about the promise of marriage in the aftermath of war ends in a statement on the inevitability of a sort of postwar karma that threatens even the happiest, most stable families, in the most common circumstances.

In a less direct way, the common family circumstance, invaded by violence, is the story of Ford's biggest hit, *Blackboard Jungle* (Richard Brooks, 1955). Most accounts of the film focus on the relationship between Ford's Richard Dadier (Daddy-O) and young Sidney Poitier's Gregory Miller. The relationship between the two characters is fascinating—and, at that point, rather unique—and Poitier's role would advance his Hollywood status immensely. Gregory is different because he is Black, but the film does not stress this as the primary reason. Actually, Gregory is portrayed as a young man with true potential, less likely to continue hijinks and destructiveness into adulthood than his working-class white fellow students. Poitier's performance, like Edwards's in *Home of the Brave* indicates a sensitivity that makes him a "safe" Black man but pushes the boundaries a bit as a sullen and angry teen. Dadier overtly cares more about "reaching" Gregory than his classmates. Gregory rejects Dadier time and again, but, ultimately, he is the best of the bunch and this relationship is a model for many white teacher/Black student sagas to come. Other relationships in *Blackboard Jungle* though depict the more malevolent students and the damage that the "delinquents" do to their teacher is often on the territory of home and family and his character's identity is enmeshed in his veteran status.

When Dadier applies to be an English teacher at North Manual High School, his interview with the principal is short but telling. Dadier had a successful Naval career in World War II, and was the Navy's middleweight boxing champion, but he changed thoroughly afterward. He attended a formerly all-girls college (because schools were having trouble accommodating the barrage of incoming ex-GIs) and became an English major; he impressively quotes *Henry V*:

> Once more unto the breach, dear friends, once more
> Or close the wall up with our English dead.
> In peace there's nothing so becomes a man
> As modest stillness and humility:
> But when the blast of war blows in our ears,
> Then imitate the action of the tiger.

Though the quote is obviously about war, it is meant to apply to teaching as much as to battle, a slippage that will recur in many conversations between teachers throughout the film. Quoting Shakespeare is apparently enough to get Dadier the job and he begins shortly, on the first day of school.

Blackboard Jungle makes the case that it is the war—even war in general—which causes these students' delinquency. When the cop visits the school, he says, "They were five or six years old during the last war, father in the Army, mother at a defense plant, no home life, no church life, no place to go. They formed street gangs. It's way over my head. Maybe the kids today are like the rest of the world: mixed up, suspicious, scared. I don't know. But I do know this: gang leaders are taking the place of parents." Elsewhere in the film, Artie West (Vic Morrow), who leads much of the aggression against Dadier, explains his own actions as a form of conscientious objection or self-protection: "A year from now the Army comes by and they say, 'Okay Artie West, you get in a uniform and you be a soldier and you save the world and you get your lousy head blowed right off.' Well maybe, maybe I get a year in jail and maybe when I come out the Army they don't want Artie West to be a soldier no more. Maybe what I get is out." And, when Dadier goes on a rant against teacher ineffectiveness, he claims that it is, in part, because men are still patting themselves on the back and coddling themselves for their part in the war.

Though Dadier is excited to begin teaching, he is immediately alerted to the difficulties in store. In his very first class meeting, he finds that he has to "get tough" with his students, even mildly threatening them. But it is not until the end of the school day that the extent of the problem is evident. When a student attempts to rape Lois (Margaret Hayes), a female teacher, Dadier rescues her and beats the student up with almost suspicious aplomb. The students are furious at his nerve, and they resolve to ruin his life. Though they attack him in an alley and frustrate him in class, their most organized effort is to convince Dadier's wife, Anne (Anne Francis), that her husband is cheating on her with Lois (of whom she is already wildly jealous). They do this through a series of anonymous letters and phone calls insisting on his infidelity, but also through orchestrating her arrival at school when Dadier is arm-in-arm with Lois (to protect her from the leers and advances of the students). Lois is indeed attracted to Dadier and flirts with him, but he resists her flirtations and cares for his pregnant wife, whose anxieties have previously led to miscarriages. She gives birth successfully and admits that her doubts were in error, though even the neighbor believes him an adulterer. Dadier gains the respect of his students when he (with Gregory Miller) defends himself against them when they physically attack him with a switchblade. Using the flagpole (with the American flag waving), he fights them off. Though he has been disturbed to find his automatic violence at other points in the film (a violence that includes latent racism), it is only in this and the rape context that the film portrays it as justified. Having found his strength in the classroom (and also having made a pact with Miller), he resolves to return the following year. Unlike Jeff in *Human Desire*, Dadier cares for the stability of postwar family and safety enough to protect it violently.

3:09: *SHANE* AND *THE BIG HEAT* IN 1953

Dadier is an upstanding married man with a respectable job and a baby on the way, but, to the women in *Blackboard Jungle*, he still exudes sex appeal. Yet, though he was briefly sexually magnetic in *The Prowler*, Heflin's lack of sexual potency and solid marital fidelity became his defining features by the 1950s. In *Weekend with Father* (Douglas Sirk, 1951), he is emasculated by the presence of a strapping shirtless Richard Denning, whom everyone thinks more deserving of female company. By 1954, he had played Peter Denver in *Black Widow* (Nunnally Johnson), whose totally asexual kindness to an 18-year-old girl gets him accused of murder, and Jerry Talbot in *Woman's World* (Jean Negulesco), who seeks the top position at his company only to find out that his bombshell wife (Arlene Dane) has offered herself sexually to the company's owner in exchange for the job. While at war in *Battle Cry* (Raoul Walsh, 1955), his Sam Huxley celibately awaits a reunion with his wife of many years, while the young men around him flirt with nurses and cheat on their girlfriends left at home. In the midst of his solid family-man period, Heflin played his most famous role: Joe Starrett in *Shane*. The story of the film, based on Jack Schaefer's novel, is well known. Joe is the head of a homesteader household and Rufus Ryker (Emile Meyer) wants him and his fellow "sodbusters" off the land. Shane (Alan Ladd), a reformed gunfighter, comes to live with and work for the Starretts as tension mounts between Ryker's gang and the homesteaders. When it becomes clear that the dispute will not resolve without violence, Shane finds and kills Wilson (Jack Palance), Ryker's gun-for-hire, as well as Ryker and Ryker's brother. Realizing that he cannot reintegrate into the Starrett household after returning to his violent ways, he rides off, leaving the Starretts to their land.

Shane's mastery over his gun mesmerizes little Joey (Brandon de Wilde) to an extent that scares his mother, Marian (Jean Arthur). The gun in *Shane* is as important as it is in *The Prowler*, and even more present. The gun and a man's response to it are proxy for his past and his prowess. In the opening scene, little Joey cocks his toy rifle, and the sound makes Shane whip around with his hand on his gun. Later, the sound of a calf moving outside jerks Shane back into action with his gun at the ready. Though Joe comments on Shane's jumpiness, he shares the tendency: "I guess I spook kind of easy these days."

Joey's fascination with guns forces Shane and Joe to make their statements about them and to prove their abilities and forces Marian to offer a "woman's opinion" on the men's actions and their impact on her son. The adults work hard to avoid discussions of violence, and they prefer to speak in euphemisms, but Joey makes this impossible by asking constant, bald questions. Throughout the film, Joey admits to the things that the adults will not acknowledge, including the fact that Shane has a masculine confidence that his father lacks. Asking Joe, "Can you shoot as good as Shane, Pa?," Joey forces his father to admit that he probably cannot. Following up, "Pa, could you whip Shane?," he further forces Joe to participate in his own emasculation, by admitting his physical inferiority. And, when Joey wants to know why Shane chose not to take his gun on a trip into town, Joe reminds his son that he does not take his gun on such trips either. Here, Joey freely admits, "But it goes with *him*, Pa." Joe's slumping body language, when contrasted with Shane's upright but mobile confidence, makes Joey's words visual.

One of the most wrenching elements of *Shane* is the mutual unconsummated attraction between Shane and Marian. Neither of them ever utters even one word to that effect, but Joey becomes the unlikely interlocutor of

Marian's passion. One night, after Marian has cared for Shane's head wound, Joey takes her aside to tell her a secret. Shane overhears the conversation:

JOEY: Ma, I just love Shane.
MARIAN: Do you Joey?
JOEY: I love him almost as much as I love Pa. That's all right isn't it?
MARIAN: He's a fine man.
JOEY: He's so good. Don't you like him mother?
MARIAN: Yes, I like him too Joey. Goodnight Joey.

She closes the door to resume her conversation with Shane, but he has left the main house and is walking toward his quarters in the barn. She watches him walk away into the dark night, allowing herself to feel the feelings that she is repressing and that Joey unknowingly expresses for her. Joe re-enters the room and asks, "What's the matter honey?" Marian, flushed with arousal, says, "Joe, hold me. Don't say anything just hold me tight." As they enter their bedroom with arms tight around each other, Joey calls out "Goodnight," first to Ma, then to Pa, then to Shane. Marian, channeling her attraction to Shane, attempts to awaken the sexual aspect of her marriage, but is immediately interrupted by her son, who cannot help but puncture the adults' illusions about the changes that Shane's presence is making the household.

While the film is, ultimately, about the profound differences between Joe and Shane, their similarities are foregrounded as well, as in Joe's observation about their shared jumpiness. On Shane's first night at the Starrett place, he and Joe work to dislodge a giant stump, which has been on the property since the Starretts claimed it years ago. As they swing their axes, Joe and Shane grimace with pleasure and effort, in alternating close-ups of each. Finally, a two-shot shows Joe, dirty in his chambray shirt, and Shane, tanned and shirtless, in their final push, as they manage to get rid of the stump, and Marian and Joey watch in awe. Later, when Shane gets into a fight at the store saloon, Joe enters with a small log and uses it to beat Shane's attackers over the head. The fight continues, and the close-ups alternate again, as the sweaty, bloody, but smiling men try to finish off a room full of tough guys. Though Joe will not follow this violence through to the end of the film, he is capable of this kind of brutal pleasure, just as he is capable of the stump's destruction; he just needs a male partner to accomplish it. Shane has reawakened this sort of masculinity in Joe, and this extends to his marriage.

On Joe and Marian's tenth wedding anniversary (which happens to be on Independence Day), he awkwardly and bashfully makes a speech about his love for his wife: "I gave up my independence ten years ago today, but no man ever gave it up so easy as I did. And what's more, I wouldn't change places with any man in this world." Shane listens and looks down in pain. Though much of the film has diminished Joe, making him seem incompetent without Shane to assist and motivate him, in this moment, Joe clearly has the upper hand. But, in an instant, Shane reclaims it, when he and Marian dance. Only while watching Shane dance with his wife does Joe realize the feelings that they have for each other. This realization leads to another: he will reclaim his masculinity—the violent, confident type that Shane represents—or die trying. He prepares to confront Ryker, though Marian pleads with him not to go.

> **JOE:** Marian, honey, it's because you mean so much to me that I have to go. Do you think I could go on living with you and you thinking that I'd showed yellow? Then what about Joey? How do you think that I'd ever explain that to him?
> **MARIAN:** Oh Joe! Joe!
> **JOE:** I've been thinking a lot and, I know I'm kind of slow sometimes, Marian, but I see things. And I know that if anything happened to me that you'd be took care of. You'd be took care of better than I could do it myself. I never thought I'd live to hear myself say that, but I guess now's a pretty good time to lay things bare.
> **MARIAN:** You talk as though I'd be glad for you to go.
> **JOE:** Honey, you're the most honest and the finest girl in the world. And I couldn't do what I've got to do if I hadn't always known that I could trust you.

At this point, Marian shows no ambivalence: despite her feelings for Shane, she wants Joe to be her husband, Joey's devoted father, and the hardworking provider he has always been. She realizes the value of his brand of masculinity. Shane helps her to stop Joe before he puts himself in harm's way. Shane and Joe get into a brutal fistfight, which Joe, surprisingly, comes close to winning, jumping on his horse when Shane is down. Shane pulls him down off his horse and beats him, punching him in the face and, finally, pistol-whipping him until he passes out. Though Shane is "doing the right thing" for the Starrett family, Joey is shocked to see his violence turned on his father and tells

Shane that he hates him. Though Marian is relieved that Shane stopped Joe, she is disappointed that Shane plans to attack Ryker's gang himself: "Shane, wait. I thought you were through with gunfighting." When he tells her, simply, that's he has changed his mind, she asks, "Are you doing this just for me?" And he says, "For you, Marian. For Joe and little Joe." Shane is not only fighting for the woman he loves, he is protecting the family that he wants but cannot have, and even the man who *is* positioned to have it.

After he kills Wilson, Ryker, and Ryker's brother, Shane surveys the scene, looking with deep sadness at the dead bodies. Walking away from his righteous crime, he tells Joey:

> A man has to be what he is, Joey. He can't break the mold. I tried it and it didn't work for me. . . . Joey there's no living with a killing. There's no going back from it. Right or wrong it's a brand and a brand sticks. There's no going back. Now you run on home to your mother and tell her everything is all right and there are no more guns in the valley. . . . You go home to your father and mother and grow up to be strong and straight. Joey, take care of them. Both of them.

Without Shane's propensity for and ability to commit violence, the Starretts would probably have to leave their land and give up on "civilizing" the new territory, but Shane cannot reap the benefits of his actions. "There are no more guns in the valley," as Marian requested. But this means that Shane must leave the valley as well, to protect Joe and Joey from his influence, to keep them "strong and straight." Like Devereaux, Shane has given his service, but now he cannot be changed and reintegrated into safe, modern, family life, he "has to be what he is."

Though Heflin had played fathers before, it is not until *Shane* that fatherhood becomes one of the themes that his "first body" immediately evokes. As the 1950s progress, fatherhood becomes a critical theme in popular film. Bruzzi notes that this "new" fatherhood is basically the province of younger men, like Heflin in *Shane*, as opposed to slightly older men like Spencer Tracy and William Powell. She provides a list of these younger fathers in mid-1950s film, and mentions, briefly (as "not particularly important"), Ford's Dave Bannion from *The Big Heat*.[29] What Bruzzi no doubt means is that Bannion is not the man that we imagine when we think of the 1950s father, whereas Joe Starrett may well be. However, *The Big Heat* is about what is beneath that wholesome image and how easily its components disappear when a man's family is ripped away.

Bannion is a local cop, whose life revolves around his wife Katie (Jocelyn Brando) and daughter Joyce (Linda Bennett). Katie and Dave Bannion are very happily married and we watch them joke with each other, share a steak and cigarettes, and discuss child-rearing books and Joyce's antics. Though Bannion is a cop with regular hours, he is a devoted father by night: he plays games with Joyce, reads her bedtime stories, and puts her to bed, only to emerge and help his wife with the dishes.

But at work, he comes into contact with organized crime, "psychopathic" rapes, murder, and robbery. Disgusted with and in hot pursuit of a local syndicate run by Mike Lagana (Alexander Scourby), he becomes a target. Dave tries to keep life normal for his family, but Lagana's men make obscene, threatening phone calls to his home and, eventually, wire his car with a bomb. But it is Katie, not Dave Bannion, who turns the key and is burned to death in the explosion. As he and Joyce move out of their once-happy home, he looks back at the empty house with tears in his eyes, which quickly turn to hardness. He leaves the police force because, though he is already on a mission to dissolve the syndicate, Bannion's craving for revenge—what his friend and boss Ted (Willis Bouchey) calls his "hate binge"—leads him to pursue Lagana outside the bounds of the law.

In the process of pursuing Lagana and his men, he becomes involved with the sexy and vulnerable Debby (Gloria Grahame), whose sadistic gangster boyfriend (Lee Marvin) has disfigured her by throwing boiling hot coffee at her face. He hides her in a local motel where he is living away from his daughter, who is also under threat. Though he is concerned about his daughter, he has abandoned the actual "family" part of his family man identity, so he can minimize her presence in his life.

Throughout the film, Bannion refuses to kill anyone, but this seems a rather arbitrary rule, as he not only harms people profligately, and, worse, sets other people up to do his killing for him. He chillingly manipulates Debby to murder on his behalf, an action she feels certain that she chose independently. In the process, she is shot. As she dies, he waxes nostalgic, not about their relationship, but about the beautiful life that he lost: "Katie used to dress up the baby like a princess. One of the most important parts of the day was when I came in and saw her [the baby] looking like something that just stepped down off a birthday cake. I guess it's that way with most families." But Debby, dying before him, would never know. Unlike Vicky, the character that Grahame would play the following year, Debby wants to escape violence, to find a normal life, but she continues to be attracted to violent men. In the process, she becomes disposable, both to her gangster boyfriend, Vince, and then to Bannion, the film's "hero" and "good guy" who refuses to commit murder. To the ultimate family man, literally nothing else matters. When the film ends, Bannion goes back to work as a cop, acting jovially, as though nothing has changed. In the perfect culmination of his ruthlessness, he asks, smiling, if the coffee is hot.

Joe Starrett, having experimented with violence in *Shane*, will certainly not return to it. He is a family man, whose slow, homely nature befits that role, and he is, we assume, smart to accept a lack of virility in exchange for family stability. But Dave Bannion shows no signs of reform. He uses and abuses a vulnerable young woman, he chokes and beats other men, he lets his likely lover kill and take a bullet for him; he is overcome with rage, but he simply returns to the police force, as though satisfied. Detective Bannion may not be that different from the criminals he prosecutes, but his family man image and pose of mourning have protected him and may protect him still.

3:10 TO YUMA

3:10 to Yuma shows no indication of war, but it is a perfect example of the extent to which the period following the war defined masculinity in its shadow. Having spent years developing their personas, their "first bodies," Ford and Heflin meet in this film for a sort of quiet battle of postwar masculinities and expectations. Ford's incumbent sexual power and violent potential beneath a cool exterior threatens Heflin's fearful family man. In this case, Ford's masculinity threatens to subsume Heflin's entirely. Ben Wade (Ford), unlike Shane, does not seem to threaten Dan Evans's (Heflin's) family or marriage in a literal sense, but will come close to usurping his position within them, partly due to Dan's own weakness. Like Shane, Ben envies Dan's life and is unable to have it. Though Dan and Ben end the film with some understanding of each other's circumstances, the message is clear: the Joe Starrett/Dan Evans type triumphs over the Dave Bannion/Ben Wade type by holding fast to moral conviction over the trappings—erotic and economic—of a different masculinity. The film opens as Dan and his boys, Mark (Jerry Hartleben) and Matthew (Barry Curtis), come upon Ben and his gang holding up a stagecoach. Mark urges his father to intervene, but Dan wants to "let the dust settle." Ben takes the Evans's horses away so that they cannot ride for help, and the boys are again disappointed in their father's inaction. They watch as Ben suavely takes the money out of the stagecoach, only to shoot and kill the driver (Bill Moons) and one of his own men (Jerry Oddo) when he sees that the former is trying to thwart his plans.

Unlike Joe Starrett, Dan seems to have entirely given up on fighting and taking risks. When his wife, Alice (Leora Dana), asks him about the stagecoach robbery, he responds:

> **DAN:** That's life. You have to watch a lot of terrible things. People get killed everyday. Lightning can kill you. 3 years of drought killing my cattle—that's terrible too. What can I do? I can't make it rain. You expect me to cool off the sun?
> **ALICE:** Dan, why are you so cross?
> **DAN:** I don't know. You just seem to expect something from me that I'm not—
> **ALICE:** No, I don't. Not really.
> **DAN:** I can't go chasing after outlaws. Not with cattle dying all over. If I don't save them, I don't know what I'm going to do.
> **ALICE:** Well, you have to do something. You can't just stand by and watch.

When Dan finds out that he cannot borrow money from his friend, he agrees to shepherd Ben Wade to the train (the 3:10 to Yuma), which will take the criminal to jail. Dan knows that this is dangerous, but he sees no other choice.

Ben is not caught immediately. His gang manages to fool the marshal and others, leading them on a wild goose chase during which Ben seduces a lonely young barmaid named Emmy (Felicia Farr). Ford pushes his usual smoldering looks and raised eyebrows to a new extreme as he sweet-talks her, but also makes clear that he longs to settle down somewhere, especially after they make love and discuss the fact that he will never be back. Dan soon arrives, shamelessly asking for money for the time that he lost tracking down his horses, and the marshal and his men swoop in and handcuff Ben.

The townsmen make a plan for getting Ben to the train, which involves a stop at the Evans's house. The scene that follows is a direct comment on

Shane. On Shane's first night with the Starretts, Marian makes a delicious meal served on the "fancy" plates (Joe notices), and eyes Shane with curiosity. Alice, too, makes a dinner that Ben can share with the Evans family. The boys, like Joey, cannot stop talking to Ben. They scold him for starting before "grace" and bombard him with family details. Like Joey, the Evans boys cannot help but compare their father to the other man and feel compelled to portray him as a hero. Dan asks them to quiet down, but he cannot help but smile when they tell Ben that, "Pa can shoot a cougar running like lightning a mile away."

The boys wonder if they should say grace with Ben, given that he is "bad," but his mother assures them that "grace is for everyone." After prayers, Mark tells Ben, "I didn't close my eyes once. I just squinted. Because you could run away." To which Ben replies, "Now why would I want to run away? Why, this is real nice. Real nice." But unlike Shane, Ben does not leave the compliment. When Dan asks him if he would like him to cut his meat for him (since he is in handcuffs), he says, "Yes, would you please? Thank you. Would you mind cutting the fat off, please?" And when Dan looks insulted, he smiles slyly and adds, "I don't like fat." While Ben's strength might seem thwarted by his handcuffed incapacity, Dan still cannot fully meet his eyes.

Moments later, when Dan has to leave the house to check on a noise, Ben begins to talk softly to Alice: "I was in San Francisco once. I knew a girl there. And she was the daughter of a sea captain too. And she had the greenest eyes. I used to look real deep into her eyes and and and they'd just change colors you know, get all firey and green and, you know, all the colors of the sea. It's funny how a woman's eyes will change color at night time." Alice begins to smile and blush. Entering, Dan is deeply upset. He leads her out of the house and asks why she was "all big-eyed and listening to him," and pathetically puts his head in his arms (as he does throughout the film).

This dinner scene becomes a touchstone for the movie. Dan has been set up as weak and demoralized. Unable to provide for his family or keep his wife's attention, he is almost completely emasculated. Ben has been cool, manipulative, and debonair, despite being captured and in handcuffs. Even more than Joe and Shane, the two are set up as opposites.

Ben and Dan leave for Bisbee as Alice, Mark, and Matthew watch them ride away in terror. The two men must wait in a hotel room until the train arrives, as no one in the town will open up their homes to a criminal. The pre-existing antagonism between Dan and Ben can then be explored for most of the remainder of the film, one-on-one and within four walls, as they watch the clock tick down to 3:10.

When they enter, Ben takes the bed and Dan a chair, in positions that they will keep through most of the film. Ben bounces on the bed and then says, "This is the bridal suite, huh? I wonder how many brides, hmmmm . . ." Seeing Dan's offended look, he continues, "Is it a little hot in here? Is it warm?" and convinces Dan to open a window, which he does carefully, leading Ben to chide, "Don't take any chances do you? Hey, where's your sporting blood?"

"Back home with my wife and boys," says Dan, and Ben is chastened.

Because Ben knows about Dan's financial troubles, he is able to manipulate him and even tries to bribe him to let him go. He tells Dan that he could be rich and more successful if he set Ben free. Ben would become Dan's "silent partner," putting up the money so that the Evanses could make improvements on their ranch and have a better life. Ben tries to pitch this in different ways. He reminds Dan that his posse will find him and that, if Dan does not have the stomach to shoot, he himself will die and leave Alice a widow. He tells Dan how "alike" they are and how much he relates to him. But nothing upsets Dan as much as this exchange:

BEN, IN CLOSE-UP: When I was having supper with you last night, Dan, I was just sitting there, I was thinking. I was thinking that maybe someday I'd like to have a wife. Yeah. Must be real nice having a couple of boys like that to ride with every morning and then a woman like that every night, to pull her close. That must be nice. I'll tell you one thing though Dan, I'd feed her a whole lot better than you do. (The camera pulls back from a close-up to a two-shot.) I'd feed her better, I'd get her pretty dresses that she'd be real happy wearing. (Returns to close-up) And I wouldn't make her work so hard, Dan. (He smiles wickedly.) I'll bet she was a real beautiful girl before she met you.

From this close-up of a smiling Ben, there is a cut to a close-up of Dan, whose eyes are bulging, tears running down his face. Now, when Dan threatens to kill Ben, Ben admits that he might believe it this time.

Marian Starrett spends a lot of the film deciding and putting on dresses, trying to look beautiful to impress Shane. Though Joe teases her about it, he admits that he appreciates it when she puts time into her looks. When she dances with Shane at the party, she does so in her wedding dress, which only adds to Joe's heartache in the scene. So, when Ben sneers that Dan cannot provide Alice with "pretty dresses," he is insulting Dan on two counts: not only is Dan an inadequate provider for his family, but this inadequacy has undermined his sexual relationship with his wife. Because most viewers would have seen *Shane*, it is impossible not to associate Alice's "hard work" and lack of "pretty dresses" with sexual dissatisfaction that would lead her to desire others, others like Ben Wade. For all of these reasons, this is Dan/Heflin's emotional climax.

Alice arrives just before 3:10, begging her husband not to take Ben to the train by himself. There are no "good guys" left to help him—they have all backed out in fear—but Wade's gang has surrounded the hotel and the train station. Because Alex (Henry Jones), the local drunk, died in the attempt to prosecute Wade, Dan feels that he has no choice but to go through with the plan, however dangerous. Ben keeps making offers until the last minute, even continuing to leer at Alice, and promising Dan that their arrangement could be kept a secret. Dan finally affirms that he will not take Ben's money, and they make the dangerous journey from the hotel through the hail of bullets from Wade's men. Ben coaches Dan the entire way there, eventually saving him, and they both end up safely on the train together, as Alice and Mr. Butterfield, the stage line owner (Robert Emhardt) watch and wave from a nearby field. Ben admits that he has broken out of jail at Yuma before, leaving his reasons for manipulating Dan and allowing his men to shoot up the town and take a man's life completely unexplained. Yet, the two seem to end the film as friends. Because they have each acted morally in some respect—Dan by not taking dirty money, Ben by keeping Dan from getting shot—they seem to share a momentary similarity. But as in *The Big Heat*, there is nothing to indicate that Ford's character is reformed, only that his violence is in remission. Ultimately, the men emerge from the situation as the same men who entered it. The dramatic circumstances in the interim have not changed who they, fundamentally, are, but both men have shown that they are more complicated than they seem: the "man who does" and the "man who doesn't" emerge from *3:10 to Yuma* as distinct types, but with unexpected sympathies. Finally, *3:10 to Yuma* may have the most optimistic take on postwar masculinity of any of the films in this chapter: both the "man who does" and the "man who doesn't" *don't* in the end.

3:11, OR FORD AND HEFLIN AFTER 1957

Heflin and Ford would go on to do other films, the latter much more than the former, but the 1940s and 1950s gave them many of their best roles. In the last years of the 1950s, Ford transitioned into comedies, including several service comedies, like *Don't Go Near the Water* (Charles Waters, 1957). Ford would become comfortable in comedy over the course of the 1960s and '70s. Heflin continued to play conflicted fathers, including Lee Hackett in *Gunman's Walk*. But Heflin's masculinity, as defined by *Shane* and *3:10 to Yuma*, as well as many of his other roles, did not easily translate into the Hollywood 1960s. Their parts were lacking, but so were their understandings of the post-studio era: both found themselves without any work at times, and other times they took jobs that only set their careers back further. Heflin and Ford were simply ill-suited for the serious films of the 1960s because the films that defined them—and that they helped define—were worse than passé. Their style, their politics, and their ideas about men were now offensively uncool. The films for their types in their era ran counter to the early 1960s *Playboy* ethos: denial of the past and flight from responsibility would soon prevail.

THREE

GETTING COMFORTABLE

—

Hugh Hefner's Playboy *in the 1950s*

Hugh Hefner's *Playboy* is among the twentieth century's most important mainstream magazines, and it has without a doubt played a significant role in shaping and manipulating American perspectives on sexuality and culture more generally. Hefner himself, as an entrepreneur, a philanthropist, and an icon, as much as an editor and publisher, is rightly identified with these changed perspectives. However, like almost any major cultural achievement, *Playboy* was surprisingly and tremendously derivative, especially in its early years. Also like any cultural achievement that lasts over decades, it changed enormously over the course of its history, only solidifying its style years on, making any generalized proclamations about the "*Playboy* philosophy" only marginally applicable to its earliest years. Critics who read the magazine as an extension of the man must therefore recognize two things: 1) when Hefner started the magazine, he was a completely "average" man of his generation and viewed himself that way, and 2) the relationship between Hefner and his readers changed dramatically at the end of the 1950s, and though it continued to change ever since, it never returned to its original form. Hefner, GI Bill–educated, married white midwestern father, taking dull desk jobs to support his family but deeply uncomfortable with the contradictions of postwar life became, in six short years, the wealthy swinging bachelor whom his magazine had hinted might be only a fantasy, might not truly exist at all. On this image, *Playboy* became an empire, and Hefner became "Playboy."

To his credit, Hefner did not claim that he was single-handedly responsible for the birth of the sexual revolution, and he was willing to admit that the magazine was hugely indebted to *Esquire*. Perhaps when Hefner acknowledged this debt, he did so assuming that those listening understand its gravity. For men of Hefner's generation, the meaning attached to this invocation of *Esquire* goes well beyond a single publication, though *Esquire* itself was *Playboy*'s biggest influence. Hefner's reference extends to a wartime culture of circulation, both of magazines and discrete images, the breadth of which informed Hefner and his early staff, as well as his readership. Building on a history of, and taking its place within, men's magazine culture, *Playboy* took the country by storm. This chapter will examine *Playboy* as a particularly postwar invention, one which critically updated the men's magazine for an environment in which it was sorely needed. *Playboy*'s necessity was obvious at the time: it was as an instrument and a handbook for coping with life after World War II and the Korean War and the attendant transitions into heterosexual monogamy and middle-class life. The notion that a magazine could have such therapeutic power and importance was not outrageous but, in the postwar era, could be reasonably accepted as fact. *Playboy*, through its Playmates, fiction, editorials, and humor, trained men in what they may have needed most in the postwar era: getting comfortable.

ESQUIRE AT WAR

On one of his many USO tours, Bob Hope famously quipped, "Our troops are ready to fight at the drop of an *Esquire*," and his joke speaks volumes about the importance of magazines to wartime culture. President Roosevelt was inordinately concerned about troop morale, and entertainment was the cornerstone of his plans to maintain it.[1] USO "camp shows," as well as the circulation of Hollywood features and radio broadcasts, were considered critical components of the war effort. So too was the distribution of magazines, including, of course, *Esquire*.

Esquire was popular, though its fortunes rose and fell more than once over the period between its first issue and the war. Nevertheless, once the war began, where would servicemen be without a handbook? Initially, government officials were reluctant to support distributing the magazine, fearing its content might cause behavioral problems amongst the men, but publisher David Smart "convinced the military that a magazine filled with pin-ups, racy cartoons, and camp humor was essential for the military morale."[2]

Like many businessmen at the time, Smart, both conscientiously and shrewdly, decided that his product should actively promote patriotism. He wrote that, "*Esquire*'s role in wartime is perfectly clear. This magazine's primary job is to purvey diversion, not as an escape but as a tonic." But, as Pendergast points out, "it was not the kind of diversion the magazine had once offered. More and more of the magazine was war-related: the stories were about brave soldiers who got the girl; there were full-color illustrations of warplanes; and nonfiction pieces educated readers about wartime production, the enemies' armed forces, and other such topics."[3] "Esky," the magazine's cartoon mascot who appeared on each cover, was dressed as a soldier or sailor on almost every wartime issue, and war themes dominated the covers during this period. Some of these covers even included advertisements for war bonds. Given the breadth of the war effort and the population that constituted its most voracious readers, it made sense, both economically and patriotically, for *Esquire* to shift focus, but, as with many American entertainment products at the time, the line between *Esquire* and the US military was sometimes unclear. Smart most brilliantly maneuvered this mutual advantage and he did so in ways that ultimately benefited his military readers.

For example, the War Production Board offered magazines designated as morale boosters ample funding for paper, but this allocation was based entirely on weight. *Esquire* used lighter paper than the other magazines, which meant that they could offer more content. Throughout the war, the publishers also printed a special military version of *Esquire* that included no advertising. In order to maximize the paper allocation, some other magazines made miniatures, but, after *Esquire* attempted one, the Special Services Division of the Armed Forces advised them to print only in full-size "because soldiers didn't want miniature [pin-ups]."[4] *Esquire* expanded their product line for the war effort, creating calendars featuring their popular Varga pin-ups and other merchandise, which they sold directly to the US military, often at little more than cost. For these reasons and others, *Esquire* shed its "elite" image as a handbook to American leisure, becoming a key "morale" publication and a favorite of American troops.

STARS AND STRIPES MEETS *YANK*

However substantial *Esquire*'s influence, in giving that magazine its due, historians have largely failed to notice the role that military periodicals, often published by the United States Armed Forces, played in magazine culture during the 1940s. These publications were distributed to men in all theaters and were published weekly (to *Esquire*'s monthly), incorporating the voices of (mostly) men serving in an array of capacities, including both on the front lines and in the "brick foxholes" of the United States. As such, military magazines were among the most-read US-based publications of the 1940s.

Stars and Stripes, which operated out of the US Department of Defense, was launched by the Union during the Civil War, but stopped printing for several decades until US participation in World War I.[5] It hit its apex in World War II, thanks in equal parts to a dramatic increase in funding and the fact that military membership was larger than ever, bringing more contributors and, of course, more readers than it had before or has had since. Its visual style owed as much to the newspaper than to the magazine, likely due to its history, but many on its staff came from the magazine world and pushed *Stars and Stripes* in that direction as much as possible.

In addition to eagerly funding *Stars and Stripes*, President Roosevelt and Secretary of War Henry Stimson, in collaboration with Edgar White, formerly of *Stars and Stripes*, developed the idea for *YANK: The Army Weekly*. Roosevelt, Stimson, and White believed that *YANK* could build coherence and a space for venting amongst non-officers, whom they feared would feel aggrieved by their loss of control and autonomy in the service.[6] *Stars and Stripes* attempted to reach officers as much as enlisted men and prided itself on hard reporting, but also on its status during World War I. *YANK* was for the enlisted men and draftees, not for the officers. As McGurn notes, "One of the few times that officers were allowed to contribute was when they spoke up in self-defense in the 'Mail Call.'" *YANK* was designed with the clear objective of boosting morale, primarily for the influx of young, inexperienced men. This objective meant that *YANK* emphasized and offered more reader letters, advice, cartoons, jokes, pin-ups, games, a somewhat more magazine-like visual sensibility, and a wittier, jauntier prose style, not unlike *Esquire*'s (though for reasons of class diversity, it was less dependent on cultural allusions). "*YANK* was a friend and colleague of the World War II soldier and was itself part of the enlisted US Army. It let off soldier steam with 'Mail Call' letters to the editor allowing troops to air their beefs at a global level," cartoons and humor to raise their spirits, and "its pinup pictures of gorgeous women back home, YANK spoke to the longings of young men who sometimes went months without seeing a woman." YANK, like New Deal–era *Esquire*, developed its readers into men who could withstand the current conditions, while offering them enough pleasure and comfort to solidify these new identities.

Also, while *Stars and Stripes* was free, YANK cost five cents, the price meant to solidify its value. The decision to charge for the magazine—the charge was unnecessary given the government's funding—likely did two important things: it classified the publication as a luxury, which may have made it more of a morale booster to those whose food, clothing, and shelter were selected for them, but it may also have led to more sharing.

Though the objectives and content of *Stars and Stripes* and YANK differed, it would be a mistake to see the publications as entirely unalike. *Stars and Stripes* boasted cartoonists who were considered some of the finest in the world, while YANK did report the war, even offering some of the earliest coverage of Dachau and critical on-the-ground accounts from infantry soldiers and others. Given the wide distribution, relevance, and content overlap of *Stars and Stripes* and YANK, it is highly likely that most men (of all ranks, but especially the enlisted) enjoyed both, and enjoyed both along with *Esquire*.

MEN'S MAGAZINES: 1945 ON

The military magazines were designed to foster collectivity. In a conflict in which those fighting were separated by continents, ranks, and the often vast differences in their backgrounds, it was critical to the war effort to construct a strong collective culture. The use of magazines during the war was itself collective. Individual servicemen tended not to have subscriptions; even when the men purchased them, it was difficult for those subscriptions to be filled, given the frequent travel and overall unpredictability of the war. Generally, magazines were sent to units or companies, meaning that the experience of consuming magazines was always, to some degree, a shared one. Servicemen read magazines to each other and enjoyed pin-ups and cartoons posted in their shared quarters, but, even alone in his bunk, the individual reader was part of a world-spanning collective of American military men, a reality to which these magazines were acutely attuned.

For this reason, men's magazines' transition to the postwar era in which men's contact with fellow readers was more theoretical than actual, seems awkward and delayed. Continuing the relationship it had built with a broader base of men during the war, *Esquire* attempted to be less elite, featuring Westerns, mysteries, and war stories, and the circulation rose at the end of the 1940s. Unfortunately, the magazine lost its reputation—and elite advertisers—in the process and became one of many men's magazines rather than the preeminent. Pendergast recognizes that *Esquire*'s newfound middle-of-the-road appeal became a sort of template for men's magazines in the 1940s, though some in the magazine industry still associated *Esquire* with its fancy roots: "Where *Esquire* led, others followed.... *True* and *Argosy* offered themselves as *Esquire* for everyman. Rejecting *Esquire*'s urban sophistication and fascination with style, *True* and *Argosy* made themselves into the men's magazines for the hunting, beer, and poker set.... In the process of recreating *Esquire*'s formula for a different demographic, these magazines succeeded in bringing a whole new class of men into the cultural logic of consumerism and modern masculinity."[7] The class implications of men's periodical publishing that Pendergast illuminates here cannot be overstated. Founder Arnold Gingrich would return to *Esquire* in 1952 (about a year before *Playboy*'s first issue), with the explicit objective of resurrecting its elite appeal, but by then the magazine had conceded many advertisers of the highbrow market. The climate of postwar men's magazines is stilted because of industry assumptions: the "beer and poker set" for the GI Bill generation was not entirely different from the imagined elite market of *Esquire*; in fact, with each passing year, these seemingly discrete markets became not only more and more similar, but more and more the same.

Hefner wanted to start his own magazine partially because he was so disappointed in *Esquire*'s less urbane postwar sensibility, though, by the launch of *Playboy*, Gingrich had already restored some of *Esquire*'s highbrow reputation. Hefner found the emphasis on hunting and the like boring, downmarket, and a particular type of old-fashioned. That Hefner was a teenager during *Esquire*'s elite period is not unimportant: his particular notion of the magazine's upper-class past was probably more myth to him than memory. Hefner believed that his generation would respond to a magazine inspired by *Esquire*, but finely tuned to these men who came of age at war. Business historian Susan Gunelias explains Hefner's early—but ad hoc—analysis of market conditions:

> From the start, the target audience was defined and consumer expectations were set. Luckily for Hefner, his instincts about *Playboy* were accurate, and consumers pulled their hard-earned money out of their wallets to buy it. Interestingly, Playboy's success didn't come from years of market research, demographic analyses, and behavioral modeling. Instead, it came as a result of one man's instinct that there were more people in the United States who thought the way he did and would like to join together in sharing those thoughts through a new magazine. Hefner has admitted he based many of his early business decisions on instinct rather than traditional business acumen.[8]

The "instinct" to which Hefner admits was based on a good deal of both observation and real data. *Stars and Stripes*, *YANK*, and *Esquire* circulated simultaneously and were part of a booming wartime periodical culture in which many servicemen were dedicated readers of all three (among, of course, many others). Hefner was working at the Publishers Development Corporation, the company released an extensive study which determined that men were rarely readers of, or even subscribers to, a single publication, but could be counted on to read several magazines marketed to roughly the same demographic. He may have learned from the examples of *Stars and Stripes* and *YANK* that a fine publication could be improved upon for a younger audience, and that they could coexist with slightly variant visions of almost the same market. Also from the comparison between *Stars and Stripes* and *YANK*, Hefner likely gathered that simply up-pricing a magazine could increase its perceived value, to some extent regardless of content.

Military publications were also a launching pad for many young men who would go on to write, report, or illustrate for major American magazines on their return and men who relied on them during wartime might follow their work into new publications. Hefner was one of these contributors. Trained as an Army infantry rifleman, the 113-pound Hefner actually ended up making a name for himself as a cartoonist and writer under the byline "Hef."[9]

Even if Hefner's ambition was for *Playboy* to be the magazine of his generation—and, to some extent, it was—he was aware that *Playboy* was entering as a participant in a large market that could accommodate many players. For this reason, *Playboy* could be marginally different; it did not need to be wholly original. Its difference, ultimately, was in its creation of a market which did not strictly exist before and which sat in the center of a Venn diagram of under-40 male readers: the men who enjoyed *Esquire* but were younger than its target audience and those who read men's adventure magazines. Many of these readers would continue to subscribe to these other publications, but would find some of their dissatisfactions with them addressed in the pages of *Playboy*.

Hefner's engagement with other postwar men's publications extended well beyond *Esquire*. After *Esquire*—his first choice—rejected his cartoons, he managed to get some accepted at *True*.[10] Not long after, when he was working for Publishers Development Corporation, a major publisher of popular men's magazines, he watched the launch of a major (though yet not discussed) *Playboy* influence: *Modern Man*.[11] *Modern Man* differed from *Playboy* in the major ways that Hefner and others describe: it was too outdoorsy, too adventuresome.[12] Nearly every advertisement in its early issues is for guns, fishing gear, camping equipment, or power tools. What Hefner and others do not mention is that the magazine devoted a lot of its content to war and military features that varied from war stories to profiles of particular heroic soldiers (almost exclusively enlisted men), Army cartoons, and even illustrated and pictorial tutorials on military maneuvers. On the contrary, though *Playboy*'s fictional characters would occasionally mention the war and a few cartoons in the 1950s included soldiers, for the most part, *Playboy* seemed to avoid admitting that the war had happened at all, though it was constantly implied or evoked.

Modern Man's celebrity cheesecake—popular issues featured photographs of Jane Russell and Rita Hayworth and, on one occasion, Marilyn Monroe—likely inspired Hefner's ingenious purchase of the Monroe photographs, which gave him a serious marketing edge for a brand-new magazine. Additionally though, the accompanying text in *Modern Man* particularly calls to mind *Playboy*'s imagined reader. For example, in December 1952 (exactly one year before *Playboy*'s first issue), the editor proclaimed the magazine's position on masculinity: "Time was when a man's man preferred the company of men. But today, in the light of changing ideas and greater 'sophistication'—call it decadence if you prefer—it seems to us a man's man had damned well better prefer the company of women. It is this real appreciation that we desire to emphasize in Modern Man. We hope you appreciate it too."[13] As in much postwar culture, men were being actively pried away from other men. The mainstream strain of men's magazine culture makes this plainer than almost any other forum. Because of the crucial role they played in the war effort, men's magazines required a much more conscious and straightforward re-envisioning. That shift which *Modern Man* and its ilk attempted, *Playboy* accomplished.

PLAYBOY LAUNCHES

Until September of 1953, *Playboy*'s title was *Stag Party*. This was not a private working title but was used on all publicity and fundraising material until just over a month before its first printing. A copyright attorney threatened Hefner with a cease-and-desist order, claiming that *Stag* magazine was prepared to sue for what its publishers felt was infringement.[14] Hefner, his wife Millie, and Eldon Sellers, his right hand, brainstormed a night away. (Sellers and Hefner shared a lot of sexual adventures and experimentation.) They came up with *Bachelor, Gentleman, Sir,* and others, but eventually settled on Playboy.[15] According to Hefner and Sellers, the 1920s feel of the word "playboy," a word that they felt was no longer common parlance, made it seemed ripe for postwar reinvention.[16] Weyr suggests that the title *Stag Party* may have helped elicit initial interest because, after all, "everyone had his own vision of what went on in them."[17] However, Hefner said himself, in an interview with Greg Jackson for ABC News, "We would not be sitting here today, if I'd called it *Stag Party*."

The collectivity implied by the title *Stag Party* did not suit the period. Notably, *Gentleman, Bachelor,* and *Sir* are also individual, but, not only do they lack the ring of *Playboy,* they also suggest divisions among men. *Gentleman* and *Sir,* moreso than *Playboy,* mark the reader as upper-class or officer-class (and, furthermore, a bit of a snob about it), while *Bachelor* indicates that the subscription ought to be canceled on the reader's wedding day. Given the breadth of *Playboy*'s readership, this would have constituted a division; for *Sir* readers, it was a perfectly-pitched assertion of their marginal—and therefore shared—status. Yet, *Playboy,* like *Stag Party,* involves "play" and "fun," not just a title. The playboy can have as much fun on his own terms, rather than as part of a group of men. In other words, the word and image of the *Playboy* straddled the complicated requirements of 1950s magazine culture:

to construct camaraderie among a broad reading public but to envision its members as individuals, reading alone and living apart.

Furthermore, the postwar era required a different role for women than during the war, as sociologists Beggan and Allison suggest: "Women are unwelcome at stag parties, except in the limited role as sex objects. They are incorporated into stag parties as strippers and prostitutes. They may appear as images in pornographic movies. But the presence of a woman as a co-participant in a stag party contradicts its core concept. As such, a stag party becomes an environment and process that reifies, for both men and women, identity as a stereotype."[18] Because both the Playboy and the Playmate have since become stereotypes, it is easy to forget that Hefner was attempting to revise—and, to some extent, undo—the stereotyped gender norms of the previous generation. One of the ways that he accomplished this was by allowing men and women to happily, comfortably spend time together in the pages of his magazine.

Playboy's co-ed environment was markedly different from *Stag*'s. Men's adventure magazines—otherwise known as "sweats"—boomed in the postwar era, and *Stag* was among them. Sweats were salaciously illustrated, absurdly sensational magazines, focused on violence, muscles, gore, and anger. Sarracino and Scott claim: "In the mid-1950s, publishers would begin to test the limits of men's ability to identify with extreme images and stories. Till then, most covers and interior illustrations depicted men in combat, against men or animals, and the blood on display often belonged to the protagonist, whom we were meant to believe would fight his way to safety."[19] It was not until 1956 that scantily clad women were consistently pictured in the sweats, but, in these magazines, women were "menaced by the same kinds of attackers that, until recently, only male heroes had to battle, thereby ramping up the level of violence involving scantily clad women." As the decade passed, "clothing became more tattered, and the poses began to look suspiciously like those of a woman during sex, despite the arms of the octopus wrapped around her. Simultaneously, the American male figure began to shrink both visually and in the storyline" (74). The menaced and assaulted women were almost all white, as were by all indications, the presumed readers. Typically, the appearances of women and men of color were in the Western-themed sweats, in which "Injuns" attacked. Though in its earlier years, *Stag* was very similar to *Playboy* in covering art, music, literature, fine food, and examinations of heterosexual relationships, by 1950, publisher Martin Goodman fully ushered the magazine into sweat territory.

Stag and its ilk indulged in the very things that *Playboy* anxiously eschewed. Collins and Hagenauer, throughout their opening essay to *The History of Men's Adventure Magazines in Postwar America*, draw a sharp contrast between *Playboy* and *Stag*, not just as publications, but also asserting that the readers and their concerns were completely different, implying that life for the working-class readers of sweats was difficult and defined by the horrors of the war, but that *Playboy*'s readers were able, through the consumerism and education enabled by the GI Bill, to forget about those horrors and to avoid daily anxieties in postwar life, particularly about their relations with women.[20] Sarraccino and Scott add that, "*Playboy*'s good life, however, seemed foreign to many working-class men. The resonant message of the [men's adventure magazines] was that American men, many of them former combat soldiers, triumphed through the power of guns and clenched fists. If 'they' want to steal your masculinity, the MAMs implied, you'll have to keep it through violence and sheer force of your will."[21] Of course, men of or aspiring to the middle class had also experienced the horrors of the war.

Like the paperback writers, the writers and illustrators of the sweats suggested to their readers that attempts to cope with the war past (and the subsequent problems of postwar life) were futile; in the end, men were reduced to that past, and the life ahead was determined by it. The sweats, therefore, forthrightly acknowledged the fears of veterans that society—and these men themselves—had. However, while coping with memories and fears about what war brought to the present, men also dealt with discomfort and isolation in the postwar environment, the uncertainties and complications of which could not be understood in the terms of the war. Adam Parfrey claims that the sweats were uniquely able to communicate to those frustrations and, atypically, sees a broad—rather than strictly working-class—readership:

> This new era lacked its means of instruction for gray flannel and blue-collar foot soldiers. After vets returned home, battles were fought daily in the expanding corporate world. Instead of being sent to Boot Camp, given uniforms and meals and taught how to make camp and murder, corporate soldiers were expected to compete in the marketplace. . . . The humiliations of the working world and romance were more subtle and devious. . . . All of [the sweats] had, among the lures of woman flesh and vicious bad guys, a lot of warnings, how-tos, and comforting memories of wartime, when decisions were black and white, the villains darker, and victories sweeter.[22]

Palfrey posits that, in addition to the "comforts" that the sweats offered, these magazines also instructed, taught, and warned. They did not simply vent men's pain; they were not simply palliative; they told them what to do. Of course, the sweats and the postwar pulps were outlets for the very emotions that they suggested could not be handled safely, albeit in opposite ways from *Playboy*. The problem was that these magazines gave advice that their readers, in reality, should and could not take or use.

While *Playboy* is a pose, and one of cool confidence at that, *Fury* and *Rage* are the *True* and *Real* emotions beneath the pose; *Peril*, the *Savage*, and the *Untamed* within are what the *Playboy* sought to escape; *True War* and *Real Combat* are what they wished to forget; the bunny, not the *Wildcat*, what they chose to project. Sarracino and Scott argue: "The revolution *Playboy* started in 1953 contrasted starkly with the marketing appeal of the MAMs. Whereas MAMs sold fear and anger, *Playboy* sold pleasure and joy, whether in the form of centerfolds or in the reviews and ads for the best new products."[23]

Playboy's readers were far from carefree, though the pose of relaxed fun—"pleasure," if not "joy"—was the editorial hallmark. According to the Editor's Note in its inaugural issue: "If we are able to give the American male a few extra laughs and a little diversion from the anxieties of the Atomic Age, we'll feel we've justified our existence." As I suggest in the introduction, using the language of the "Atomic Age" may also have allowed middlebrow writers to more casually allude to the stresses of the era without acknowledging their roots in men's wartime experiences. Since so few interacted with the Bomb, and it was not used until the end of World War II, the "Atomic Age" may have couched war trauma in depersonalized abstraction. The violence perpetrated by or trained for by individual veterans that the sweats forthrightly acknowledged in their dirty treatments of combat, *Playboy* slyly glanced at sidelong.

As Smart said of the wartime *Esquire*, *Playboy*'s "primary job is to purvey diversion, not as an escape but as a tonic," and, as Gingrich said of New Deal *Esquire*, this diversion would train readers who "hadn't the faintest idea" how to negotiate a new era. This diversion, through which *Esquire* offered a hopeful cure to the Great Depression and the tonic that kept soldiers in fighting shape, was called for once again. Diversion, in the particular form offered by *Playboy* magazine, was actually fashioned as a road to health, maybe even a cure, for the ills of postwar American men. Given the abiding faith of Roosevelt and his public in entertainment as a combat coping tool, it was reasonable that Hefner, with former Army Air Force pilots Art Director Art Paul and co-publisher Eldon Sellers, would see the potential of *Playboy* as medicine for postwar men.

THE NAKED AND THE SICK

In addition to and within Roosevelt's "prescriptions" of USO shows and magazines for the troops, women were an enticement and motivation to fight. As Marilyn E. Hegarty discusses: "Morale building and morale maintenance emerged as significant concerns of the state apparatus; the military must be fit to fight both physically and psychologically. Government officials assumed that women would provide [sexual] services to the military, and they did. . . . The subject of male sexuality was both present and absent in these discussions. Since many authorities took as a given the male need for sex, their concern was not to prevent men from sexual liaisons but rather to ensure that they would be protected from venereal disease and fit to fight."[24] Though publicly defensive of the servicemen as "good boys," government and military officials were conflicted about the issue of prostitution. As Hegarty discusses, "officials believed that 'prostitution was inevitable,'" and "were generally convinced that 'a segregated district with medical inspection was the answer to the problem.' The army was willing to support 'added protection' by means of increased attention to prophylaxis."[25] Condoms were liberally distributed, and the American Social Health Association (ASHA) passed pamphlets that cautioned men to wash thoroughly after a sexual encounter and to report to a prophylactic station immediately for a thorough internal and external chemical cleansing.[26] As Hegarty aptly puts it, "The postcoital procedures maintained a link of sex-sin-dirt-danger that not only supported the women-disease connection but also can be seen as both deterrent and incitement to sex."[27]

The military and the media also constructed careful racial and classed boundaries around acceptable and "healthy" sexuality. The original ASHA anti-venereal disease propaganda generally featured women coded as working class, but those campaigns began to change, as awareness of "khaki-wackies" and "patriotutes" increased. Women—usually young, white, or Black (though generally not integrated), and frequently middle-class—patriotically attended USO dances and servicemen's balls, but some number would later have sexual contact with the soldiers and sailors. Having previously attributed the spread of VD to Black servicemen and sex workers, military officials and the ASHA were forced to realize that men might contract VD even from white and Black "good girls." In response, they developed new anti-VD campaigns, including the famous "She May Look Clean . . . But . . ." posters and pamphlets which read "You are badly mistaken if you think you can tell whether or not a girl has Venereal Disease by her looks or her clothes or by listening to her story."[28] In a film made specifically for Black soldiers, *Easy to Get*, two characters experience the consequences of unprotected sex. One, Private Anderson, misjudges a sex worker. According to the narrator, "Whores are supposed to keep clean, aren't they?" More dramatically, Colonel Baker, back from furlough, suffers the consequences even of a "homefront girl" who "looked clean all over." Clearly, these "suggest[ed] that appearances could be deceiving." Even the iconic girl next door could be dangerous. By making inferences about the girl next door, conservatively dressed and made-up, "the official stance once again blurred the line between the good girl and the bad girl."[29]

Some scholars have concluded, then, that female sexuality was particularly pathologized, as women of all races and classes became associated with disease.[30] However, it may be equally appropriate to say that sexuality itself was pathologized, and that it was male sexuality which was considered "out of control"; after all, women's sexual advances were out of some sense of patriotic "duty," while men's were biological subversions of that duty.[31] In Hawaii, for example, Bailey and Farber note that residents near Army bases called for a "buffer of whores"—presumably Native Hawaiian—which would isolate the "innocent," young, white or Black middle-class women from the base desires attributed to soldiers of all races.[32] As a result, brothels near military bases were tolerated, or even approved of, by government and military personnel at many levels, to the point where some servicemen were given phrasebooks to use with sex workers in their stationed countries, some including as many as fourteen ways to say, "goodbye."[33] Women who were non-white and "professionals" could be merely "outlets," which would keep men from being distracted by their libidos, rather than companions who might distract them from their duties. According to Hegarty, "the military, as well as many citizens, approved of the brothels for the simple reason that, given 'unstoppable urges and acts,' regulated prostitution kept venereal disease rates down." Some feared that, if they were not able to patronize sex workers, the servicemen would prey on "our young girls and women," meaning middle-class white and sometimes Black women, whether through seduction or sexual assault.[34]

Amid all of these attitudes, "married women also continued to receive a variety of messages that reinforced their obligation to maintain sexual allure by remaining the same women they had been when their husbands went to war," sending homemade pin-ups and yet staying faithful to their fighting men, as much for the health of the nation as for love or commitment.[35] These married or betrothed women were urged to "be his pinup girl" by the military and advertisers alike.[36]

PINUP GIRLS

Obviously, many servicemen did not have frequent access to, or chose not to engage in, sex with sex workers or local women. Presumably, pin-ups supplied much-needed sexual and romantic succor. American writer and World War II hero Kurt Vonnegut had this to say of the pinup: "The American male's capacity to make do with imaginary women gave our military forces a logistical advantage I have never seen acknowledged anywhere. Commanders of other armies and navies had to try to arrange, however cumbersomely and often cruelly, for some sort of female companionship, in a manner of speaking, for their fighters from time to time. But American soldiers and sailors simply brought their own undemanding and nearly weightless paper dolls along."[37] Vonnegut is inaccurate in that, as I discuss, the American military did not completely avoid contact with sex industry, but also in that other militaries encouraged the use of pin-ups. Furthermore, the pin-ups created or supported by rival militaries became treasure for Allied captors and vice versa.

However, Vonnegut's experience with and appreciation for American pin-ups is both typical and warranted. Pin-ups were so critical to morale that soldiers themselves advocated to get their needs met. Black soldiers, unsatisfied with the mostly white pin-ups, went so far as to reach out the NAACP requesting pinup images of Black women to help them get through the war.[38] The American pin-ups, the women men "made do with," were not all the same, and the degree to which they were "imaginary" varied from picture to picture. Although the term "pinup" is largely associated with the illustrations of Alberto Vargas, *Esquire*'s wartime pinup artist, the pinup circulated in several simultaneous incarnations during World War II. In addition to the extremely popular Varga Girls, the aforementioned homemade pin-ups joined celebrity and model pin-ups distributed through the USO and *YANK*. Many women who rose to their prominence in postwar Hollywood began their upward trajectory as a result of being *YANK* pin-ups (like Rita Hayworth and Betty Grable), while others felt responsible—to their country and their studios—for providing pin-ups based on their pre-existing or current fame (like Jane Russell and Lauren Bacall).

There was certainly slippage between and amongst these three categories, but the variety of these images attest that pin-ups were not "one thing," but served a range of men's desires. The Varga Girls and the models looked more sexually experienced, even aggressive, while the homemade pin-ups tended toward innocence, with Grable offering a blend of both.

As art historian Maria Elena Buszek points out, Vargas was "indebted to the proliferation and popular acceptance of the professional, sexually self-expressive woman that Hollywood had been glamorizing since the First World War."[39] Indeed, Vargas's early work was as a poster and portrait artist for Hollywood studios, creating images of Barbara Stanwyck, Marlene Dietrich, Dolores del Rio, and many other unabashedly sexualized stars, before the Production Code required him to "tone down" his illustrations.[40] Not long after, *Esquire*'s David Smart, against the objections of Arnold Gingrich, employed Vargas to work with artist George Petty in order to illustrate "The Types of American Beauty."[41] Vargas's particular "type of American beauty"—glamorous, exotic, seductive, airbrushed, and impossibly proportioned—quickly overshadowed the silly blond Petty Girl as *Esquire*'s representation of women. Unlike the Petty Girl, the Varga Girl followed the fashion of Stanwyck and del Rio, flaunting her appeal and thusly pursuing her pleasure. There was no mistaking the Varga Girl's intentions, nor *Esquire*'s intentions in printing them. As the *New Yorker*'s "Talk of the Town" read, Vargas "could make a girl look nude if she were rolled up in a rug" and the women he drew were "faultless in limb and shaping, curved with strange magics."[42] This strange magic was in Vargas's departure from realism, his pursuit of a purely sexual ideal. As Buszek describes: "Vargas embellished freely upon his renderings of the female body in order to exaggerate their sensuality. The Varga Girls' impossibly long legs ran derriere-lessly into their waists; their ample breasts spread irrationally far across their chests; their doll-like and fetishistically detailed feet teetered on pumps rendered with equally lavish attention. . . . [And] adding to the Varga Girls' unsettling perfection was Vargas's airbrush technique."[43] This air of unreality, the smooth glowing skin, the fantasy proportions, the "freakishly faultless" body, and the come-hither look of the Varga Girl seem to contradict the common notion that pin-ups were designed for men fighting abroad to feel something of home. I attribute the Varga Girls' popularity to their isolation of sex from obligation, guilt, homesickness, and fear. They were not touched, they did not touch back. They were alone, often without even a background, and few props, making them tough to locate, and therefore entirely sexual and entirely fantasy. Buzcek continues: "The Varga Girls didn't seem to like company of any kind: during Vargas's six-year association with *Esquire*, they appeared only once as a duo, once as a trio, and once with a man. Engaging viewers with their forward, even predatory gazes and beckoning gestures while distancing them with the shimmering solidity of their impossible figures and spectral surroundings, they aimed to entice but not necessarily to invite" (206). Buszek, Westbrook, and other scholars of pin-ups claim that these "faultless," "magic," airbrushed women were "liasion[s] to the homefront" and "metaphor[s] for the American girl" (210). On the contrary, though these liaisons to the home front were necessary, they were not embodied by the Varga Girl, though during the war, her image was unavoidable. According to Pendergast: "It was the Varga Girl who most commonly graced the nose sections of U.S. Warplanes; the Varga Girl whose pinup traveled across enemy lines with U.S. Soldiers. She soon became the subject of calendars, playing cards, drinking glasses, and a variety of other products. The Varga Girl soon replaced Esky, the pop-eyed playboy who graced the cover of *Esquire* through the 1930s, as the magazine's dominant image."[44] Pendergast rightly points out that Varga Girl seemed to be everywhere and, for that reason, her image has understandably eclipsed other pin-ups in the popular imagination. Rita Hayworth, Lena Horne, and Betty Grable may, however, be exceptions. Hayworth and Horne's images owed much to the Varga Girls and were in keeping with the seductive celebrity and model pin-ups at the time, though their expressions were modulated because of their race and ethnicity.

As with the Varga Girls, the argument that celebrity pin-ups were direct invocations of home is overly simplistic, though the Varga and celebrity pin-ups differed in many important ways. While the Varga Girls were often in almost strangely nondescript locales, many of the celebrity pin-ups featured the women within the war context, especially in the Pacific, or with military gear. Unlike the pin-ups that Westbrook discusses, these images do not conjure the home front, but bring a woman into a sex-segregated environment. Unlike the sweetheart at home or the wholly imaginary Varga Girl, celebrity and model pin-ups were there and in the here-and-now. Mostly, this idea is constructed, but there is some tangible truth to this image: celebrities and "starlets" did visit the troops abroad and provide them with entertainment through the USO, both live and through film. Of course, the fact that many of the most popular of these pin-ups were virtually unknown before is equally important, making these women of the war itself.

The role of race and ethnicity in the composition of celebrity and model pin-ups—and the changes therein—shows the extent to which the pinup needed to change toward the end of the war. The early softening of Horne's image due to her race was not entirely consistent. Early in the war, so-called exotics were nearly as common as "all-American girls." What is perhaps most interesting about these particular pin-ups is the fact that some of the same women made the transition from "ethnic" to "white" or "Black" as the war came to its end.

So, Rita Hayworth, dark-haired and explicitly "Latin" at the beginning of the war, became a white redhead in American-style lingerie by the end. Lena Horne, once in brightly-colored garb with "Gypsy" jewelry, became once again a light-skinned Black woman draped in glamorous Hollywood gowns. Dorothy Lamour was no longer the woman of the South Pacific wearing Hawaiian flowers, but a standard white movie beauty. In this way, the pin-ups anticipate both *Playboy*'s Playmate and *Ebony*'s postwar ideal, both of which relocated sexual desire to home front women and away from the dangerous "exotic" zones in which white and Black American men engaged with local women. Nevertheless, the celebrity and model pin-ups maintained a similar style, with highly suggestive looks and glamorous clothing, even as the "exotic" trappings disappeared.

But Grable was enormously popular—nearly as popular as the Varga Girls—though her image was surprisingly multifarious. The "cute" end-of-the-war Grable is the most recognizable, but she was highly glamorized in earlier pin-ups. This certainly enabled her popularity among men, but also made her an ideal model for home front women to copy in producing their own pin-ups because she willingly embodied multiple forms of sexuality, all of which they could try on. Referring primarily to the "cute" images of Grable and her imitators, Robert Westbrook claims that servicemen viewed them "not only as objects of sexual fantasy but also as representative women, standing in for wives and sweethearts on the homefront."[45]

Like the disappearing "exotics," Grable's image changed over the course of the war. By the end of the conflict, Grable's marriage to Harry James was well known and, as Westbrook points out, seems only to have added to her popularity. There begins the sexualization of intimacy, a reinvestment in monogamy which was required on the home front. Seemingly contrarily, Grable's popularity after her marriage points to the sexualization of the "other man's woman," which Hefner would capitalize on in *Playboy*. The "taken" woman—featured throughout the war in the homemade pin-ups—was the woman at home, the woman to whom these men were returning.

Home front women were encouraged to make their own pin-ups. Some photographers—men and women—offered free or low-cost services to young women who wished to pose for their partners. overseas. There was a tremendous range in homemade pin-ups, but these circulated as much as the mass-produced imagery.[46] Some pin-ups were posed at the aforementioned photo studios, but they were more often shot in familiar locales, places that men would recognize. The homemade pin-ups were also frequently very tame, especially when compared to the Varga Girls. The censorship of the more risqué of these images depended upon the servicemen's locations. Because the threat of censorship was ever present, and presumably out of modesty, it is difficult to find many nude homemade pin-ups, though they do exist. Women's legs, however, were almost always on display.[47]

PLAYMATES AND POSTWAR SEXUAL CULTURE

American men, having been told both that sex was dangerous and that titillation was a boost for morale, that their own sexuality was risky but uncontrollable and that experts were trying to assure that it was appropriately channeled, understandably needed guidance to understand the place of sexuality in life after the war. For certain, in the era before *Loving v. Virginia*, this meant an orientation not just away from "exotics" and "foreign" women but toward intraracial sexual contact, designed to exist inside domestic spheres segregated in postwar America. Sex experts flooded booksellers and popular magazines with information meant to ground postwar sexuality.

The supposed increase in extramarital sex and sexual desire might seem likely to occasion outright repression, but the concurrent popularity of Freud among postwar psychiatrists and Alfred Kinsey's best-selling *Sexual Behavior in the Human Male* and Havelock Ellis's *Sex and Marriage* paved the way for a therapeutic culture centered on safe sexual expression.[48]

From Freud and Ellis, Americans learned that sexual repression was not a cure for, but actually caused illness. As Petigny notes, "According to the leading psychologists and psychiatrists at midcentury, sexual repression was a major source of human neurosis. . . . These concerns went well beyond the academic writings of psychologists . . . throughout the culture of the 1950s, Americans were being urged to 'ease up' sexually."[49]

Freud and Kinsey in particular became mainstream cultural touchstones but were merely leaders to a wider marriage improvement industry, which included marital therapy but also yielded a flood of marriage advice manuals.[50] Despite the exhortations against "repression" and the encouragement of sexuality, complications and contradictions remained. Marriage counseling and marital advice were hugely popular and were rife with these complicated demands.

In Clifford Adams's best-selling advice guide, *Preparing for Marriage*, for example, he sets up the contradictions of marriage in the postwar era:

> For ten years, war, or its threat, has made normal living impossible. Constant insecurity and uncertainty do not promote healthy attitudes in young people. A desire to make every minute count has impelled many of them into unorthodox behavior. Many men inducted into military service have been tempted into promiscuous associations. A good many veterans saw so much of war and its destruction that they became cynical of the value or standards and ideals. This put them into an extremely poor mood to think of marriage. Others, returning to civilian life, have colored the thinking and behavior of their friends and acquaintances.
>
> Yet to millions of other veterans war has made marriage seem terribly attractive. After leading a shifting existence where nothing seems real or permanent, the lasting unchanging things in life appear more significant than every before. Marriage, ideally, is one of the most permanent things in life. It gives a person a chance to sink roots.[51]

Though he acknowledges the difficulties of marriage, and even its drawbacks, Adams is fervently pro-marriage because, as he puts it, "Marriage must have something to offer. If you doubt it, consider these facts: —Married people normally live longer than single people . . . —Fewer married people go to jail than single people —Fewer need confining in mental institutions —Fewer commit suicide" (17). Marriage is, in short, healthy and its medicinal value is more urgently necessary for veterans.

In chapter XVI, "Is Your Mate a Veteran?," he explains that the problem is inevitable: "There is no need to discuss the question, 'Should a girl marry a veteran?' because most girls have married veterans anyhow." But these girls must realize that "the standards of fighting men are those of men living without women, of men who have temporarily forgotten many of the moral values of our normal living. If they hadn't lost them they wouldn't have been good killers. Some of them have feelings of guilt and remorse from cheap women they have known" (168–69). But despite the pressure for openness and sexual honesty and freedom, Adams is clear: "Questioning him about his 'past' . . . will only upset him and add nothing either to present adjustment or future happiness" (170). Because he acknowledges that these marriages are "unstable," "the past is the past" and should be kept there in order to preserve or forge a union (191). In order to move past the shame of wartime transgressions, husbands and wives must develop into sexually healthy and mature companions. Adams believes that "sexual health and maturity" have three components:

> There is freedom from repression and inhibitions concerning sex.
> There is no disgust or aversion as far as sex is concerned.
> Likewise there is no abnormal curiosity or longing for sexual information or experience. (38)

The abnormal was defined broadly, though Adams would occasionally mention specifics, including: "-Homosexuality;—Voyeurism;-Fetishism;—Pedophilia;—Sadism and masochism" (68–69). Those were the key themes of pornography in the early twentieth century, and this was the image that *Playboy* needed to shed. Adams next cautioned readers that "Unhappy Husbands" tend to be "more radical about sexual morality," and to "like recreations that take them away from home" (69, 83).

Adams sounds rather like *Playboy*. After Mike Wallace interviewed Hefner, *Playboy* published a transcript of the program in the December 1957 issue, in celebration of the magazine's fourth anniversary. Before the Playboy Philosophy, published in installments from 1962 through 1966, this interview is perhaps Hefner's clearest articulation of his vision for the magazine. Wallace consistently and critically questions Hefner about the place of sex in the magazine, to which Hefner responds, "Sex always will be an important part of the book because sex is probably the single thing men are most interested in. We're quite honest and open about it—we think that's a healthy way to be." He later says: "There's nothing dirty in sex unless we make it dirty. A picture of a beautiful woman is something that a fellow of any age ought to be able to enjoy. If he doesn't, then that's the kid to watch out for . . . The deviates, the perverts, the serious delinquents, they're not interested in healthy boy-girl relationships. It is the sick mind that finds something loathsome or obscene in sex."[52] In short, Hefner's supposed "radical" reappraisal of 1950s sexual morality is, in fact, very much in keeping with the contemporary discourse. Men and women both should enjoy and desire sex, and be free of "hang-ups," but also of "perversions." The "kid" who does not like a *Playboy* pictorial ought to be "watched out for," for he may have a "sick mind." In fact, because *Playboy* portrayed "healthy boy-girl relationships," the magazine actually fended off the "perverts" that observers like Wallace wrongly presumed it would attract. Wallace, it is implied, simply misunderstands postwar sexuality and boundaries of sexual health.

For servicemen with spouses and committed sweethearts at home, it was important to believe that only certain women—certainly not their own—craved sex. The Varga Girls and most celebrity pin-ups represented an active, assertive, glamorous sexuality, the realization of which did not overtly threaten men with concerns about their mates' fidelity. After the war, these same men had to readjust to the notion of their own partners as sexual beings. Most critics have read the Playmates as relocating heterosexual male desire outside the home during a period of increased domesticity, but they can equally be read as re-importing this desire into the safe confines of home and neighborhood. Desire for "dirty girls," whether sex workers, women of more sexual experience, or women of other races or nationalities, as well as desire for other men, had to disappear. It was important that the girls around them, the non-threatening girls they knew, became the locus of their desire.

Furthermore, for years, heterosexual desire had become an almost exclusively homosocial experience: lusting over the pin-ups—whether Varga Girls, celebrities, or buddies' wives—was something that men not only did together, but they did mostly to the exclusion of real sexual interactions with women. Even in seeing sex workers, male bonding experience defined the encounter. Given the number of men who joined the service as adolescents, it is likely that, for many, these were formative sexual experiences (as the letters from servicemen in the prologue suggest).

Playboy's Playmates were the result of these many competing and conflicting needs: they liked and wanted sex but seemed innocent about it, they were gorgeous but not overly glamorous ("girls next door"), and they seemed like they "belonged" to someone, conjuring up the experience of shared sexual interest to which men had become accustomed. Their images—criticized as sanitized or dumb (and therefore not sexy enough)—made sexual desire safe and comfortable in the postwar period, which was no small feat.[53] On the heels of Betty Grable and the homemade pin-ups, Playmates redefined "sexy" for postwar America.

Though Hefner brilliantly chose Marilyn Monroe's image for *Playboy*'s first issue (at this point, the feature was called "Sweetheart of the Month," rather than Playmate), he shifted gears immediately to his original interest: publishing cheesecake of "the girl real to the reader."[54] Hefner has since congratulated himself on "put[ting] an end to the Madonna-whore complex that has been very harmful throughout the centuries," but the breaking down of this complex was being undertaken throughout much of American culture, including film, literature, advertising, and psychology, as I have discussed. What Hefner was able to do was bring that sensibility to an adult entertainment context, which had theretofore been dominated by what some have called "whore-ish" representations.[55]

First of all, Hefner's Playmates were less dressed than most pinups, but more dressed than the women in under-the-drugstore-counter pornography. The pubic area was entirely off-limits and even nipples were often obscured.

Partly because *Playboy* wanted "amateurs" who had never before posed nude, some critics have described the 1950s Playmates as looking "awkward." Sometimes the poses were themselves awkward, but other times the women seem awkwardly imitating celebrity pin-ups and having fun doing it. Again, this may have added to their "nakedness" and to the sense that they wanted sex too, not just cash in exchange for their images, nor did they seem to be demanding of any kind of service or evoking any guilt. They were interested in doing the very same things that the reader was supposed to be interested in. Similarly, another aspect that stands out against other erotic photography before and since is the genuine smiles on many 1950s Playmates.

In addition to the fact that the Playmate pinup shots were not entirely nude in many cases, the fact that they were printed alongside fully dressed pictures of the same women made the nude women look more dressed and the clothed women more naked. The photos could evoke the experience of wanting to know what a particular woman looked like with her clothes off—not just any woman naked, but *this one*—making even the nude photos romantic, not strictly "dirty." *Playboy* promoted the fact that they found their models just anywhere and one, in particular, stands out. Miss July 1955 was Janet Pilgrim, a woman Hefner met working in *Playboy*'s (then quite small) subscription department. Among *Playboy*'s most popular 1950s Playmates, the circumstances of her discovery undoubtedly added to her appeal. As with all the Playmates, Pilgrim's feature included clothed shots, in this case at her typewriter in the magazine's office. Pilgrim was not only the "office girl," but she was also pictured "dolling up" for the evening, powder puff in hand, with a man waiting for her in the background. The presence of men in Playmate photos is surprising and was part of almost every pictorial.

Much has been made of the fact that the man in the background of the Pilgrim photo is Hefner, but readers were not privy to this information. Hefner suggests that it was not important that he was identifiably tied to the pictured Playmate, even in Pilgrim's case, where he is visible: "I tried to suggest the presence of a man, something to suggest that what we were really looking at was a sexual situation of some kind, because what I was trying to say, quite frankly was that sex was a natural part of life, and that nice girls liked sex too."[56] Given the marked similarities to many wartime homemade pin-ups, the notion that the reader was looking at a "taken" woman might have had a nostalgic resonance. While the Varga Girl was purely sexual and the celebrity or starlet was incorporated into the wartime environment, the homemade pinup (and mass-produced pin-ups of this style) included the promise of home: security, love, and a certain type of monogamous, "healthy" sexuality. The shared sexual desire for Jane Russell on the wall was only one sort; men shared desire for the women in the homemade pin-ups, developing desire even for the letters, the families, the lives that came with them. In this way, the Playmates not only revise sexuality for the postwar world; Hefner uses them to tap into men's own feelings of romance and innocence, their prior knowledge that they had the capacity for healthy sexuality, even love.

It is no secret that Hefner felt stifled, even under attack, by what he saw as the repressive nature of American sexual mores. Despite the prominence of Freud and Kinsey, the post office threats against *Playboy*, the opprobrium of people like Wallace, and his unsuccessful attempts to "liberate" his own sex life proved to Hefner that the current environment was actively hostile to sexuality, male and female. Well beyond publishing the Playmates, *Playboy* regularly bemoaned this harmful "repression" and "Puritanism." Though the magazine developed an increasingly evident "personality," the advocates for further sexual openness in its pages were not just upwardly mobile heterosexual men, and their arguments were not always in the editor's notes. Fiction, cartoons, and commentary by *Playboy* outsiders evinced this same point of view, but in sometimes radically different forms.

A CROOKED MAN: CHARLES BEAUMONT IN *PLAYBOY*

Playboy's publication of "The Crooked Man," by up-and-comer Charles Beaumont, is an important example of their emphasis on thwarting repression. Beaumont initially submitted his short story to *Esquire*, but *Playboy* eagerly printed it when the other magazine's editors had second thoughts. *Playboy* was clearly a better fit, as Hefner encouraged science fiction writers (the staff at *Esquire*, especially after Gingrich's return in 1952, considered the genre beneath them) and, in fact, its apocalyptic sexual scenario appeared quite appropriate in the *Playboy* context. Science fiction scholar Valerie Broege summarizes the story:

> A further step toward what most would consider technologically abetted perversion is taken in Charles Beaumont's "The Crooked Man." In a future society under heavy electronic surveillance, homosexuality has become the norm and heterosexuals are deemed unhealthy criminals, misfits, and animals. Because everyone is born from a test tube, nursed by machine, and raised in Character Schools, old-style mammalian reproduction and family life are obsolete and thus considered abnormal. When the story's main characters, a fugitive man and woman in love, are apprehended, they will spend a couple of days in the hospital, have one short session with the doctors, have a few glands removed, receive a few injections, have a few wires attached to their heads, be placed under a machine, and—voila—they will be cured of their affliction: They will be gay like everyone else.[57]

Playboy historian Carrie Pitzulo mentions Charles Beaumont's "The Crooked Man" in her *Bachelors and Bunnies,* and Hefner himself discusses publishing the piece in Brigitte Berman's documentary, *Hugh Hefner: Playboy,*

Activist, and Rebel. One possible reading—the most attractive to Pitzulo and to Hefner himself—is that the publication of the piece was a sort of pro-gay activism. In fact, to reader complaints, *Playboy* responded, "we saw it as a plea for tolerance—shoe-on-the-other-foot sort of thing."[58] It is only this response that both Pitzulo and Hefner cite. There is undeniable truth to the contention that "The Crooked Man" had an activist potential and, obliquely, echoed the sort of arguments that Harry Hay and other important gay activists had begun to use in 1950 for ending the oppression of homosexuals.[59] However, just before the letter that Pitzulo cites and to which *Playboy* responds, another reader's letter offers a different interpretation of the story. Herbert Tuthill of Sunol, CA writes: "Charles Beaumont's 'The Crooked Man' is quite a story and may well be more prophetic than we think. In my opinion, the hypocritical heritage of Blue Laws and Puritanical ideologies which permeates our era is certainly giving us a decided push in that direction."[60] Tuthill's interpretation may well be representative of other readers', especially those of subscribers whose reading had already been conditioned by *Playboy*. For example, Tuthill's recourse to our American "heritage" as "Puritanical" is a move redolent of Hefner's media talking points and articles in the magazine in the two years prior. The notion that male heterosexuality—including that described as "natural"—was under attack was an enormous part of *Playboy*'s message. Yet, the story itself is remarkably more complex in its negotiation of sexuality and gender than critics generally acknowledge. Context, of course, matters a great deal in interpreting the story; its publication in *Playboy*, a flamboyantly heterosexual men's magazine, demands a closer reading of the piece, rather than mere summary.

It is not just casual heterosexual sex and sexual commerce that are abolished in Beaumont's dystopia, but true love and intimacy between men and women, reproductive sexuality, and family life. Jesse, the story's heterosexual male protagonist, and Mina, his female lover, long for monogamous heterosexual and romantic love, and even consider each other "fiancées," though they cannot legally marry. They are saddened not only by the restriction of their recreational sex lives, but by the use of artificial reproduction rather than biological birth, and the reduction of sexuality to a sort of sleazy, self-interested activity which centers entirely on physical pleasure, to the exclusion of companionate love relationships. In the world of "The Crooked Man," shame around, pathologizing of, and repression of "healthy" heterosexuality has perverted all forms of sexuality and, furthermore, led to an extreme divide between the sexes. "The Crooked Man," though ostensibly about the particular stigma of homosexuality in the postwar era, actually endorses *Playboy*'s forms of sexual expression.

The story takes place at a mainstream nightclub tellingly called The Phallus, and its patrons are mixed: young attractive "Hunters" and older unattractive "Beasts" who are reduced to winning the young men over with money and gifts. The partners are described as somewhat hostile to one another. The wait staff are dressed only in gold-sequined trunks and their muscles are oiled, which they clearly dislike. Rather than speaking to one another, Beasts and Hunters communicate largely through "desire symbols"—physical gestures which indicate sexual interest. Jesse is particularly unsettled by their dancing: "pressed close together, dancing with their bodies, never moving their feet, swaying in slow lissome movements to the music, their tongues twisting in the air, jerking, like pink snakes, contracting to points and curling invitingly, barely making touch, then snapping back." What could be a fun and even skilled recreation becomes a lewd display.

The patrons and staff revolt Jesse, but so too does The Phallus's decor. After expressing concern that citizens would be trapped in same-sex dormitories, no longer able to have private homes, but also "no more parks, no country lanes," he casts a look around at the walls filled with "carved symbols and framed pictures of entertainment stars—all naked and leering." This paragraph matter-of-factly combines three concerns—homosocial dwelling, the absence of "home" in the form of suburban and/or rural markers, and pinup decor—suggesting that all are related and distasteful, and that the entire world would resemble military barracks. Also, two things stand out about Beaumont's description of the pin-ups. First of all, they appear alongside "carved symbols," indicating that the photographs are primitive or even savage expressions of sexuality. Second, these pin-ups are not the homemade sort, nor the Playmates, but more in the style of the provocative wartime celebrity pin-ups, even though the models are male in this case. Their "leering" as much as their nudity sickens Jesse. As such, their presence in a story in *Playboy* implicitly authorizes Playmate-style imagery as less primitive, more evolved erotic portraiture.

The story frequently portrays male semi-nudity as repulsive, whether in photographs or in reality, and regardless of their particular appearance—pale or tanned, fat, athletically-muscled, or thin. All the men at The Phallus are mostly undressed. However, when Mina meets Jesse there, she is dressed in drag to infiltrate the gay male world in which her lover is trapped. This requires her to be mostly covered to hide her feminine body. He looks for her breasts beneath her clothing, while also hoping that her shape will remain invisible so that they are not caught. Here again, the hidden female body and the exposed male body represent a dangerous inversion of the "norm" to which Playboy readers are accustomed, but this conflict may also signal that public demands for the magazine to forgo female nudity are harmful and confusing.

While Jesse is appalled by the behavior and imagery of The Phallus, it is not only the "normal" homosexuals who perform such vulgar sexuality. Jesse remembers visiting "Crooked Clubs," at which heterosexual people met other heterosexuals for sex. Jesse was looking for love, but "it was no use" because "there was a sensationalism, a bravura to these people, that he could not love. The sight of men and women together, too, shocked the parts of him he could not change, and repulsed him." By removing reproduction and family from sexual attraction, and by stigmatizing desire between men and women, heterophobes have essentially required a particular performance of sexual identity, which makes Jesse uncomfortably aware of his "black desires." His internalized heterophobia makes him disgusted at himself; the "crooked" people that he sees at these clubs also experience this shame, which further denaturalizes their sexualities. Perhaps ironically, Jesse seems to believe that more (hetero)sexual openness mitigates this distastefully overt behavior.

Even without the eroticized "Battle of the Sexes," men and women are antagonistic in this society on both personal and political levels. The shift in preferred object choice has forced the genders into entirely separate camps. When two women enter The Phallus arm-in-arm, their same-sex object choice is not adequate for them to fit in; they are seen as "dirtying up" the place and wished away to "their own clubs." This disgust for, or disinterest in, the opposite gender is built into the political structure: senators are elected not to serve the greater good, but each to represent the interests of her or his own gender. Heterosexuality has, perhaps unexpectedly, been the crucial link between men and women and sex segregation has jeopardized social coherence.

Politicians, particularly heterophobic Senator Knudson, have capitalized on the rampant fear of heterosexuals, saying: "The disease that throws men and women together in this dreadful abnormal relationship and leads to acts of retrogression—retrogression that will, unless it is stopped and stopped fast, push us inevitably back to the status of animals—this is to be considered as any other disease. It must be conquered as heart trouble, cancer, polio, schizophrenia, paranoia, all other diseases have been conquered." Though heterosexuality has been criminalized, in large part due to Knudson's efforts, heterosexuals are also told that they are "sick" and "diseased," not just breaking laws. This notion of "sickness," like Adams's and others' in the postwar era, denies people's sexual agency. When they are arrested, they are not imprisoned for their crimes per se, but are subjected to physical cleansing to remove their very desires. There are clearly parallels to discourse on homosexuality, but postwar psychiatrists mostly believed that the theory of being "born that way" was debunked by psychological advances which proved that homosexual activity was the result of "conditioning," rather than a physical problem. Adams is typical: "It was once believed that homosexuals were 'born that way.' But now it is known that the great majority of them, male and female, are normal in a bodily sense. Their interest in persons of the same sex is clearly the result of unfortunate conditioning" (68).

Given the common pathologizing of so many sexual behaviors and desires in the postwar period, Knudson's speech is redolent of more than postwar homophobia, though that is certainly prominent. Again and again, Jesse and Mina have been made to feel "dirty," a word which signals similarity to the discourse around "dirty magazines," and the "dirty pictures" within them, a discourse in which Playboy was, in 1955, the major focus. Of course, the "clean" versus "dirty" dichotomy around sex during wartime would have weighed heavily on readers' reactions to the words, as well.

Toward the end of the story, Jesse and Mina embrace in a dark corner booth, racked with fear and guilt. Addressing her ambivalence about their feelings for each other, Jesse tells Mina that he has read books that tell the "truth" about sexuality and that they are not sick, not truly abnormal. The comfort that Jesse takes in these books, their portrait of his "normalcy" and his eagerness to share their messages with Mina would undoubtedly ring true to a variety of *Playboy* readers in the post-Kinsey world. Hefner felt that *Playboy* was that book for the 1950s, a place in which "healthy" heterosexuality is given free rein.[61]

Though the controversy around "The Crooked Man" made it Beaumont's most famous story for *Playboy*, Hefner enthusiastically published a number of others in the 1950s. The stories vary quite widely, ranging from humor to thrillers, but each sheds light on the logic of "The Crooked Man." The

Beaumont story that *Playboy* published just before "The Crooked Man," entitled "The Hunger," most suggestively registers men's concerns about their own sexuality, as well as their sense that women looked on them with fear.

"The Hunger" takes place in a town driven to panic by a serial rapist and murderer. The story alternates focus between the deranged culprit and Julia, an "old maid" of thirty-eight who, with several of her widowed friends, has become obsessed with him. As Julia and her friends desperately try to determine who would do such a thing, they keep coming back to the notion that any man—given the right circumstances—is capable of such violence. As Maud says, "this here maniac is only doing what every man would like to do but can't . . . It's a man's natural instinct—it's all they ever think about." Maud does not specify whether what men think about is rape, murder, or the combination of both. Julia does not want to believe Maud but feels that since she and Louise have been married, they must understand men better than she does. She imagines what it was like for them, believing these awful things about men even when "soft words have been spoken to them, and strong arms placed around their shoulders." Attempting to sympathize with him, Julia determines, but does not say aloud, that the killer must be especially lonely. She too is lonely, so she walks out late at night, planning to sacrifice herself to him. Meanwhile, the killer stalks the streets, overcome with "the hunger." He fights with everything in him to be a good man. Unfortunately, "the hunger grew: with every step it grew. He thought that it had died, that he had killed it at last and now he could rest, but it had not died. It sat inside him, inside his mind, gnawing, calling, howling to be released." Repeating nursery rhymes, attempting to inhale the beauty of nature around him, he is unsuccessful. The story ends just as the attack is to begin and Julia hopes that, after the assault, he will allow her to live, but the reader knows better: his eroticized hunger requires him to kill as well as harm.

This story is like so many of its time in its characters and its assumptions about masculinity: however average, men are rapists and killers, even when they wish not to be. The closer women are to men, the more certain they are in this belief. So, while many of the messages in "The Hunger" are interchangeable with those of other fiction at the time, it's important that Beaumont and *Playboy* were also susceptible to these portrayals of masculinity. The killer and Julia, in their loneliness, develop sexual desires which are unsafe and socially unacceptable, inarguably "perverse" under *Playboy*'s definition. In "The Hunger" it is their lack of sex appeal, rather than the social stigma of "The Crooked Man," which keeps Julia and the killer from having consensual sex with others; however, as in "The Crooked Man," unexpressed sexual desire is channeled into unhealthy and dangerous activities, rooted in shame and desperation. Though Maud and Louise assume that all men are capable of or want to commit violence, Beaumont does not actually confirm that belief: though presumably Maud and Louise knew their own husbands well, the fact that Julia herself wants to be victimized indicates that loneliness and the social distance between men and women may have triggered the killer's actions. Were Maud and Louise's husbands satisfied? Or were they too on a continuum of "hunger," of which their wives were marginally aware and which heterosexual monogamy kept in check? Again, as in the case of Jesse finding solace in his books, perhaps *Playboy* can provide the comfort and release that would have kept the killer's hunger at bay.

ARE AMERICAN MEN ASHAMED OF SEX?

As Pitzulo points out, the Playmate features allowed young women a rare opportunity to voice their own sexual desire, not just cater to men's.[62] Women writers also found space in the magazine to champion a new sexual morality. Pamela Moore's "Love in the Dark: Are American Men Ashamed of Sex?" is a most fascinating example.[63] Like a number of *Playboy* writers in the 1950s, Moore makes a comparison to Europe to suggest that Americans held inferior sexual attitudes. Moore's essay—which occasioned furious debate in the Letters section of the following issues, equivalent only to "The Crooked Man" in its response—includes the usual inveighing against sexual repression, but Moore's take on it is unmistakably a woman's. The repression of male heterosexuality, she argues, creates an environment in which women and girls feel uncomfortable, men become neurotic, and family is imperiled.

For example, Moore tells of a thirty-year-old woman and a twelve-year-old girl arrested for wearing "too short" shorts: "Their arrest implied that the average American male, witnessing such a display of feminine anatomy, would go instantly berserk, and that rape was uppermost in men's minds, controlled only by the vigilant police force and a 'moral' insistence that women of all ages, including children, display only that part and that amount of their anatomy as will not drive men to these desperate and violent acts"

(55–56). In other words, American culture paints men—average men—as so damaged that women's bodies actually have to be concealed for their own protection. To Moore, it is not that men are biologically disposed toward rape, but that the stifling sexual culture of the United States both conditions and assumes it, like Maud and Louise in "The Hunger." Rape is considered "uppermost in men's minds," and these "average" men become defined in American society as rapists. Women too are oppressed as a result: not only are they arrested for wearing shorts, but they develop shame about their bodies.

Men's inappropriate and disrespectful behavior toward women, Moore argues, is also rooted in the repression of male heterosexuality, but one mode of "repression" that she acknowledges is surprising in the pages of *Playboy*: "Another thing about American men that has always fascinated me is the way that they collect pinups of movie stars and naked women; the way they whistle at a pretty pair of legs. I had accepted that as part of 'what men are like' until my trip abroad," during which Moore emerged nude after skinny-dipping in front of a group of men and was not cat-called. Well before Gloria Steinem and others criticized *Playboy* for dehumanizing and objectifying women through the Playmates, Moore implies that sexualized imagery of women leads to what we now call sexual harassment and, what's more, she clearly does not wish to experience that harassment. Jesse, in "The Crooked Man," is appalled by sexual imagery of a very certain type, but Moore reproaches not only nude pin-ups, but also men's conditioned reaction to women who are not trying to arouse an erotic response. For Moore, the "healthy" sexual individual most able to experience true erotic satisfaction does not fixate on an image, nor dehumanize his object, reducing her to a "pretty pair of legs." On the contrary, it is through true engagement and intimacy that both parties find honest pleasure. She describes what she believes American men are missing in the words of an Italian professor whom she met on a train: "To make love—anonymously—when the whole meaning of love and loving lies in the fact that this is a person you love, whose eyes you watch, whose body you cherish, whose mouth has meaning because it expresses love—for you. Yet you close your eyes, you say. You isolate yourself. You do not dare to say, 'It is you and it is I and we are here, together, making love.' Instead, you say, 'I am an island of Blackness, receiving anonymous sensations. You are as personally involved as a radar set.'" That men and women suffer lost sexual satisfaction, discomfort, and neurosis due to sexual repression is not the extent of repression's harms. Moore also sees this American attitude toward sexuality as toxic to family life: "Years and years of repression, of being taught that sex is evil, that it is something carried on in the dark, can, and often does, lead to impotence. Yet, young fathers continue to pass this hypocritical attitude from generation to generation." And later: "The guilt-ridden, convention-ridden American male will be a better father when he's no longer ashamed to be his wife's lover." Children grow up not only ashamed of their own sexuality, but with a view that sexuality does not take place within the security and intimacy of a marriage, but outside of it, in desire for pin-ups or scantily clad women.

Liberated sex exists, but it is actually loving, monogamous, and domestic. Like Beaumont, Moore argues that it is this sort of sexuality that is being pathologized, not just "perversion." In fact, Moore sees 1950s America as very near the dystopia of "The Crooked Man," in which only "unhealthy" sexuality can be expressed due to widespread shame and censure. Though she points to different manifestations of and problems with men's sexual repression, Moore's take is in keeping with *Playboy*'s general treatment of male sexuality: managed expression is the closest thing to freedom.

Later in his interview with Mike Wallace, Hefner goes on to say, "For us, sex is neither dirty nor is it a sacred cow. A society that is able to laugh at itself—sex included—has a pretty healthy attitude." So, for Hefner, the magazine's role is not as simple as normalizing "normal sexuality": *Playboy* treats the subject with humor and the humor is part of the medicinal effect.

LAUGHING AT LIFE

The notions about sexual health and perversion discussed above were widespread, but there was certainly a class component to the *Playboy* manner of addressing them, and this manner was often humorous. And as the discussion of the sweats suggests, there was at least the appearance of a class divide between the readers of *Stag* and those of *Playboy*, even if those men were often, in fact, the same. *Playboy* was addressed to the striver. Unlike prewar *Esquire*, which positioned its ideal wealthy, fashionable, and educated reader against a mass of men struggling within the economic climate of the Great Depression, *Playboy* was addressed to the man in the middle, the man on his way up, in a way that could accommodate a much wider swath of

American men. Osgerby contrasts *Playboy* to *Esquire* and earlier men's magazines: "While the masculine culture of leisure and personal consumption celebrated in *Playboy* was not unprecedented, the sheer scale of the magazine's success testifies to the growing pervasiveness and acceptability of male identities predicated on hedonistic consumerism. More broadly, the magazine furnished an ideal for living that corresponded with the cultural orientations of the 'new' middle class—a rising faction whose habitus (like that of Bourdieu's 'cultural intermediaries') eschewed production and self-denial in favor of consumption, style, and an 'ethic of fun.'"[64] So, whereas the pre-war *Esquire* had been said to include "an unholy combination of erudition and sex," *Playboy*'s content was rather more eclectic and middle-class. The "ethic of fun" required that these middle-class men refuse to confine themselves to the highbrow, taking pleasure and style from everywhere. Speculative and noir fiction like Beaumont's fit beautifully in the magazine, which, while quite literate, could hardly be called erudite. While *Playboy* often failed at the sophistication that Hefner and his staff sought to attain, it did not fail as ultimately as it might seem. Hefner, Sellers, and Paul—and here I am exempting literary editor A. C. Spectorsky—envisioned a particular type of reader who, like themselves, did not need a strict diet of any one sort of entertainment to enjoy life. In an advertisement to subscribers, an attractive, thirty-ish man is pictured beside the following caption: "The suave citizen relaxing here is our idea of A Real Man. . . . His eyes can scan the profound pathology of Sigmund Freud, Jean Paul Sartre—or Professor Mickey Spillane."[65] The joke, "Professor Mickey Spillane," signaled to readers that they were in a certain company: this company liked Spillane's pulp novels, but knew that they were just that. To the imagined *Playboy* reader, as to Hefner and his staff, eschewing Spillane due to some allegiance to Sartre and his ilk was to be phony and to deny oneself pleasure. If *Playboy* was central to the "making of the good life in modern America," as Fratterigo argues—and I agree that it was—"the good life" was being redefined for the GI Bill generation.

This "ethic of fun" was to extend not just to fun sex with fun women, fun pulp literature, or fun concerts wearing fun clothes, but also to making fun of the lack of choices that men felt that they had. Like *Esquire* helping men who felt duty-bound to take advantage of opportunities ushered in by the New Deal, *Playboy* taught men how to be married and middle-class, whether they wanted to or not. Unlike *Esquire*, which functioned as a rather literal etiquette manual and advice guide, *Playboy* made fun of the entire enterprise of advice on etiquette. The best examples of this style of humor are in Shepherd Mead's monthly satires, starting with his famous "How to Succeed in Business Without Really Trying." "How to Succeed in Business" is a parody of an advice guide, the purpose of which is to point out how utterly absurd the steps are to success in business. More relevant for our purposes is his subsequent, "How to Succeed with Women Without Really Trying," which, fascinatingly, is not a primer on getting a woman into bed, but a parody advice guide to dealing with women at all stages, including and especially one's own wife. As members of the emergent middle class, *Playboy*'s readers would find the ridiculousness of its rules and guidelines transparent and frustrating. And, as the Playmates gently redirected men's anxieties and frustrations into safe zones, Mead and the rest of *Playboy*'s satire channeled their cynicism and bemusement.

For most men, the fantasy of upward mobility and sexual license could only go so far and, for that reason, the Playmates and satires functioned as containers for those desires and even justifications for never making those fantasies reality. However important the pretense of the good life was to the magazine's popularity, its inability to fully realize its aspirations to sophistication was an asset. David Halberstam writes in *The Fifties:* "Hefner's great strength was his lack of sophistication. If he was square, he still longed to share the better world, which was now increasingly available around him; in that he mirrored the longings of millions of young men of similar background, more affluent than their parents, wanting a better and freer life."[66]

Hefner famously left *Esquire* when he learned that he would have to move to New York in order to continue in his position. He wanted to stay in Chicago. Obviously, Chicago is an urban center and, historically, has bested New York's reputation in some eras, but in the 1950s, Chicago was not envisioned as New York's peer in sophistication, especially in the magazine industry. The choice to stay in Chicago can be read in many ways: his unwillingness to step outside his comfort zone (evinced later in his life by his reticence even to leave the house), his desire to maintain family stability with Millie (who was pregnant with Christie at the time) in his hometown near his mother, or a sort of acknowledgment that he would not fit into the world of New York magazines. Hefner was ambivalent, and this ambivalence is evidenced throughout the magazine.

Hefner himself was unsophisticated, even philistine. While the pages of the magazine were filled with fine cuisine and wine, he largely lived on ham sandwiches and Pepsi. His experiences with women were few when he started *Playboy*, and most were with his wife, Millie, to whom he lost his virginity. A magazine business colleague remembers Hefner just before *Playboy* talking "a lot about becoming a publisher himself, but I don't think anyone took much notice. I thought he was very immature for his age. He was totally unsophisticated, but he had an obsession with sex."[67] When asked about his former boss, famed *Playboy* contributor Ray Russell sneered at the notion that it was Hefner who contributed to the literary quality of the magazine, saying that he had all the "sophistication of Dennis the Menace."[68]

When he started the magazine, he was this unsophisticated white midwestern boy, bored with his work, unsatisfied in his marriage, unfulfilled by fatherhood and homeownership. These dissatisfactions, quite simply, led to the magazine. By 1959, Hefner's life had changed dramatically and *Playboy* changed with it. Divorcing Millie and cavorting with innumerable beautiful (and very young) women, Hefner became the enviable swinging bachelor; dressed in, driving, listening to, and living in the finest, Hefner was the consummate story of "succeeding in business." He escaped from his suburban house into the ultimate Playboy Penthouse apartment.[69] He rose not just to the middle class, but to wealth and fame, not just to successful marriage, but to success with women past marriage. Hefner created *Playboy* as a tool to help men cope with quotidian postwar family life. He did not intend it to be a way out, but a way through. For him, it had been the opposite, so he was no longer its original reader.

With the drastic changes in his own life came changes in his aspirations for *Playboy*. The magazine, which had eschewed politics, became a place for major political figures to debate and pontificate. Two of its major features—the Playboy Interview and the Playboy Advisor—began. Originally imagined as a one-off joke, the Advisor was exactly the sort of mainstream and sincere advice column that *Playboy*'s earlier readers were trained to look at with suspicion. The Interview was, more than anything in its history, the feature which allowed *Playboy* to fully enter the realm of respectability.

Playboy and Hugh Hefner's progressive politics have become part of its legend. In-depth and sympathetic interviews with the likes of Malcolm X and Eldridge Cleaver were better reasons even than the centerfolds to purchase the magazine. As *Playboy* was able to offer more and more money, its contributors became increasingly willing to provide them with their best material, rather than sending pieces rejected by *Esquire*, *Look*, or *Life*. And rather than breaking or helping junior writers, *Playboy* easily published the most well-regarded writers of its day, including James Baldwin and Norman Mailer. *Playboy* got serious.

While Hefner's political commitment to racial integration was real, he was also attuned to the shifts around him. One such shift was the launch of *Duke*, a men's magazine pitched to an African American audience. Unlike *Ebony* (launched in 1945) and *Jet* (launched in 1951), *Duke* (launched in 1957) was meant for men alone and a majority of its features and cartoons were nearly (even comically) indistinguishable from *Playboy*'s. Some applied a sort of Black "spin" on *Playboy* perennials, like the style feature, "Evolution of the Conk." As Fraterrigo points out, since whites had long perceived Black men's sexual desire as a threat, leading, in some cases, to horrific crimes against them, *Duke*'s "Duchesses," their answer to Playmates, did not even bare their breasts; their styling however was very much of the late-50s *Playboy* model. Though the magazine folded after only six issues, Hefner would likely have seen the introduction of *Duke* as a mild critique or the realization of an opportunity to which he'd been blind. Though the magazine began to work harder to integrate Black men into its readership (even while *Duke* was in print and later *Players*, *Playboy* was the magazine most subscribed to by Black men), it took years for Hefner to realize women of color as objects of desire in the pages of *Playboy*. In 1964, China Lee became the first Asian American Playmate and Jennifer Jackson, the magazine's first Black centerfold, appeared in 1965.

In 1959, *Playboy* ceased to be a magazine and became a brand. Hefner himself has connected the expansion of *Playboy* beyond the magazine to these changes in his own life, though most fail to do the same: "[The Jazz Festival] was when Playboy became a mainstream brand. And that was when I came out behind the desk and literally reinvented myself and started living the life that I was espousing in the pages of the magazine. And became, in effect, Mr. Playboy." After developing the Jazz Festival, a live event which brought some of the finest jazz musicians together for a night of music, Hefner went on television in *Playboy's Penthouse*, a show in which he mingled with the "elite"—entertainers, intellectuals, and their dates—in a half-hour meant to feel like a party. These parties were racially integrated, even though this limited the syndication of the show in the South. *Playboy's Penthouse*, in fact, highlighted Black artists, including women like Sarah Vaughn and, with great reverence, Ella Fitzgerald. White women were treated differently on the show: Spectorsky subjected writer Rona Jaffe to a dressing down which we might now call a particularly harsh version of mansplaining (Hefner followed by saying that the "feminization" of which her work was evidence of "what was wrong with society today"). White wives were also the ones who could ruin the party, imitated cruelly by white male comedians. White Playmates were on hand not just to perch prettily on the steps, but also to learn about new kitchen devices. In this way, gender, the divide most important to Hefner was maintained and, in fact, exacerbated.

Most importantly of all, the first Playboy Club opened in Chicago in February 1960. This was when Playboy became what Gunelias calls an "experience brand": "By offering opportunities for consumers to experience a brand's promise, consumers can personally connect with it and develop relationships with it. That connection becomes more powerful when consumers can share those experiences with others."[70] The magazine ceased to be a point of connection between individual men, painfully dispersed, but an element of a brand that brought men back together. That this transition in the Playboy brand was concurrent with the rise of the Rat Pack is certainly no coincidence and Hefner's public adulation of Sinatra is no secret. Joel Dinerstein writes that Sinatra "became the primary avatar of cool renewal for the wartime generation and shifted its imagination from past to future with the onset of economic prosperity. . . . The Rat Pack was a twist on World War II infantry units, with its variety of regions and ethnicities represented."[71] Hefner claims that his goal in opening the clubs was to "create the fantasy that we promoted in the magazine," and he did that with not only the best food and drink, excellent live music, and Bunny waitresses, but also with exclusivity: membership to the Playboy Clubs was required for entry. As Nadel argues, "sexual license was a class privilege."[72]

At the same time, these spaces were racially integrated. Though Black men, especially in the South, were likely wary of joining or fully participating in the clubs, Hefner made clear that it was class and gender which offered entry. Of course, Jim Crow interfered with his best intentions and he had to fight for integration in the franchises located in New Orleans and Miami. One way he did this was to emphasize that clubs were now employing women of color, possibly to manage white concern that Black patrons would interact "inappropriately" with the (still almost all) white Bunnies.[73] In his own words, "anyone who can afford to join our club is welcome," though women of any race were barred from membership.[74]

The Playboy Clubs were not for the man on his way up, but for the man who had arrived. Simultaneously, the natural aura of the Playmates—who were clothed like "real girls" in "regular surroundings"—was replaced by the stylized "Bunny dip" and the derriere cottontail. While the Playmates were everyday girls with their own sexual desires, the Bunnies were there to serve.

Within the magazines, much about the Playmates in the magazines remained the same or similar for a bit longer, but the "man's mark" disappeared—being "unattached" became the default for men and women alike.[75] In 1964, Robert Benton and David Newman sneered at *Playboy* magazine in their piece, "The New Sentimentality," as part of a decrepit old style of American culture. By 1965, *Penthouse* was to *Playboy* what *Playboy* had been to *Esquire*: the energetic upstart, claiming to "free" sexuality from its presumed "Puritan" bondage. By 1973, *Players* magazine was *Duke* for the Baby Boom, but with the literary and editorial sophistication of *Playboy* and, by the 1980s, an admitted focus on "soldiers and prisoners." In the meantime, Playboy the "experience brand" became, simply, the Playboy brand, with Hefner (in his own words), "the symbol for the swingingest, the heppest cat around" or, alternatively, the symbol of the creeping uncool of Greatest Generation's grasping. Or worse, its falsity.

FOUR

THE HORROR OF "HONEY, I'M HOME!"

1950s Domestic Sitcoms in the Twilight Zone

In the late 1970s, both Rick Nelson (*The Adventures of Ozzie and Harriet* [ABC, 1952–66]) and Desi Arnaz (*I Love Lucy* [CBS, 1951–57]) hosted NBC's late-night sketch comedy show, *Saturday Night Live* (NBC, 1975-present). *SNL*'s baby boomer writers used sketch comedy to comment on the culture and politics of the 1970s, and often their satire was meant to undermine the hypocrisy and sanctimoniousness that they saw in the older generation. As symbols of an earlier period in American television in which this older generation controlled the images that held young baby boomers in thrall, Nelson and Arnaz's appearances offered the *SNL* writers ideal opportunities to further their critique, even to rip out this "hypocrisy" by its roots. Nelson was just a bit older than the boomers and had been portrayed as a "nice boy" role model (if an "irrepressible" one) on *Ozzie and Harriet*, while Arnaz's Ricky Ricardo—though utterly individual in some ways—was among the prototypes for the domestic patriarch that came to define television in the 1950s. In the years during and after their television heydays, both of their personal lives careened out of control, and, by the late 1970s, both had been associated with substance abuse, reckless spending, criminal activity, and infidelities. So, when *SNL* solicited the talents of Nelson and Arnaz, the men shared a remarkable capacity to both evoke the past and register its troubled passing, virtually on sight. In 1979, Dan Ackroyd—impersonating *Twilight Zone* (CBS, 1959–64) host Rod Serling—introduced a sketch, itself called "The Twilight Zone": "Meet Ricky Nelson, age 16: a typical American kid in a typical American kitchen in a typical American black-and-white TV family home. But what's about to happen to Ricky is far from typical unless you happen to live in the Twilight Zone." Nelson—now Ricky again, as he was called on *Ozzie and Harriet*—finds himself lost in a suburban neighborhood, trying to locate his house in time for dinner. He enters a generic kitchen, reaches into the refrigerator for a bottle of milk, and meets June Cleaver of *Leave It to Beaver* (CBS, 1957–58; ABC, 1958–63), who offers him a brownie and an invitation: "I don't care who you are, you must stay for dinner," but encourages him to wash up first. Realizing that he is in the wrong house, Ricky begs off, and Ackroyd's Serling interrupts: "Submitted for your approval. A sixteen-year-old teenager walking through Anytown, USA, past endless Elm Streets, Oak Streets, and Maple Streets, unable to distinguish one house from the other, for he's just entered a strange neighborhood, a neighborhood known as the Twilight Zone." Having escaped the Cleavers, Ricky now finds himself at the Andersons' of *Father Knows Best* (CBS, 1954–60), where he is also offered a brownie, dinner, and the suggestion to wash before the meal. The pattern continues, so that, having politely excused himself from the Andersons, Ricky realizes that he has mistakenly visited the Williams family of *Make Room for Daddy/The Danny Thomas Show* (ABC, 1953–57; CBS, 1957–64), and finally ends up in the midst of one of Lucy Ricardo's raucous kitchen meltdowns in *I Love Lucy*.

This skit's treatment of the 1950s domestic sitcom is typical of popular representations of them: the upper-middle-class family comedies are treated as interchangeable, milquetoast, fantasias of conservative suburban social norms. Though the other characters have never met Ricky, and Ricky himself is mystified as to how he got into their homes, his strange appearance barely phases the Cleavers, the Andersons, the Williamses, or the Ricardos, so trapped are they in their routines. The episodes proceed almost seamlessly through their usual tropes: Eddie Haskell is obnoxiously obsequious, Betty Anderson has a date, the Williamses make fun of Danny's nose, and Lucy spectacularly fails to satisfy Ricky's expectations for her domestic management. "The Twilight Zone" skit takes for granted the repetitiveness of these shows; in fact, this repetitiveness and interchangeability are what make the sitcom universe "the twilight zone."

But however predictable its elements—from the ruined dinner to the celebrity guest—*I Love Lucy* is portrayed as exceptional amid these other sitcoms. It is a vehicle for a woman who fails to fall in line with the brownie-bearing sitcom wives, expresses emotion, and is actually funny. Television critics' assessments of these shows have largely failed to differ. It is unsurprising, then, that Arnaz, unlike Nelson, was given the chance to perform a bolder parody of *I Love Lucy* when he appeared on *SNL* in 1976.

Arnaz introduces the skit, explaining that, before he, Lucille Ball, and his producers developed the *I Love Lucy* format, they tried other ideas, and he shares these old films with the *Saturday Night Live* audience. Though several of the ideas are absurdly tame—"I Love Asparagus," for example—others comically explore the underbelly of *I Love Lucy*'s humor. The most poignant of these is "I Loathe Lucy," which begins like an average *I Love Lucy* episode. Ricky comes home from the club and the Ricardos embrace and engage in cute chit-chat, only for Ricky to suddenly turn on Lucy, shoving her, throwing a drink in her face, pulling her in for a kiss only to violently push her to the ground, berating her all the while, as the live *SNL* audience roars with laughter. The remarkable thing about the "I Loathe Lucy" skit is not that it is so dramatically different from *I Love Lucy*, though that is clearly its intent. On the contrary, "I Loathe Lucy" only hyperbolizes one of the original show's most oft-recurring themes: Lucy is afraid of Ricky, who is frequently abusive.

LUCY THINKS RICKY IS TRYING TO MURDER HER

It is instructive to compare "I Loathe Lucy" to "Lucy Thinks Ricky Is Trying to Murder Her," an early episode of *I Love Lucy*. Due to production problems caused by the use of four cameras, "Lucy Thinks Ricky Is Trying to Murder Her" was not actually the first episode aired on CBS, though it was the first one shot. After its problems were resolved, "Lucy Thinks Ricky Is Trying to Murder Her" was the fourth episode aired. In "Lucy Thinks Ricky Is Trying to Murder Her," Lucy Ricardo is absorbed in a lurid mystery novel. Becoming increasingly influenced by the book, she begins to believe that her husband is plotting her murder. Ricky, for his part, playacts and narrates a murder scene in bed with her. He weighs his options: "A gun?—too noisy. A knife?—too sloppy," before settling on a scarf, with which he playfully threatens to strangle Lucy. Though viewers see that Ricky is kidding, only dramatizing his annoyance with Lucy, Lucy lays awake, eyes wide in fear. Her suspicions build when her friend Ethel's fortune-telling experiment portends her death. Then, Lucy overhears Ricky on the phone with his agent as they discuss firing his female singer: "I'm going to get rid of her. I have been wanting to do it for a long time.... I'll miss her at first, but soon I'll have another one just as good." He mentions that he has "the gun" concealed in his desk drawer. Lucy is terrified, and Ethel soon joins in her panic. When Ricky loudly slams the door, Lucy even believes that she has been shot, feels around for a bullet wound, and is relieved that "he missed" her. Lucy and Ethel read Ricky's blotter with a mirror and, finding a list of women's names, they assume that Ricky is already looking for her "replacement." The list ends with the name Theodore, which leads Lucy to stare wide-eyed at the camera in shock, believing that Ricky is bisexual. Since Lucy is acting strangely anxious, Fred suggests that Ricky "slip her a mickey," and hands him a packet of sedative. Lucy enters just in time to see Ricky pour a powder into her drink, which naturally she assumes is poison. After Ricky leaves, she believes that she is dying, but decides to confront Ricky at the club in her last moments. When she and Ethel arrive, the situation is clarified and the women are relieved: the performing dogs go by human names ("Oh, *that's* Theodore!") and the gun is actually a harmless prop for Ricky's act.

This episode of *I Love Lucy* sets up most of the major conflicts that will dominate the show's six-year run. Lucy is afraid that her husband will hurt her, that he will become involved with other women, and that he is hiding a shocking secret. Lucy fears and reacts to her husband's anger, as the audience—of both *SNL* and *I Love Lucy*—laughs with and at her. And in these concerns, however differently she acts on them, Lucy is no different from the other housewives on 1950s television—in fact, she is the prototype.

That the domestic sitcoms of the 1950s presented an idealized picture of the American family is a truism that almost no one disputes. This truism has permeated not only mainstream accounts of the genre, but also the work of a surprising number of scholars. Despite the fact that shows like *Leave It to Beaver* are syndicated and broadcast every day in America and throughout the world, our discourse about these shows (or our allusions to these shows as a shorthand in place of discourse) is terribly misleading and proves that few ever watch and consider them seriously, even if their alleged ideologies are subject to insistent critique. Shows which—to varying degrees and in myriad ways—were about the terrors of the home, the violent and erotic negotiations of power in the domestic sphere, are popularly remembered as completely safe havens. Furthermore, many critics and viewers actually blame these shows for masking or deflecting attention from the very conflicts that they repeatedly broached.[1]

Scholarship on 1950s domestic sitcoms—what David Marc refers to as the "benevolent Aryan melodramas"—has often been surprisingly light, even when written by the most sophisticated critics.[2] Take Judy Kutulas: "We see in the Cleavers (*Leave It to Beaver*) and other television families a vision of perfection, the embodiment of security, stability, and togetherness that haunts us as we grapple with our real, less-than-perfect, families. At the heart of these television families is the clear articulation of roles and responsibilities and gentle lines of authority that flow from wise dad and understanding mom to obedient children."[3] Kutulas's notion that viewers are "haunted" by the memories of these sitcom families is not hers alone. The 1950s domestic sitcom is decried not only for being uncreative, boring television, but has habitually been blamed for setting up unrealistic standards for American families. The genre is not just bland, these accounts argue, but is actually harmful.

Studies of particular 1950s sitcoms—rather than of the genre at the time—have commonly avoided some these pitfalls. *I Love Lucy* and *The George Burns and Gracie Allen Show* have been read through a feminist lens. *The Honeymooners*, too, has received attention from scholars. Finally, *Beulah*—groundbreaking and problematic at once—has rightly been treated separately from other sitcoms of the era because having a Black protagonist makes it so.[4]

Neither does this chapter entirely dispute the notion that the domestic sitcom presented an "idealized" American family. However, it departs from prior scholarship in one significant way: it argues that these sitcoms show the very *limits* of the ideal in the period. For Americans in the postwar period, the "ideal" American family was not one in which the man of the house was free of violent urges, or extramarital sexual impulses, nor was it one in which other family members were free from fear of the husband/father. On the contrary, the "ideal" family was one in which these dangerous impulses were *usually* reined in, the very real fears of the man of the house remained *mostly* unrealized, and the worst outcomes were only imagined: husbands did not leave or cheat on their wives even if they came close, men did not actually murder or irreparably injure their families even if they did harm them, and the secrets that they kept did not tear the fragile society to shreds. That is the ideal that these sitcoms promulgated.

The 1950s sitcoms showed that violence and sexual threat awakened by the war were newly replanted in the domestic sphere and, thus, highlighted the vulnerability of women and children in their own homes. These shows drew both explicit and implicit connections between military service and domestic violence within families. Sometimes his military past makes a man incapable of good, compassionate parenting, while, other times, it is the key component in a good father's child-rearing strategies.

Even when the men in these shows were not actively violent, their homes were filled with uncertainty, wariness, confusion, and suspicion: children and their mothers were on guard constantly for signs that men were going to lash out. Mothers and children were not only afraid of being physically harmed but were also worried that fathers might endanger the family in other ways, through committing sexual infidelity or crimes outside the home. Because the men often stopped short of violence or were exonerated of suspected sexual indiscretions, women and children in the programs sometimes appear paranoid, but, more routinely, they are simply lucky to experience seemingly random mercy. Sitcom men, for their part, grant these moments of random mercy, and sometimes feel entitled to and enthralled by their own power, but they also experience erratic mood swings and alternate between self-loathing over and utter denial of the impact their unpredictability has on their wives and children. Sitcom women, children, and men all understand family happiness as both painfully hard work and a masquerade in which each family member, however victimized, must participate. Though the shows hyperbolize them, these very conflicts were animated in the popular literature on marriage and parenting in the postwar era.

The domestic sitcom, because of its chronological mirroring of American family growth, its formal reliance on repetition and circularity, its physical proximity to the family, and the visibility of its biggest stars, was an ideal form through which to visit and revisit concerns about marriage and family in the postwar era. Yet, it is precisely these attributes that have allowed most popular and scholarly analyses of the domestic sitcom of the 1950s, as well as "memories" of the period and genre, to languish and become themselves repetitive, circular, bland, and indistinguishable. Since *I Love Lucy* is generally exempt from these criticisms, considering its key differences from the other programs—primarily the visibility of the real-life Arnaz marriage—allows us insight into the genre as a whole. Finally, this chapter, like those preceding it, deals with the above issues on two fronts: how the people living in the postwar era experienced their lives and the art and entertainment designed to reflect and manage them, but also their legacy.

CAN THIS FAMILY BE SAVED?: THE DOMESTIC SITCOM IN CONTEXT

Many popular and scholarly critics of 1950s sitcoms complain that the families seem indistinguishable from each other, as illustrated in Rick Nelson's *SNL* sketch.[5] Though many recent scholars have pointed out the diversity in postwar experience, there was, in fact, one element of striking uniformity: the majority of men under forty had served in either World War II or Korea.[6] In light of both the experiential chasm and the long physical separation between men and women, the postwar rush to marriage and children both makes perfect sense and is suspiciously—and perhaps impossibly—abrupt. Many, if not most, marriages were marked by serious gender divisions, in part because the postwar marital unit was a rapid suture, inevitably crude and with visible seams.[7] The television domestic sitcom did not cover or erase these seams, and did not write around the conflicts inherent in this defective suture, but repeatedly explored the tensions that this new family unit produced in ways that the genre, format, and medium were particularly suited to do.1950s sitcoms appear to echo basic black-and-white ideas about appropriate norms for marriage and parenting in the period; in fact, the shows display the contradictions therein. The postwar popular press was inordinately concerned with the establishment and stability of American families, as the nation's best hope for readjustment and security after the tumult of the war years. As Weiss points out, divorce actually surged during and immediately after World War II. The pressures of distance between men and women, as well as women's earning power while men were away, enabled this surge, but the trend reversed quickly, and divorce rates were at an all-time low by 1947. Reversing this trend took an abundance of cultural support for marriage, which took many forms, including an outpouring of marriage advice films, manuals, and columns, notably *Ladies' Home Journal's*

"Can This Marriage Be Saved?" Couple's counseling ("marriage analysis") became far more common and simultaneously more secular. According to Kristin Celello, marriage counseling emphasized keeping the marriage together at all costs, and counselors "direct[ed] much of their advice to women to hold them accountable for their marital successes and failures."[8] At the same time, the "permissive parenting" movement, most closely associated with the best-selling work of Dr. Benjamin Spock, became entrenched in child-rearing discourse.[9] Though ascendant, "permissive parenting" was not the only perspective represented in this discourse. Andre Fontaine, for example, urged parents to remember that their sons would likely be soldiers and that their duty was to prepare them for that eventuality.[10] Yet, the manner in which this preparation was to take place was surprisingly benign: rather than preparing boys for the brutality of the battlefield, Fontaine's ideal mothers and fathers would encourage their boys' headstrong independence and risk-taking behaviors, but would not be harsh disciplinarians. Even Spock himself offered a more nuanced perspective than that with which he is usually credited: "spoiling the child" was dangerous and, though he was not in favor of spanking per se, he was not firmly against it either.[11] The notion that marriage and child-rearing were difficult and needed to be worked at, studied, puzzled over, and fought for was perhaps the most consistent element of discourse on the American family at the time.

While we imagine the postwar *Playboy* and pulp reader alone in his workshop or garage, and the film viewer in a theater full of friends and strangers, the 1950s sitcom viewer is not a viewer so much as one among a *family* of viewers, which makes it an ideal form through which to explore the aforementioned family theories and concerns. Because television advertising actually suggested that the new technology could offer families more time together, interior design re-centered "group space" around the television rather than the kitchen, and TV dinners emerged, foregrounding shared consumption of entertainment over pressured conversation at a time when this buffer was sorely needed.[12] But, though a handful of homes had televisions even before the war, most Americans waited until the early 1950s to buy a household set. Taverns were among the first places to purchase television sets in the 1940s.[13] Geared toward these taverns, 1940s television emphasized sports (especially boxing) and variety shows, which meant that the adults seated at the bar were essentially transported from one adult environment to another. As TV—for the most part—moved from outside to inside the home, programming changed to reflect the viewing environment. By the end of the decade, television geared toward children and women slowly began its takeover, as assumptions about the place of the television set shifted.

Marc notes that this shift was not immediate, but that a number of programs operated in a middle ground in which "vaudeville schtick [was] embedded into dramatic structure" and older forms were otherwise awkwardly integrated into newer ones. This confused and halting transition came partially from public ambivalence about what should be in the home, ambivalence rooted in worries about "innocent children" and tempted husbands.[14] The controversy surrounding talk show host Faye Emerson (*Paris Cavalcade of Fashion* [NBC, 1948–49]; *The Faye Emerson Show* [CBS and NBC, 1950–51]; *Faye Emerson's Wonderful Town* [CBS, 1951–52]) exemplifies this ambivalence. CBS received hundreds of letters decrying her low-cut gowns, and television journalists in major newspapers leeringly joked about her cleavage. When rumors spread that she would be taken off the air because her breasts were so distracting, she offered viewers the chance to vote: should she continue to dress as she wished or should she dress more demurely? Even after all the anxiety, 95 percent of viewers—male and female included—voted that she should continue her own styling, exactly as she saw fit.[15] As a network censor aptly put it, "'on matters pertaining to sex . . . America as a whole proclaims itself to be one way and acts another.'"[16]

Most popular programs of other types operated in service of this ambivalence. Milton Berle toned down some of the risqué elements of his act, but still appeared in drag.[17] Western gunfighters shot, but only when shot at.[18] CIA agents infiltrated international spy networks, encountered Soviet snipers and seductresses, but returned safely to their families at the end.[19] Television's profitability was dependent upon ratings, which meant that this ambiguous stance was the only way to do business. Sponsors did not want to be associated with risqué entertainment, nor were they willing to foot the bill for the sort of dull programming that fell to the bottom of the Hooper barrel. If there is truth to the notion that the 1950s were television's "Golden Age," this tension between sponsors' maintenance of respectability and their flirtations with more sophisticated fare may well be at the core of it. In a circumscribed landscape in which only four (and quickly three) networks offered the programming that captured the American imagination, and before the magazine format of television advertising allowed companies the benefits of TV spots with a less risky "stake" in the program's image, this tension was at its height.[20]

Domestic situation comedies, as much as, or perhaps more than, any other genre of programming, danced carefully between adult enticements and bland sentimentality. Though the domestic sitcoms of the 1950s have since become synonymous with dullness, the spark of danger was equally important to the popularity of these programs, such as *Father Knows Best*, *Leave It to Beaver*, *Make Room for Daddy/The Danny Thomas Show*, *The Adventures of Ozzie and Harriet*, and *The Donna Reed Show* (ABC, 1958–66). As "Lucy Thinks Ricky is Going to Murder Her" demonstrates, *I Love Lucy*—television's first runaway hit—ideally illustrates this complicated balancing act, incorporating violence and sexuality in relatively daring ways, while deflecting their seriousness at the end of the episode.

Television scholars have noted that the sitcom went through at least two important phases in the 1950s. I join scholar Michael V. Tueth in defining the first phase as the marital sitcom, which included programs like *I Married Joan* (NBC, 1952–55), *Life with Elizabeth* (syndicated, 1953–55), and *My Favorite Husband* (CBS, 1952–55) (as well as, by some accounts, *The George Burns and Gracie Allen Show* and *I Love Lucy*), defined by the "zany women" for whom the shows were named. In the case of *Beulah*, the title character is not so much zany as witty in comparison to her boyfriend Jack (whose frequent marriage proposals she never accepts) and the rather dim white family by whom she was employed and for whom she works not merely as domestic help but as a sort of marriage and family counselor. But as the genre and decade wore on, the "zany women" fad mostly receded; in fact, the wife's role was subordinated to the husband and children's roles (in most episodes).[21] Many feminist TV critics have commented on the obvious therapeutic functions of these zany woman sitcoms for other women—the vicarious rebellion, in particular—but the inexplicability of these comparatively childlike women must have equally rung true to some male viewers who were becoming re-accustomed to women whose relatively benign, homebound antics bore no resemblance to the day-to-day life of war, nor to the concerns of even the women they met while serving. For both women and men, Lucy and Joan's antics were likely cathartic, but they may also have equally appreciated the context within which they occurred; after all, it was the domestic context—not the zany antics—that remained as sitcoms progressed and viewers of both genders kept watching.

This timeline—through which the marital sitcom turns into the family sitcom as the decade and genre progress—is useful, if self-evident: in the postwar era the shift from the marital to the family unit was one of the most important transitions to take place in the domestic sphere. Because the war produced such unprecedented semi-conformity in this respect, the generic transition followed the transitions that were happening in many American homes at the time. But even as children began to claim the "zaniness" once ascribed to their mothers, and fathers gained prominence, these men's roles and personalities actually changed relatively little. Sitcom men continued to berate, threaten, and punish their wives, but, in many cases, their children became their additional or preferred targets.

"BUT THIS ISN'T THE ARMY!": THE WAR AT HOME

Sometimes the sitcoms explicitly connected men's volatility or insensitivity to the war, suggesting that men's abusive or indifferent parenting is linked to their service. On *The Donna Reed Show,* the Stone family takes in a "problem child" for Thanksgiving when he has nowhere else to go. Determined to "get to the bottom" of the child's hostility, Donna is enlightened by a letter the boy leaves on his desk. His father, a Major in the US Air Force, has written him a cruel, critical answer to his pleas to come home. Donna shows the letter to her husband, Alex, but he fails to make the same connection between the boy's behavior and his father's response, saying with a shrug, "Reminds me of every answer that I got in the Army." Donna is shocked: "But this isn't the Army, this is a father!" Alex has so normalized the brusqueness of military culture that he unthinkingly imports its sensibility into the domestic sphere; Donna, like most sitcom wives and mothers, vigilantly polices the boundary between military life and a more compassionate vision of domestic normalcy in keeping with the parenting philosophies of the time. This conversation between the Stones is uncommon because Donna admits the gulf between the spouses' experiences of the war. Many wives seem intent on diminishing the difference between their own experience on the home front and their husbands' experience in the military, as though this divide imperils family unity and happiness. Because the wives efface these differences, their children often unwittingly participate, assuming their mothers' perspectives on their family's war history. While Donna responds directly to Alex's conflation of family and Army, insisting immediately upon the distinction between these two spheres, *Leave It to Beaver*'s June Cleaver and *Father*

Knows Best's Margaret Anderson simply ignore or leave the room when their husbands bring up their service, treating it as boring, immaterial, or irritating. June is occasionally forced to acknowledge Ward's Navy experience, but always underplays it. For example, when Beaver asks his mother's help in writing a biography of his father for school, June breezily mentions that "he was in the Seabees," but emphasizes the aspects of his life, like marriage, career, and family, which she considers worthy of or safe to mention. When Kathy Anderson similarly writes a biography of Jim, his service is not mentioned at all, though committed viewers know that he spent years away from Margaret, Betty, and Bud fighting in the Pacific. In other instances, June and Margaret incorporate themselves into the war narrative. In "Perfect Father," Ward begins to recall his wartime activities, but June cuts him off: "We all contributed to victory in our own ways." Presumably because of her disregard, her posture of boredom, and her eagerness to lay equal claim to the war experience, most of Ward's rare mentions of the Seabees take place with his boys or among men, when June is absent. As such, the women's effort to expunge war references from their homes actually solidifies the divide between them and their husbands.

The sitcom wives are never entirely successful in banishing the war from their homes, which means that their opinions on disciplining children often collide with their husbands'. Perhaps no episode more clearly invokes the dangerous permeability of military life and family life than *Make Room for Daddy*'s "Parents Are Pigeons," in which parental discipline is managed through the metaphor of war throughout the episode. Danny, whom his wife Kathy refers to as "General," explains that the two parents must be "allies" against a common "enemy": their children. Kathy initially laughs weakly at the war metaphor, but Danny is committed to it, saying that it's not meant to be funny, but is a strategic way of viewing their parenting responsibilities. When Kathy fails to immediately agree with his opinions about family discipline, Danny accuses her of being a bad mother. The two come to an agreement to let nothing "undermine parental authority," though Kathy begs Danny to say goodnight to his son, hoping that he won't consider it "giving aid and comfort to the enemy." As the episode comes to a close, Danny takes off his belt and grabs another, holds both out to Kathy, and says, "Men, choose your weapons," and they hide their belts behind their backs. Now that they are armed, he calls mock-sweetly to the children, "Little angels, come along my sweets!" When they emerge from their bedrooms, Danny and

Kathy ambush Rusty and Linda, brandishing their belts. The kids take off running and the adults run after them, until Danny swings the belt in the corner of the frame (while Rusty is hidden from view behind the door).

Danny sees this harsh militarized discipline as his parental duty (though he positions his children as the enemy, rather than under his command). Likewise, the conversation between the Stones over their charge's letter implies that, in Alex's opinion, such parenting is harmless, if not actually good for the boy. Domestic sitcom fathers often encourage their sons to develop boot-camp-like discipline in activities ranging from boxing to basketball to boy scouts. Many of these fathers do not limit their encouragement to athletic or civic endeavors, but demand that their sons adopt a military attitude in everyday life. What looks to these fathers like good parenting, preparing their boys for the harsh realities of masculinity, sometimes looks sadistic to the children themselves. For example, when Beaver is scared to have his cavity filled, his brother Wally explains to June that Beaver is not actually afraid of the pain, but of Ward's reaction if he winces. Beaver's concerns are well-founded: when Ward and a trembling Beaver arrive at the dentist's office, Ward irritably tells his son to "be a good soldier," not a baby. Beaver, who has grown up hearing about the ways of the military, has a telling response: "If I was a soldier, I'd shoot the dentist." Beaver's line may be among the most important uttered in 1950s sitcoms because it puts into words the assumption underlying much of the tension on these shows: to Beaver, as to many sitcom children (and even wives), being a soldier is not about self-discipline, respect of rank, or taking orders, but about perpetrating conscious, chosen violence, rooted in personal motives. The conflation of "soldiering" with this type of violence explains why these fathers and husbands are so terrifying: they could be triggered by anything.

"I TOLD YOU SHE WAS GOING TO GET IT!": ANTICIPATION IN THE SITCOM PLOT

While the war is often present in these shows, most episodes do not invoke it directly. So, Beaver's assumptions about a soldier's conduct align with sitcom children's ideas about many adult interactions, especially those between husbands and wives. Kathy Anderson's first puppet show is a Punch-and-Judy comedy about a man beating his wife with a bat as she begs him to stop.

Jeff Stone shares Kathy's frightening view of marriage. After Donna's friend, Alice, and her husband quarrel, Jeff is confused and says, "I didn't see any marks. Did he do it with a rubber hose?," and when his own parents argue, he expects them to "slug it out." Beaver is equally confused when June jokes about Ward's seduction technique, saying that, "He came in my cave and hit me with a club." He takes it literally until Ward assures him that his "mother was being a facetious female." Though Kathy's puppet show and Jeff and Beaver's remarks get laughs, the laughter occurs partly because, within the universe of the domestic sitcom, the children's "confusion" is quite insightful.

After all, television wives had been running from (and sometimes getting caught and hit by) their husbands from the earliest television sitcoms. Though their fear generally arises later in the episode as the husband's day of work comes to an end, other times, this dread lasts for most of the episode. Arnaz and his writers worked toward building that sense of dread, as he put it: "It's good for the audience to be anticipating you. Then, when it does happen, they say, 'See, I told you so. I told you she was going to get it." For example, for most of "Lucy Wants New Furniture," Lucy and Ethel anticipate Ricky's coming rage. Ricky chases Lucy around their apartment when he arrives home, catches her and says, "Do you know what I'm going to do?" Lucy replies, "Do you mind if I close my eyes? I can't stand the sight of blood." Despite the expectations that Lucy, Ethel, and the audience share, Ricky is merciful this time and forgives her.

While Ricky, Bradley, Jim, Danny, and others sometimes actually hit their family members on screen, these moments of mere anticipation are more plentiful. The aforementioned scene in which Rusty and Linda run from Danny and Kathy's belts is one of many in that and other series; some of the most evocative scenes of these sitcoms feature children running or hiding from their fathers' wrath. By foregrounding the running, hiding, and anticipation, the writers insist that it is a climate of anxiety—rather than the violence itself—which is traumatizing the women and children in these homes.

For example, in "Jim the Tyrant," Kathy Anderson—having been mildly spanked and very harshly scolded earlier in the episode—is terrified of her father's coming home. Jim, feeling that he has lost control of his family, threatens at the dinner table, "If I have to be a tyrant, I'll be one. And if discipline has to be enforced around here, I'm just the fellow who can do it. And what's more, I intend to do it." Margaret begs the children to be on their best behavior, fearing that her husband will act out. After Kathy breaks a window, her mother and siblings begin to worry for her safety and Kathy pleads with them not to tell Jim what she has done. When Jim arrives home from the office, Kathy takes off running. In an almost cinematic sequence, ominous music accompanies extreme close-ups of each of Jim's slow, pounding footsteps as he makes his way up the stairs to Kathy, who is hiding under her bed. With teary eyes squeezed shut, Kathy imagines that her father is preparing to beat her to death with a baseball bat. Just as he raises the bat above his head in her imagination, she returns to reality, where Jim stands next to the bed. She screams, "Don't do it!" and runs down the stairs to her siblings, with Jim in hot pursuit: "Where is she? Where is that fat little girl?" Almost immediately, Jim acts as if the children are confused and deluded to believe that he might really harm her, even as he chases, threatens, and bellows, but Margaret tellingly explains that his "chickens are coming home to roost." Indeed, the children might be remembering any number of incidents. The last time that Jim thought Kathy had broken a window (in "Boy's Week"), she also ran upstairs from her father's visible fury, accompanied by ominous music, but the audience was not privy to what happened next—that was the end of the episode.

"YOU KNOW WE NEVER HIT YOU": THE PERFORMANCE OF FAMILY NORMALCY

As in this episode of *Father Knows Best*, many sitcoms imply a history of abuse, but then emphasize that it is hidden from the outside world: men, women, and children all view their family happiness as a constant performance. This performance is especially painful and confusing for the children who seem less invested in its success. These children's recurring confusion about the state of their homes and families suggests that "the performative quality of middle-class family life" operates on multiple levels at once and that its audience includes the on-screen characters as well as home viewers.[22] In *Leave It to Beaver*'s first episode, "Beaver Gets 'Spelled,'" Beaver climbs a tree after his expulsion from school, and, like Kathy Anderson, is terrified of his father's response. His fear is proven justified when Ward yells up the tree in full view of the town. Beaver explains, "I'm not coming down. You'll hit me." Ward angrily begins to take off his belt and starts, "Well, you just better bet—" but he looks around at the people surrounding the tree and trails off, then adds with strained benevolence, "Beaver, you know we never hit you." As Beaver begins to dispute this with some examples, Ward quickly tells him to "never mind," and changes his tone, coaxing Beaver out of the tree. Though Ward does not hit Beaver that night, this scene and others prove that, in the Cleaver household, hitting is certainly not off-limits.[23] Moreover, Ward's performance serves multiple goals and reaches multiple audiences: he tries to convince Beaver to come down by assuring him that it is safe to do so, he pretends for the benefit of the townspeople that he does not use corporal punishment, and the home audience is meant to find humor in his layered deception.

Indeed, *Leave It to Beaver* periodically intimates that the Cleavers are hiding the inner workings of their household, perhaps even from the viewing audience, but the show also makes clear that a disjointed performance of domestic happiness occurs within the family itself. When Beaver asks how he would handle June in a fight, Ward starts, "You mean last Thur—" before quickly covering, saying that he and June simply "don't have fights," an apparent lie which he shores up in other episodes, denying that he ever screams at June, even when he has just done so. Between watching their parents perform for others and hearing their parents lie to them, the Cleaver boys seem confused, half-heartedly performing for other people, while questioning the foundations of their performances. When Beaver tells another child that he comes from a happy family, Wally asks him, "What'd you go and make up all that junk for?" Wally allows that "maybe" the Cleavers are relatively happy in comparison to other families, to which Beaver responds, "That's good because sometimes I can't tell." The Cleaver boys simply cannot fully distinguish the performance of family happiness from "the real thing." In admitting this, Beaver and Wally invite the home audience to ask the same questions: are we watching a happy family? If so or if not, how can we tell? And, finally, is the "happy family" merely the one who puts on the best show?

Those questions come up equally in the other 1950s domestic sitcoms, many of which are invested in a more obvious form of performance. Spigel in particular notes that "theatricality" was a key part of many 1950s sitcoms, including but not limited to *Make Room for Daddy*. So, while in "Beaver Gets 'Spelled,'" Ward performs paternal calm and compassion in front of the town of Mayfield, Danny Williams gives his performance literally, on a nightclub stage. In "Danny the Performer," Danny threatens to beat Rusty early in the episode for not adequately appreciating his success as an entertainer. Later, Danny jokes in his nightclub act about his weak discipline as a father: "You know what the worst punishment in our house is? Go to your room!" He goes on, "My father used to say 'go to the woodshed, I'll be right there.' And he always showed up!" The television audience shares our knowingness with Rusty who sits in the nightclub audience that evening, laughing at this very routine. Though it is true that Danny doesn't "always show up," or follow through on his threats, Rusty, Linda, and Terry have faced far worse than being sent to their rooms, a fact of which any viewer—even a casual one—would be aware. Furthermore, since Rusty risks a beating if he does not show adequate enthusiasm over his father's act, he is essentially forced to laugh publicly at Danny's jokes, which misrepresent their relationship as one in which mercy—however reluctant—is typical, rather than random.

"A MONSTER OR A WEAK-KNEED JELLYFISH?": THE SITCOM FATHER'S SENSE OF SELF

Apparently random mercy—shown above in "Lucy Wants New Furniture," "Jim the Tyrant," and "Beaver Gets 'Spelled'"—is the most common outcome of sitcom conflicts, but, in each case, it is clear that this mercy is inconsistent and unpredictable. As Beaver says when Ward asks him what he is afraid he will do to him, "Well, that's the thing, Dad. We never can tell." Though we, the home audience, mostly see occasions in which these men hold back from the severest acts, the dialogue in many episodes implies that, in other instances, such control is not exercised. Therefore, sitcom wives work tirelessly to manage households in which provocations to their husbands' rage will be rare. But it is not just the wives and children who work to protect themselves. In fact, many of these men try very hard at times to keep from acting on their violent impulses. Of course, the contradictory expectations for husbands and fathers—to be "permissive authorities" as Dr. Spock and *Ladies' Home Journal* prescribe—make it impossible for these men not to fail. Most of these husbands and fathers evince a great deal of guilt and self-loathing when they do not manage to control their violent urges. Not only are husbands like Bradley, Ozzie Nelson, Ricky, Stu Erwin (*The Trouble* with Father/The Stu Erwin Show [ABC, 1950–55]), and Albert (*Ethel and Albert* [NBC, 1953–54; CBS, 1955; ABC, 1955–56]), abject and painfully apologetic after hitting their wives and children, or even just severely berating them, many fathers begin to see themselves as "ogres," "beasts," or "monsters," and are even afraid to look in the mirror. Jim, Danny, Ricky, and Ward all lament that their relationships with their wives and children are strained, sometimes recognizing that they are at fault and attempting to change. Ward often hurriedly sends Wally or Beaver away as his fury rises. When June pleads with Ward not to, as he puts it, "wail the tar" out of Beaver, he keeps her near him to avoid what he feels is otherwise inevitable, vowing sternly to June and to himself that, "I won't resort to physical violence." Ward's feelings and methods seem tame in comparison to Jim Anderson's. He is frequently worried about his "nerves" and sometimes excuses himself during stressful moments with lines like, "I think I'll go to the den before I succumb to a rather primitive impulse that I have." In later episodes, he takes more serious steps to avoid lashing out, including downing handfuls of unidentified pills to "simmer down" when he is "like a caged lion." Danny does not consume pills, but takes showers to "cool down" or bangs on the piano when he is tempted to beat his wife and children. Having solemnly promised Lucy that he will not hit her over her latest mishap, Ricky occasionally will pantomime beating her right before her eyes in order to get it "out of his system," while, in another case, he destroys a hotel room as Lucy says to Ethel with relief, "[taking] his anger out on the bric-a-brac."

Though viewers are often privy to these men's attempts to maintain control—and these are, indeed, a source of laughter—they are rarely central to the episode. Though it is more outrageous, "Danny Roars Again" is a notable exception. In this episode, when prompted by a concerned psychiatrist (who is a family friend), Danny imagines being married to himself. Dressed and made-up as Kathy, he lives through breakfast as his own wife, being screamed at, belittled, and threatened. Overwhelmed by guilt, he vows to keep his temper under control. Holding in his anger actually makes Danny physically ill, and he has to see a doctor, who tells him that his illness is psychosomatic. Because it is unhealthy to resist his natural emotions, Danny's effort to stay cool is unsuccessful, as it was in several other episodes in which he makes a similar vow. Alex, Jim, and Ricky also make these promises and, in each case, the men fail to stay rational and even-tempered, lashing out at the end of these episodes. When the men try but fail to contain their anger, this failure is usually presented as "for the best." Their wives and children try to provoke them, afraid that the men no longer love them because rage is their most common form of self-expression. When the men resume their old habits, order seems to be restored, and the men scream, yell, and threaten their families with "love," as in: "What do mean I no longer love you.?! I've known some feather-brained dames in my life, but you're out of your cotton-picking mind! What do you mean I don't love you? I love you more than life itself. Why you pretty nitwit, you're the whole world to me! Don't you ever dare say it again, you understand, or I'll pin your ears back!" Men's performances of kindness are merely gestures and are unsustainable. In the end, women and children must adhere to their own roles more strictly to retain the man's "natural" affection.

When these sitcom men do not harm or threaten to harm their wives and children, they often express frustration that social norms work against those actions, likely because this leaves them with no clear alternative form of fatherly self-assertion. Ward and Jim are fond of recalling how their fathers would use "old-fashioned discipline," and they clearly feel stifled, though they also admit that "reason" is often the best approach. Similarly, Danny encourages a local man to use "reason" with the neighborhood children, but, when their misbehavior continues, he recants: "Fortunately, I had a father who knew how to handle me. When my father hit you, you were hit. And you knew why you were hit. And you remembered it. My father never gave me the courtesy to bend down when he slapped me, he picked me up by the hair and held me at eye level and gave it to me there. That's how these kids should be treated." Danny's narration of his own childhood is telling: it is not enough, he argues, for a child to be spanked, but he must be treated utterly without respect and hit in a way that "you know you were hit." He not only veers from the permissive parenting paradigm, he disposes of it entirely. Moreover, he makes this speech outside the home, and it is itself a performance of caring fatherhood toward the neighborhood children as well as his own.

Ward, Danny, and Jim all partially attribute their personal and professional success to their fathers' severity, so they feel a responsibility to use this style of parenting, even when doing so is painful for all parties. The use of the "woodshed" in so many of these examples—though obviously a common trope—also indicates that this discipline needed to be hidden, even in the alleged "good old days," in which fathers could supposedly rule openly with an iron fist and discipline as they saw fit. The other men seem to accept that this style of discipline must be concealed, but sometimes Danny defiantly admits that he uses corporal punishment and asserts that he would "rather be a monster than a weak-kneed jellyfish." Despite Danny's spells of guilt and self-loathing, being an emasculated father is worse than damaging his closeness with his children because it sets them up for future failure.

"THE KIND OF TRAUMATIC EXPERIENCE THAT DOES SOME GOOD!": SITCOM CHILDREN AND TRAUMA

Though some of these cases vindicate a harsher approach as more "authentic" parenting or marital relations, the shows generally portray physical discipline as unfortunate. While most sitcom episodes appear geared toward helping viewing parents cope with their roles as partners and parents, occasionally the impact of these parents' confusion on their children is given attention. Several sitcom children actually appear to be deeply affected by their fathers' harsh discipline. In addition to the running and hiding examples above, they or their parents sometimes narrate a kind of post-traumatic distress. At one point, Jeff Stone has a "broken spirit," and becomes "too good," leading Donna to ask Alex to be gentler with his son because "we tried to instill discipline, but instead we instilled fear." Jeff explains to Donna and Alex that "the kind of guy who did everything the first time you asked" is merely acting nicely out of fear, rather than because he learned a lesson. So, by the end of the episode, Jeff appears to be cured.

Unsurprisingly though, Rusty—the most abused child in 1950s sitcoms—never appears cured. These scenes are meant to be comical because Danny desperately wants Rusty to love rather than fear him, but his actions do not reflect that. For example, as Danny chases Rusty with scissors, he yells, "You're not afraid of your own father, are you?" to which Rusty breathlessly replies, "I don't know why, Daddy, but I am!" And when Rusty comes home from school, acting anxious, Danny begs him to tell him what's wrong.

RUSTY: I'm afraid to.
DANNY: What are you afraid of? Daddy's your best friend.
RUSTY: I'm afraid that my best friend is going to kill me.
DANNY: What's that? If you can't talk to your father, who can you talk to?
RUSTY: The police.

Rusty sees safety outside the home, away from his loving father. Rather than protecting him, his father is the threat against which Rusty needs protection. Alex, Donna, and Danny see this damage at home, but others outside the home also claim to see these children's trauma. When Betty Anderson goes through a depression, her friend Dottie alleges that Betty must have had a "traumatic experience" with Jim in her childhood (and Jim responds by threatening to hit Betty, saying, "That's the kind of traumatic experience that does some good"). Like Rusty, Betty must leave the home for protection and care even when she is most vulnerable, so she spends part of the episode finding comfort in other adults at the train station. The performance of the happy family, unfortunately, does not satisfy these children's needs for real supportive, trustworthy adult authorities, whether police or simply safe strangers in a public place.

While Jeff and Rusty try to avoid being punished in the above episodes, other times they and other sitcoms mothers and children volunteer themselves as victims: these children have internalized the notion that the postwar family requires their performance as much their parents' and that their roles are as victims. Some see masochistic self-offering as a way to alleviate their own guilt or to provoke guilt in the men, others as an offering of love, others as an act of defiance, and finally others as a means to their own desires. When Bud Anderson disappoints his father, who tries desperately to handle him with restraint, Bud says that he feels that "something is missing" until Jim threatens to "tan your backside until you can't sit down for a week!" Seeing Jim's apparent relief at having released some frustration, Bud smiles broadly and says, "Yes sir." While Jim's response is merely to threaten Bud, Rusty and Terry explicitly make themselves available for Danny's actual violence. Observing his father's frustration one afternoon, Rusty martyrs himself for the family, volunteering to be an outlet for Danny's rage: he hands him a baseball bat, hangs his head, turns his back to his father and says, "Beat me. Go on, if it'll make you feel better." When his sister Terry wants any sort of independence or privacy—taking a phone call alone in her room, going on a date, having a co-ed party, choosing not to audition for the school play—she knows that Danny will react in anger, so she offers to take a beating in a pre-emptive trade. The Williams children are not atypical: many wives and children are willing to face violent punishment to "help" their families as a whole or in some other exchange. Not only is their role to take punishment, but the punishment is actually their only source of power in a performance which, however complicated, seems directed by either their fathers or an unseen source.

"THE EYES OF A STRANGER": THE UNSAFE SAFE HUSBAND

Episodes in which violence is merely suspected, but are not acted on, are perhaps the most important episodes of these series because they not only register the climate of dread that is evoked in the episodes of anticipation, but also suggest that no man is innocent, and no home is safe. While Ricky (Cuban) and Danny (Lebanese) were marked as ethnic others likely to be "hot-headed," the less ambiguously white sitcom dads' motivations were at times portrayed as mysterious, even unknowable.[24]

Though Harriet works hard to avoid his disapproval, Ozzie is noticeably nearly absent from the above discussion of violence. He does get into altercations outside the home on occasion, so the locus of his (nominal) violence is, unlike the other men's, in the public sphere. However, Ozzie is the ideal example of another trend in the domestic sitcom, in which even a man's appearance of nonviolence is suspect. In "Honest Face," David learns about reading faces in psychology class, only to determine that Ozzie's marks him as dangerous. In "Ozzie's Double," a criminal who looks exactly like Ozzie terrorizes the town. Though these and other episodes of mistaken identity and suspicion eventually restore Ozzie to his position as the mild, slightly daft head of the household, their repetition registers a disturbing theme: despite Ozzie's consistent composure, his wife and children are concerned that he might, deep down or secretly, be dangerous. Donna and Margaret Anderson both have to comfort and reassure female friends who are on the verge of marrying or recently married when these women become anxious that their men are "strangers" or claim to have seen the "mask slip" to reveal a "cruel, hateful beast." Donna herself has explicitly fretted about Alex's being a "stranger" and Jim tells Margaret, "you don't know your husband," and that what is "on the surface" should not be believed. Given that neither Donna nor Margaret genuinely trusts her own husband, the reassurance that they provide their friends is only that this state of dread and suspicion is the unavoidable condition of marriage.

Ozzie and Harriet uses the mistaken identity trope more than any other sitcom, but wariness of the man of the house is part of every program mentioned here, especially *Father Knows Best*. Like David's face-reading experiment, Betty's handwriting analysis suggests that Jim is not what he seems. Far more striking, however, is Kathy's seemingly irrational fear that Jim is a criminal. Though, by all appearances, Jim is a model citizen, Kathy is certain that Jim is hiding some unspecified pattern of lawbreaking. When she sees police, she yells, "Run Daddy, run! Run Daddy, run!" though there is no indication that they are after him. Again, with no evidence to suggest that Jim is guilty of anything, Kathy worriedly says to her mother, "Maybe Daddy did something we didn't know he did and the cops found out about it and now they're going to put him in the clink!" As expected, Jim is always restored to his status as a law-abiding resident of Springfield. However, "Bud's Encounter with the Law" does not resolve this concern by its end. When Jim is wanted by the police chief and doesn't know why, he is panicked, though Margaret assures him that, since he is not the type to commit a crime, he should be able to sleep without worry. Jim mysteriously stops short of agreeing with her, and, as soon as he lays his head down on the pillow, sirens sound, a police car stops at the Andersons', and Jim's eyes open wide with terror. The episode ends without explaining Jim's interaction with the police, if indeed there was one at all, and this incident is never referred to again. This strange ending places the viewer in the role of the sitcom wife: we are forced to suspect Jim of *something*, but we will not get confirmation of our worst fears.

"RED-BLOODED AMERICAN MEN": SEX AND THE SITCOM HUSBAND

Wives' suspicions are even more animated around the issue of adultery and, in these cases, men seem to believe that their performance should suggest their wandering eyes, not their trustworthiness. David Tucker, discussing *I Love Lucy*, claims that no other show "derive[d] so many plots from the heroine's fears that her husband might be sexually attracted to other women."[25] Tucker is correct, but most of the era's other domestic sitcoms did include frequent variations on that theme. Though scholars and viewers seem intent on claiming that these shows portrayed little or no sexuality, each of the couples mentioned here have moments of clear physical passion. Alex and Donna and Lucy and Ricky in particular have very frequent scenes of unmistakable verbal foreplay, which end as they recline while kissing and the music swells. Entire episodes of *Make Room for Daddy* revolve around Danny trying to get Kathy into bed (and the children are threatened when they get in the way) and, other times, Kathy tries to lure Danny into bed with lingerie to get her way. Also, while many assert that television couples could not share beds on television, two of the couples—the Nelsons and the Ricardos—do because the actors were married in offscreen life. But sleeping in the same bed is not required when a man can simply join his wife in her twin bed as Alex does. The fact that they are so amorous with each other does not diminish the women's jealousy. While the women seem to want only their husbands, the men lust after other women, and their desires are explained to be "normal" for "red-blooded American men." When it comes to their sexual pasts, these husbands can be carefully circumspect with their wives and consider this circumspection integral to their roles in the performance of domestic bliss, advising other men to do the same. While Margaret tells her young friend that suspicion and anxiety is normal in a marriage, Jim simultaneously cautions her young lover that one's past with women should be "taboo, verboten, off-limits." Though Jim tells Margaret that he has only been with her, he shares his "taboo" past when alone with male friends. Ozzie and the Nelson boys also frequently discuss Ozzie's past as a "ladies' man," who "knows all about women." Margaret and Harriet married as adolescents, so viewers are likely to assume that their sexual experience is minimal. Alex and Donna met after college, so more experience on each of their parts is presumed. When Alex meets up with a college friend, they trade laughs about Alex's womanizing ways. Donna overhears this conversation just as Alex is about to attend a "bachelor dinner," so she spends the episode in a panic that he will cheat on her. Donna's panic is women's most common emotion in the 1950s sitcom: the threat of infidelity is ever present and more episodes revolve around this anxiety than any other.

While the men are ashamed of and guilty over their brutality, they appear to derive pleasure from their sexual power. These men know that the very threat of sexual infidelity allows them to dominate their wives, and several of them see no shame in using it to their advantage. Ozzie, for example, lies to Harriet when he is irritated with her, telling her that he flirted with a "blonde" or a "redhead." He also makes a show of keeping secrets from Harriet: when she asks simple questions about his whereabouts, he shames her and tells her not to give him "the third degree." His friends, Joe and Thorny, join in, embarrassing their wives for their suspicions but showing up late, disappearing, and whispering with other women. Clearly, sitcom men feel that these actions are their prerogatives, that they should be trusted, and they play mind games to "prove" they deserve these prerogatives. When Joan admits that she does not trust him, Brad also uses a "redhead" to teach her a lesson. This counterintuitive strategy by which men "reassure" their wives by convincing them that they *are* cheating comes up again and again. The men's pattern of inflaming their wives' insecurities, only to inspire later relief and gratitude, also comes up in other ways. The "other woman's" relative youth is repeatedly invoked to exploit the wives' insecurities. Ward, for example, jokes that June's looks might be fading and that her only remaining beauty is because of pancake makeup, until she becomes insecure. She compares herself to the teenager sunbathing in a bikini next door, which Ward encourages, but, by the end of the episode, Ward says (in what is meant to be benevolence) that he thinks that June "has a few good years left." Ozzie and Jim shamelessly check out the young women around them, even their sons' dates, some of whom suggest that they "like older men." When other women flatter their husbands in this way, June, Harriet, Margaret Anderson, Kathy Williams, and Donna especially become almost hysterical. Of course, the men reaffirm their monogamy at the end of these episodes. Moreover, though these husbands often intentionally inspire their wives' jealousy, the women are portrayed as "crazy" for believing their deceptions.

But, as in "Lucy Thinks Ricky Is Trying to Murder Her," we must ask why these women and children are so ready to believe the worst of men, even those that they have known their whole lives. For these women, there is obviously a lot at stake. None of them earns her income outside the home and, though Margaret Anderson inherits a house from her parents, these women do not generally appear to have other assets. Donna and Kathy Williams were nurses prior to marriage and Harriet was a performer, but even they are mostly depicted as "silly," "idiotic," and incompetent at anything beyond cooking and cleaning. Worse, June struggles even with her relatively simple household chores, turning to frozen dinners (for which Ward, of course, criticizes her), and domestic help, while Margaret Anderson cannot drive, so she relies on her husband and children for anything outside the home. Lucy, Joan, and both Williams wives are clueless about money; yet, while Elizabeth, Margaret Anderson, June, and Donna seem fairly competent, their "allowance" is never quite adequate. Given this extremely precarious position, they are understandably petrified that their husbands will jeopardize the family's survival. For this reason, when Ozzie spends the "day in bed" shirking his responsibilities and threatens to do "whatever he wants" for as long as he wants (even if it means getting arrested), or Jim suddenly quits insurance sales in order to be a farmer, their wives are disturbed and frantic. However, it is integral to their performances as wives and mothers that they constantly reassure the children, many of whom fear that their fathers will simply leave. The Anderson children are most prone to this anxiety, but June puts on a veneer of complete denial when a frightened Beaver asks how she would react if Ward did not come home after they had a fight: "Well, I'd keep his dinner warm for him." Even having assured their children that the men will return home as usual, sometimes these mothers leave their company to cry, believing that they have finally "pushed [them] too far." But even when the men are sorely tempted, they have never been "pushed" past the point of no return: none of them ever actually cheats or leaves his family permanently. After all, the series could not continue if they did.

"A SENSE OF CONTINUING STORY": SERIES NARRATIVE AND EPISODIC SITCOM FORM

"Bud's Encounter with the Law" and "Boy's Week" leave viewers uncertain about their outcomes and, in this, they are unusual: most domestic sitcoms resolve conflicts within a single episode, even if similar conflicts eventually or commonly reappear. Several early television scholars identified this pattern. Kaminsky and Mahan explain that for "the continuing television narrative, there is a series of narrative units, little segments in which the narrative action takes place. Those units are tied together . . . even if there is a dramatic resolution in each segment, the audience has a sense of a continuing story." Lawrence Mintz refines this idea of the "unit" for the sitcom, specifically: "The program opens with the characters in a state of normality . . . the 'situation' of the sitcom is the interruption of this normality, attempts at coping with the intrusion or problem, and the resolution of it, allowing for what we *could* call 'the return to normality.'"[26] Mintz is, of course, careful to clarify that the "intrusion or problem" is "always a minor threat." The resolution of conflict by the end of nearly every episode, or this "return to normality," when paired with "a sense of a continuing story," partially accounts for viewers' and critics' insistence that these shows are idealized portraits of American families, when clearly the homes that they portray are filled with strife, rage, and even danger. That the sitcom abandons the linearity associated with narrative in favor of circularity—as in Mintz's "normality–intrusion–return to normality" schema—makes its format *seem* like a safer terrain. The family had to survive because it was the basis of each series. Even when Betty goes to college and David marries, they remain major characters and life for their families appears to go on relatively unchanged. This certainty allows for a less-threatening exploration of family strife because it will inevitably be resolved in some form. However, this circularity does present a danger: it makes the sitcom ripe for the sort of readings that essentially ignore the texts' interiors. Because conflict derives plot, "happiness" cannot, per se, be narrated as plot, so the viewer who claims to see happiness and tranquility, is seeing that which is *not* narrated. As such, when viewers "remember" the domestic sitcoms of the 1950s as the stories of happy homes without "real" problems or tensions, they are reading the presumed *spaces between* the episodes, assuming that the conflicts that these shows make visible are the only conflicts that occur, that the state of resolution to which these families return is the default position, and, most consequentially, that this resolution is trustworthy.[27] Take Castleman and Podrazik's take on "Lucy Thinks Ricky Is Trying to Murder Her": after describing the premise, they write, "Like any misunderstood situation, the mix-up took only a few words of explanation to clear up at the end.... Strong performances by each character turned such silly fluff into engaging comedy." There is little "fluffy" about a "mix-up" in which a woman sincerely believes that her husband is planning to kill her, is drugged by him, and thinks that she has been shot and poisoned, but the very premise of the episode is obscured by the fact that viewers know how it will conclude. However, the repetition of these conflicts, their similarity to each other, and the reactions and assumptions of the characters within them, suggest that these problems might be viewed as just as "normal" as the calm family hugs, laughs, and dinners that append them. Furthermore, acknowledging the exceptions—the episodes in which the show ends mid-spanking, pre-punishment, or without otherwise resolving the conflict, and the episodes that rely on suspicions, rather than on actual actions or threats—proves that the "idealized" sitcom of "perfect" family relations is a construct as pervasive as the one that many claim the sitcoms themselves perpetuate. If men are dangerous and cannot be trusted, even with all evidence to the contrary, the frame of an "episode" certainly cannot contain women's and children's daily dread and unease interacting with them.

PLAYING THEMSELVES: LUCILLE BALL AND DESI ARNAZ

This extension of dread and unease beyond the episode explains why critics and viewers often feel that *I Love Lucy* is exceptional, even though the popularity of *I Love Lucy* first led to the explosion of domestic sitcoms, and it eventually fell into line among them. Other shows featured rowdy female comic talent, and many *I Love Lucy* episodes were recycled from, or identical to, other television and radio shows in the surrounding years, and it was certainly not the only funny or risky show at a time when Milton Berle was "Mr. Television." However, unlike in the other domestic sitcoms, the presumed "space" of domestic bliss between the episodes of conflict was constantly threatened, if not completely undercut, by the public's knowledge of the Arnaz marriage.

Because the sitcom writers, performers, and producers claimed to strive for "realism" whenever possible, their stars were, more or less, believed to be facsimiles of their on-screen characters.[28] John Ellis argues that the "narrative regime" of television actually requires that "the performer's image is equated with that of the fictional role (rather than vice versa)" and his contention is borne out in reports of fan behavior in the 1950s.[29] Many viewers assumed that all actors who played married couples were married off screen as well, sometimes resulting in embarrassing accusations of infidelity. *TV Guide* tried to set the record straight in 1954 in "Honest, She's My Wife! But Most TV Viewers Are Still Baffled," clarifying that Danny Thomas and Jean Hagen, William Frawley and Vivian Vance, Joan Davis and Jim Backus, and William Bendix and Marjorie Reynolds were *not* married. Most viewers could basically separate fact from fiction, but, "Honest, She's My Wife!" aside, most media portrayals of sitcom actors worked against this separation, implying that they were generally "playing themselves." Many in the industry complied with or furthered this mythology: Eugene Rodney and Robert Young, Lucille Ball and Desi Arnaz, Ozzie and Harriet Nelson, Joe Connelly and Bob Mosher (creators of *Leave It to Beaver*), and Danny Thomas all claimed repeatedly that their episodes were drawn from their "real-life" family experiences.

When they saved *Father Knows Best* from cancellation, Scott Paper Company said that viewers wrote to them expressing that the show "represents the American family as it really is and not how some TV scriptwriter thinks it is—or should be" since Young, Rodney, the writers were working from their own lives.[30]

The Nelsons and the Arnazes had an extra burden: because these actors were married, as were their characters, much press focused on the permeability of their on-screen and offscreen lives.[31] *Ozzie and Harriet* appeared to add only the most minimal layer of artifice, in that the actors went by their own names and their characters lived in a home modeled off the Nelsons' own. However, the Nelsons were known to have had a stable marriage and professional partnership before the war.

On the contrary, Ball and Arnaz attracted tabloid scrutiny from the early days of their courtship, starting more than a decade before *I Love Lucy*. Though there was much speculation that their marriage would not last, their early romance appeared constantly in *Movie Life*'s "Tables for Two," and Hollywood gossip columns. Their very public near-divorce in 1944, precipitated by Arnaz's absence during the war, only fed the appetite for Arnaz gossip, making the couple more famous than their film careers might ordinarily have warranted.[32] Though they reconciled just short of divorce, the issue continued to come up, with especially renewed vigor once *I Love Lucy* made them America's most fascinating pair.[33] The press never allowed the tension in the marriage to rest, and it was integrated into, if not the subject of, nearly every account of the couple. Ball was frank about the hard work it took to keep her marriage together, the pressure of fame on their relationship, her jealousy, and their fights about the home and finances. Most of these accounts reassured audiences that these fights were "normal," that they "hold up a mirror to every married couple in America," and, further, that seeing their arguments replicated on television might actually help to "save the marriages" of both the performing Arnazes and the presumably strained viewing couples nationwide.[34] Because of this background, Ellis's contention that the performer's image is subordinated to the character's image is somewhat more complicated, and this more complicated shared "star image" may have even broadened their appeal in both arenas: not only were their ratings high, but they sold out issues of *Time, TV Guide, Cosmopolitan*, and other publications, and had box office success playing married couples in movies who were not the Ricardos or the Arnazes. Their offscreen image and on-screen image as a married couple changed the way that they used and were used in "subsidiary forms of circulation." The usual "straightforward" resolution of Ellis's "basic enigma: 'Is there a person different from the role in the fiction?'" was not so straightforward at all.[35]

In 1955, Arnaz appeared on the cover of *Confidential*, a hugely successful Hollywood tabloid, in which it was revealed that he was cavorting with "door-to-door dames" or "vice dollies" and that audiences could "bet your last dollar that cameras are not around," emphasizing the falsity of the life lived on a soundstage. In a section subtitled, "Something Special in Army Maneuvers," *Confidential* reveals that, according to one of the women involved, Arnaz attempted to orchestrate a ménage a trois while stationed at an Army hospital. Despite the fact that the article is clearly meant to shock readers, it ends by implying that the Arnaz marriage is just like so many others: "Desi most certainly loves Lucy. It's just that, *like a lot of other husbands,* he's got a little extra—to go around" (emphasis mine). According to biographers of Ball and Arnaz, this revelation was—despite Lucy's knowledge of previous affairs—cataclysmic for both their marriage and working relationship.

The following year, the Arnazes made several television appearances outside of *I Love Lucy*, including on *The Bob Hope Chevy Show* (NBC, 1956–57) and *I've Got a Secret* (CBS, 1952–67). On Hope's program, Ball plays Lucy Ricardo, Hope plays Ricky, Arnaz plays Fred Mertz, and Vivian Vance, as usual, plays Ethel.[36] This tangle allows some of the conflicts brought to light in the press to come out on-screen. Hope as Ricky gets angry with Lucy and is delighted to be a "hot blooded Latin," so that he can grab and shake Lucy and generally react toward her mischief as Ricky might.[37] Arnaz as Fred flirts heavily with Ethel, even hinting that they were physically intimate in the Ricardos' closet and are planning to go to bed together. As Desjardins puts it, "Lucy Ricardo keeps slipping into Lucille Ball every time Ethel/Vance appears to be enjoying Desi-as-Fred too much," desperately but unsuccessfully trying to keep them apart, grabbing and pulling Ethel away, and screaming at them to "break it up!" Since Arnaz is supposed to be Fred, the audience relies on their understanding that Ball and Arnaz are actually married to understand the joke, which would undoubtedly bring to mind his rumored infidelities. The skit ends with Lucy's deception unmasked and Hope/Ricky, cuddling with Arnaz/Fred on the Ricardos' couch, again hinting at bisexuality. This episode comes after Arnaz's 1952 appearance in "Stars in the Eye: The Dedication of CBS Television City," in which he ends up in the shower with Jack Benny, who, as Alexander Doty notes in his work on the comedian, was frequently read as bisexual or gay.[38] On another occasion, when Lucy thinks that Ricky is cheating on her, he says, "If you don't believe me, ask the boys in the band. They were all there." Lucy replies with insinuation: "Well, that must have been a cozy gathering." "The boys in the band" come up as sexual threats numerous times on *I Love Lucy*.

The Hope appearance specifically though reveals some of the complexity of their so-called star image, which both facilitated, and was caused by, the incredible popularity of *I Love Lucy*, but the Arnazes' 1956 appearance on *I've Got a Secret* offers a glimpse into their relationship which more simply extends the dynamics between the Ricardos. Ball and Arnaz appeared on the program to promote *Forever Darling* (Alexander Hall, 1956), their second feature film together as a married couple. The host, Gary Moore, reveals that Arnaz has fixed the program so that Ball alone will have to determine the "secret," which the panelists, the studio audience, and those watching at home already know. (Arnaz's secret is "I love Lucy.") This cute premise devolves quickly into a troubling scene in which Arnaz embarrasses Ball for struggling to find an answer:

ARNAZ: Why you going to come and sit on a panel if you don't know how?
BALL: Because you told me to.
ARNAZ: I told you to come and plug the picture, not to make a fool of yourself! Play the game, ask some questions. Come on dear, there are a lot—millions—of people watching this.

Ball pauses, looking hurt and stunned.

BALL: I did plug the picture. If I happened to make a fool of myself in the middle of it, I can't help it. Forever Darling, Forever Darling, Forever Darling.
ARNAZ: You did that already. Now play the game. Be smart now. Up, up, everybody up!

When Ball finally comes to the answer, Arnaz laughs derisively, "How about that? She did it!"

As Moore thanks the couple for appearing, Ball looks down, fiddles with her belt, and averts her eyes from Arnaz. Having been introduced as a

"Lucille Ball-Arnaz, a well-thought-of wife and mother," she does not have recourse to Lucy Ricardo's exaggerated facial expressions or other physical hijinks to take the edge off the spousal conflict. Instead, her face records a very real feeling of humiliation, discomfort, and fear. Coming almost exactly one year after the fateful *Confidential* cover story, the "star image" that Ball and Arnaz worked hard to build and rebuild and rebuild would seem to have crumbled, though it had been crumbling since 1940. In fact, the reverse is true: their "star image" was dependent upon and defined by their constant conflict, always portrayed as "normal." But, as in the unresolved sitcom episodes, the *I've Got a Secret* audience is left wondering what happened between Ball and Arnaz on the way home from the studio, or whether they went home together at all.

The Arnaz marriage was not anomalous on a game or panel show. Just weeks before this particular episode of *I've Got a Secret* aired, *Do You Trust Your Wife?* (CBS, 1956–57), hosted by Edgar Bergen, premiered on CBS. Though many episodes of the show also showed happily married couples, the show's very premise—that the wife might not be trusted to answer difficult quiz questions—set up marital conflict between ordinary spouses, marked by women's fear and dread and men's irritation and contempt, as entertainment. In that context, the Ball-Arnaz episode of *I've Got a Secret* should not be seen as aberrant or illustrative exclusively of the Arnaz marriage—viewers in 1956 might well have seen it as typical of postwar marriage. Whereas Carini suggests that Ball's "gender conservatism" or "'anything for my man' ethos" likely "strained the sympathies of 1950s female fans hungering for a plucky Lucy on and off camera," it seems equally possible that female fans were sympathetic exactly because she was not unusually "plucky," because Ball and Arnaz corroborated the "performativity of family life" more baldly than the fictional Cleavers (or Andersons or Stones) ever could.

Carini also argues that establishing similarities between the Ricardos and the Arnazes such as "assigning the Ricardos the same anniversary year as theirs," and "using the Byram River Beagle Club in Greenwich, Connecticut, as the site of both marriages and the site for recommitment ceremonies for both couples," (and, I would add, giving Little Ricky and Desi Jr. the same birthday, celebrating their thirteenth wedding anniversaries with a party at the same nightclub in Hollywood, and many others) were "insurance measures used to give the marriage the appearance of solidity," but, even if that was the intention, this certainly had the opposite effect. The more that the Ricardos seemed like the Arnazes, the less solid their marriage seemed to be. Furthermore, if Carini is correct that "Ball had conceived of *I Love Lucy* as the ultimate rewrite of their marriage—the final chance to register perfection," meaning that Ball and Arnaz strove for the "perfection" of the Ricardos; 1950s marital "perfection" is a rather tragic notion.

By contrast, appearances by the Nelsons, *Father Knows Best*'s Robert Young and Jane Wyatt, and *Make Room for Daddy*'s Danny Thomas on other game and panel shows during the same timeframe went smoothly and resolved soundly. These other appearances seemed designed to put the domestic sitcoms in safe perspective, and star interviews, like the game and panel shows, offered actors the chance to participate in the extratextual situating of their own vehicles (which were, in many cases, their own properties as well). Like most interviewers, Edward R. Murrow urged Danny Thomas to connect his own home life with the happenings on his series, when Thomas and his family appeared on *Person to Person* (CBS, 1953–61) in 1955. Thomas and his wife, Rose Marie, came across as generally quite companionable, but grievances between Thomas and his children came up several times, sometimes as inspirations for the television show. To illustrate, Thomas tells the story of his son, Tony, writing on the walls with crayon. Thomas chases him, removing his belt, until Tony looks at him and says, "You wouldn't hit your own son, would you?" Thomas claims that his child's reaction stopped him short and reassures Murrow and those watching at home that Tony was not punished. This anecdote indicates that those "moments of mercy" described above in *Leave It to Beaver*, *Make Room for Daddy*, and *I Love Lucy*, are intended to seem like more than a norm, but a constant: in "real life," even when fathers threaten, children have the power to talk them out of it. Also, this anecdote, which is relayed humorously to Murrow (who laughs), allows that these programs are not episode-after-episode of idealized domestic tranquility, but are actually *about* the comic thwarting and avoidance of violence. Thomas indirectly says something analogous when he recalls Phil Foster's take on his comedy: "You bum, you ain't funny. They're just relieved to know you don't mean it." Unfortunately, the public knew that Desi Arnaz/Ricky Ricardo meant it.

1950S DOMESTIC SITCOMS IN THE TWILIGHT ZONE

The place of the sitcom in postwar family life can only be conjectured, and speculation on the subject has been seemingly contradictory. In the 1950s though, psychologists and the public shared a consensus that television generally, and domestic sitcoms particularly, could serve a therapeutic function. *TV Guide* assembled psychiatrists and other "experts" to explain the popularity of certain programs and themes. These experts (and the viewers that they cited) invariably said that audience members sought vicarious experiences of their deeper desires. It is possible that viewers did not look to television to provide this acting out of urges, but, rather, they may have sought the resolution of conflicts week after week. It was not that these conflicts, suspicions, and fears did not exist—either in "real life" or on-screen—but that viewers were given that final, fleeting moment of escape from those concerns at the end of each episode. More than that, perhaps it was the promise that they were, in their daily dysfunction, like the Cleavers, the Andersons, the Williamses, the Nelsons, and the Stones—or the Ricardos and the Arnazes—normal. The spaces between episodes could therefore be read as strife-filled, complicated, and fearful, as Ball and Arnaz made clear in their time, and Rick Nelson, Lauren Chapin, Billy Gray, and Robert Young would later, themselves afflicted with substance abuse, legal, and mental health issues. Ball and Arnaz were unable to control the space between the episodes, which revealed more than their own personal shortcomings: *I Love Lucy* exposes the fact that the happy space between sitcom episodes was nothing more than viewers' willful collective projection, a self-protective strategy from the everyday fears and dangers of family life in the postwar era. But, like Rusty at the nightclub show, many children probably felt forced to laugh at the violence and suspicion on-screen when seated in their living rooms with their parents, compelled to participate in the performance of the happy family. For that reason, they may have resented those concluding moments of happiness for the ways that they overwrote the rest of the shows' content. Television history, as we have come to accept it, has largely been written by these baby boomers, the hostages in front of the television, not the people who created or managed 1950s programming, or the other people in front of the set. As Kompare points out, baby boomer executives started "Nick at

Nite/TV Land, by far the most significant site of rerun culture on American television," which, in its infancy, emphasized the 1950s (24). Almost immediately, programming was shifted toward the 1960s, with the conspicuous exceptions of *I Love Lucy* and *The Honeymooners,* allowing conjecture about and parodies of 1950s sitcoms—like those on *SNL*—to stand in for the programs themselves.[39] Baby boomers read the texts on behalf of their parents as well as themselves when they claim that 1950s domestic sitcoms were portraits of perpetually happy people without real problems; they impose their childish readings on texts that were produced to—and indisputably did—speak to everyone in a household. Even the actors on these programs are divided generationally.

Take, for example, Billy Gray (Bud Anderson) who angrily calls *Father Knows Best* "a hoax," whereas Robert Young (Jim Anderson) and Jane Wyatt (Margaret Anderson) say that the show was not meant to depict life as "a bowl of cherries," but was, in fact, "realistic."[40] Domestic sitcoms are blamed for perpetuating an impossible model of domestic bliss, they actually critiqued this model and proved its failure. The "Greatest Generation" that is commended for their "strong silence" is expected to stay that way and is, retrospectively, expected to have been that way. Like cinematic Westerns and *Playboy,* the 1950s sitcom has been so strictly defined by baby boomers that the texts' meanings have been all but closed for later interpreters. The men and women who built lives and families after World War II may have admirably struggled to do so, but they were not exactly silent about it, to which all these texts attest. 1950s domestic sitcoms, however derided in the years since, were not only rife with the inevitable problems of reintegrating men into postwar life, making partners out of people who could not understand each other, and bringing up children in a mess of radical change and confusing expectations: that is what they were actually about. Helen Gurley Brown and Betty Friedan spoke more directly than Lucille Ball and Lucy Ricardo but were heard because, by the 1960s, the baby boomers were old enough to hear. In the epilogue, I will discuss this extension of women's concerns during the 1950s into the apparent explosion of women's texts in the 1960s.

CONCLUSION
THE "LOVING LITTLE STOIC" SPEAKS

After *The Best Years of Our Lives*, this book analyzes literary and pulp fiction, drama, Hollywood film, *Playboy* and entertainment gossip magazines, domestic sitcoms, game and panel shows, and only in *Act of Violence* is a man's veteran status defining enough to land in a mainstream summary. Combat literature, films, and television isolate the war experience, and the post–World War II era includes some of their finest examples. Other important texts in these mediums and genres are more direct about the war: films like *Bad Day at Black Rock* (John Sturges, 1955) and *The Blue Dahlia* (George Marshall, 1946) bring postwar anxieties about wartime decisions into Western and noir visions of the era. Many of the texts in this book rely on characters' wartime pasts without ever acknowledging it; most acknowledge it briefly, treating it as normal, because it was. By the 1960s, only a minority of men would serve in the military in any way. The very notion that men *should* serve in the armed forces became an outlying opinion over time; President Richard Nixon, who served in active duty in the Naval Reserve during World War II, made ending conscription an important part of his campaign in 1968. No men were drafted into service after June 1973. Popular culture reflected these changes in unexpected ways: some of the most memorable works of art set in combat came out during and in the aftermath of Americans' service in the war in Vietnam. These works include *Apocalypse Now* (Francis Ford Coppola, 1979), *Full Metal Jacket* (Stanley Kubrick, 1987), and Oliver Stone's Vietnam War Trilogy: *Platoon* (1986), *Born on the Fourth of July* (1989), *Heaven & Earth* (1993); Tim O'Brien's *The Things They Carried* (1990) and others in his oeuvre. Other films about veteran reintegration like *Coming Home* (Hal Ashby, 1978) and *Rambo: First Blood* (Ted Kotcheff, 1983) remain classics. In recent years, films set in wars in Afghanistan and Iraq, like literary adaptation *Jarhead* (Sam Mendes, 2003) and *The Hurt Locker* (Kathryn Bigelow, 2008), emphasize this abrupt transition from combat to homefront. All of these works rely on the idea that servicemembers and veterans are *different*.

In this way, assumptions about veterans' tendencies toward violence and sexual "deviancy" became assumptions about men as a group. Beginning in the late 1940s as a way to make sense of the postwar transition, many examples of popular culture protected veterans by making them "normal," which meant that "normal" men might not be able to control their impulses and certainly couldn't all the time. All men became versions of the "man who does" and the "man who doesn't": a "good" man is not one without urges, but one who generally holds them back. A "free" man, then, gives in to some of these urges.

The backlashes against feminism in its many waves may have felt justified. Americans were cleaved apart by gender during World War II and some men in that generation—as this book shows—expressed resentment toward women for "having it easy." By the end of 1959, *Playboy* diminished or dismissed women as sexual objects or nuisances. Baby Boomer men witnessed the indulgences afforded their fathers' generation; women's liberation came as they prepared to exercise such latitude.

Even as women—especially white upper-middle-class women—began to rise professionally and in the public eye, doing so required making allowances for men. President Jimmy Carter could admit to *Playboy* that he had "committed adultery in my heart many times," President Bill Clinton could admit to infidelities on *60 Minutes* before the Super Bowl, and both were elected with majorities among women. Celebrities like Sean Penn and Chris Brown could physically attack their equally famous female partners (pop singers Madonna and Rihanna, respectively) without losing popularity with their female fans. In fact, all four of these men's female partners at some point defended them, even at personal cost.

Because this transition from the veteran-focused popular culture of the late 1940s to more contemporary forms took place glacially, this conclusion can only be speculative, but is worthy of serious consideration: it may have far-reaching implications, some of which remain pertinent to toxic gender relations which we are still dismantling today. Most recently, women involved in the #MeToo and #TimesUp movements have been the public face of this activity. What activist Tarana Burke began as a post on the defunct social media network MySpace in 2006 was taken up by celebrities including Alyssa Milano on Twitter in 2017, after the allegations of sexual assault against Hollywood mogul Harvey Weinstein and the election of admitted sexual abuser Donald Trump. All acknowledge that #MeToo would not exist without decades of other brave women, from Carmita Wood to Anita Hill, many of whom were denigrated and pushed back into the shadows.

Inspired by and as part of #MeToo, Black Women's Blueprint published "An Open Letter to *Playboy* from Black Women" on the website for *Ms.* magazine in the summer of 2019.[1] In this piece written after Hugh Hefner's death, Black Women's Blueprint takes him and his brand to task. They systematically undermine *Playboy*'s progressive bone fides. Referring to the many vaunted "Playboy Interviews" with Black leaders, Black Women's Blueprint writes, "this attempt to use interviews with Black leaders as 'woke' credits, is an evasion of their own responsibility to the many survivors of violence at the hands of *Playboy* (both literally and through their perpetuation and creation of rape culture)." Nor do they take the inclusion of Black women in its pages as a sign of an enlightened masthead or readership: "whether they have graced its pages spread-eagle at one time or have been strategically kept out of those pages, is not our concern. Mere representation is but a moment if it does not uproot marginalization and does not change the course and discourse around power." Hefner and *Playboy* may have a track record of supporting some women's causes in the 1970s, primarily the right to choose, but Black Women's Blueprint also interprets Hefner and his colleagues' response to rape in the 1970s: "'We've all done it!' they proclaimed. 'I don't know a single man who hasn't!' they exclaimed." Succumbing to at least *some* urges is here the default, is "normal," every man does it. Black Women's Blueprint argues that normalizing of these perspectives on women—especially when they pertain to Black women—and men's sexual license resulted from self-proclaimed progressives' "sitting with the devil." It is time, they assert, "to think and act critically and proactively to prevent the generational and intergenerational ramifications of glamorizing that which aims to destroy our very lives—patriarchy, misogyny, sexism in all of the aggressive and incessant ways. . . . What we would hope is the script that Gloria Steinem flipped when she went undercover into *Playboy* in 1963, be taken a step further."

Black Women's Blueprint makes it clear that they are not fighting something new: it's intergenerational, developing out of long-past incarnations of *Playboy*. At the same time, the struggle against what feminists call "rape culture" in *Playboy* has a lineage too. In defiance of *Playboy*'s pose of "cool," situated against what Hefner once called the "militant feminists," Black Women's Blueprint asserts a powerful agenda: "Our purpose is to distinctly (re)member the bodies (beyond a single story, beyond any individualistic agenda) of all women that are too often forgotten, caught in the crosshairs of an omnipresent and exploitative racist, patriarchal, misogynistic gaze. . . . Thus this letter is an intentional exercise in reasserting the humanity of survivors, giving them honest, unexploited unbought, uncontrolled right to tell their own stories; resisting in a way that contemporary rape culture does not allow." This word, "resist," has become a generational clarion call for feminists and Black activists, among others. But, as Black Women's Blueprint makes clear, this particular struggle is as old as the early 1960s, when Steinem published her famous expose of her time as a Bunny in a Playboy Club.[2]

In 1963, when Gloria Steinem published "Bunny Tale" in *Show* magazine, Betty Friedan's *The Feminine Mystique* hit the shelves and Helen Gurley Brown's *Sex and the Single Girl* was only a year old. Lorraine Hansbury's *A Raisin in the Sun* had been produced for the first time four years later and had now been adapted for the screen. Several years later, Jacqueline Susann's *Valley of the Dolls* would add to this conversation.

Exactly twenty years after Mickey Spillane penned *I, the Jury* (1947), a new novel broke its record as the twentieth century's bestseller. In both hardcover and paperback, Jacqueline Susann's *Valley of the Dolls* leapt past *I, the Jury*, but also other bestsellers of the 1950s, including *Betty Crocker Picture Cookbook* (1950), James Jones's *From Here to Eternity* (1951), and Grace Metalious's *Peyton Place* (1956), creating a national sensation for its frank treatment of show business, sexuality, and drug abuse.

Set beginning in 1945, *Valley of the Dolls* tells the stories of three white women connected to the entertainment industry, all of whom succumb to "dolls"—pills to help them cope with the difficulties in their lives. Jennifer, a beautiful, buxom blonde, finds that she is loved only for her body, though she has a sharp mind and a loving heart. After marrying the sexually violent singer Tony Polar, she finds out that he has a congenital brain condition, which will lead to complete dementia. Jennifer has an abortion, leaves Tony, and, after being abused by the French art film industry, meets and becomes engaged to Win Adams, a Republican senator. When Jennifer's doctor tells her that she will have to have a mastectomy to remove a cancer, she stops short of telling her fiancé because he claims that her breasts are indispensable to their relationship; Jennifer commits suicide.

Her friend, Neely, begins the novel young and ambitious, angling for a career in show business, which she quickly assumes. After conquering Broadway, Neely moves to Hollywood and becomes a star in film musicals. Her demanding career and unsatisfying personal life lead her to take "dolls" in order to wake in the morning, sleep at night, lose weight, and deal with her anxiety and depression. Under the influence of drugs and alcohol, she becomes an unreliable prima donna, which leads to fewer jobs and a terrible reputation. After attempting suicide and being institutionalized more than once, she begins an affair with the dashing but self-involved agent and author Lyon Burke, who never commits to her but re-launches her career. By the end of the novel, her drug abuse and mental health lurch into a final spiral.

Lyon has a more extensive love affair with Anne, who is arguably the novel's protagonist. The relationship between Anne and Lyon anchors the book, beginning and ending it tragically. Though all (but one) of the men in the novel are selfish, cruel, even bordering on sociopathic, Lyon is the irresistible villain of *Valley of the Dolls*.

Anne begins the novel as the pretty and plucky secretary to a high-powered agent. She falls madly in love with Lyon in a matter of pages when he returns to work in the agency after nearly four years in World War II. Anne's boss, Henry, asks her to find Lyon an apartment. Lyon claims that, "after some of those bombed-out places I slept in during the war, anything with a ceiling will look like the Ritz," but Anne insists on finding him a comfortable home.[3] Within moments of meeting him, she is already trying to anticipate ways to help him recover.

When she takes him to see the place, the two have their first conversation alone. Lyon's erratic nature, his sense of entitlement, and his resentment are immediately clear; so too are Anne's typically postwar ideas about relationships. When Lyon tells her cryptically that, "we all have different sides that we show to different people," she smiles and says, "You mean that even Hitler could be soft and playful with Eva Braun" (33). Anne fantasizes about finding the "soft" beneath the hard man. Lyon responds, "Something like that. And King Henry didn't kill *all* of his wives. If I recall correctly, the last one actually henpecked him." While Anne is able to offer a measure of humanity even to Hitler, believing in the romantic capacity of all men, Lyon uses the opportunity to take a swipe at women.

Lyon continues to confuse and mesmerize Anne. Admitting that he has "a touch of battle fatigue," he tells her that his dream is to "have several beautiful girls who look exactly like you to look after me and knock out a best-selling novel about the war," then doubles back, saying that actually, "I'm not sure there's anything I particularly want" (35). After another "quick change of mood," he says, "there's one thing I do want. I want to be aware of the minutes and the seconds, and to make each count"—though he does not describe what it would mean to make each moment count. Ever sensitive, Anne says that she understands his feelings: "It's a natural feeling for anyone who's been in the war" (37). Though Anne's statement seems innocuous, Lyon reacts angrily: "Oh? I was beginning to wonder if any females over here recalled there was a war." Anne is not angry at his overreaction, but protests quietly, "I'm sure everyone felt the war." Lyon "can't agree," and, the feeling of coming home to a postwar New York City in which "death and bloodshed seemed so remote," he continues to berate American women for their inability to understand their men's sacrifices: "Last night I was out with a beautiful creature who spent hours telling me about the hardships she had endured during the war. No nylons, plastic lipstick containers, no bobby pins . . . it was awful. I think the shortage of nylons affected her the most. She was a model, and her legs were important to her. She said she was terribly glad we finally discovered the atomic bomb—she had been down to her last six pairs when it hit." Even though Lyon is bitter at women, presumably including Anne, for not serving in the military, when Anne hears his voice turning "soft, remembering," she tries again to understand his feelings. Recognizing his receptive audience, he tells her a story about his comrade's death. Anne is moved and encourages him to tell her more, but he stops shortly and "look[s] at her strangely. 'I've said a great many things today . . . things that probably should have stayed locked away in my mind,'" before simply leaving. He leaves Anne thinking that though he is "inscrutable," when "he talked about the war—he seemed accessible, capable of caring. He had cared about the corporal. Who was Lyon Burke, really?" Like the women Lyon so despises, Anne does not understand the realities of war for him. The fact that he "cared about the corporal" says nothing about the potential of a relationship between them: the love he feels for his fallen comrade will never extend to her. In fact, he will keep many parts of himself "locked away" from her always.

Immediately in love with Lyon, Anne decides to break off her engagement with another man and do everything in her power to be with Lyon. So, she is shaken to see him laughing at the Stork Club with another woman and she chides herself for having "gotten him all involved so he remembered the ugly things in his past" (61). Though, before that, she was proud of herself for being someone with whom he could speak openly about the war, she now feels inadequate. She is determined to handle him differently the next time around: though his willingness to talk about the war is what attracted her to him, and though she is immensely curious, she decides that her role is to distract him and give him a good time. Next time Anne gets him alone, she is on edge. After he spends the first few minutes of their date insulting her, "her eyes suddenly flash in anger" and she says, "The war is over. Life goes on. Are you going to fight again?" (111). He becomes quiet and says to her, "I'm fighting right now." Guilty, she tries and fails to make him laugh and the two get drunk, muting their tension. From then on, her role is to cover up that tension between them.

Though he continues to be unpredictable, Anne's feelings for Lyon only grow deeper. She loses her virginity to him on a business trip, and their lovemaking is an intense experience in which Anne finds self-worth: "When the pain came, she clenched her teeth and made no sound. . . . All at once she knew—this was the ultimate in fulfillment, to please a man you love. At that moment she felt she was the most important and powerful woman in the world. She was flooded with a new sense of pride in her sex" (126–27). Anne finds pride, importance, and power in concealing her pain from Lyon in order to please him. She does not see this reaction as her own, but feels it on behalf of women: she believes that she has now felt the power of her gender. This feeling of power, of course, diminishes because it relies on Lyon's consent, which he quite quickly revokes. She does not hold back her emotions: "I feel closer to you than I've ever felt to anyone in my life. I want to know everything about you. . . . I don't want us to have any secrets. We're one, Lyon, part of each other. I belong to you," and Lyon replies, "I wonder if I can ever measure up to that kind of love, Anne. I don't want to hurt you . . . I've given all I might ever be able to give you" (139). Anne is hurt at first, but, like many women trained by postwar propaganda, believes that this is indeed the best she can get. She tells Lyon, "Of course you can't love me like I love you. I don't expect it.... Love me as much as you can. And let me love you" (140).

In this conversation, Lyon is honest. He is incapable of truly loving Anne. His heartlessness and instability cause problems for Anne as long as they are together. Even that evening, he abandons her in New Haven because she wants to go to a friend's party, leaving her to find her own way back to New York. She offers to support him with her modest inheritance so that he can write his war novel, but he keeps thinking back to "the old Lyon Burke" bemoaning his loss of "that Lyon Burke [who] was killed in action" (159). Even though she supports him through his anxieties, misery, and writer's block, he chooses not to marry her and, in fact, encourages her to shed every part of the identity she has constructed for herself as a young adult. She tells him that she won't live with him until they are engaged, but she quickly changes her mind, offering to type his manuscripts and make his breakfasts, all while working at the agency. Still, Lyon breaks off their relationship when she says that she does not want to move back to her childhood house in her hometown and become a housewife for him, which he insists would better "suit her" (215). He leaves her with a "Dear Jane" letter, telling her that he intends to marry the first woman "who will cook and tend for" him, saying "I shall concentrate on my writing—at least in that way I can hurt no one but myself" (220).

He does not keep his word. Many years later, Lyon returns to Anne's life—his war buddy reintroduces them after she has found a new relationship and livelihood—and he convinces her to give up her new life so that they can marry and have a child together. Having abruptly taken up the domestic life he has so long claimed to need, he is bored almost immediately. While Anne is pregnant, he begins his relationship with Neely, and each woman is aware that he is involved with the other. When his daughter, Jennifer, is born, he leaves town with Neely, essentially abandoning his wife and child for the first few months of her life. Though he never admits it, it appears that Lyon cannot maintain a home and family. Anne loves Jennifer and decides to protect her from men like Lyon, Win, Tony, and so many others: that is all she has left.

In the novel's last scene, Anne overhears Lyon with yet another woman, nineteen years old—the same age she was when they met in 1945. Admitting to herself that Lyon will never reform, she thinks, "each time it would hurt less, and afterward she would love Lyon less, until one day there would nothing left—no hurt, and no love . . . from now on, she could never be hurt badly. She could always keep busy during the day, and at night—the lonely ones—there were always the beautiful dolls for company" (442). Anne ends the novel wishing for lifelong numbness because she believes that her man will not, and probably cannot, ever change.

Though Jennifer, Neely, and Anne together comprise a compelling portrait of postwar white American femininity (if in the rarefied environment of entertainment), Anne's story is clearly written to be the most "relatable"—she is both the reader's and author's surrogate. The reader is privy to her interior life more than to the minds of the other two characters, and her rise to fame is far less dramatic—though she models for a cosmetics company, she never becomes an international star at the level of her two closest friends, one perhaps the world's most beautiful woman and the other a world-class entertainer. Jennifer and Neely fall in love and get their hearts broken throughout the novel as well, but neither sets her sights on an individual man for good, whereas Anne's heart belongs completely to Lyon. If the novel were any less bleak, Anne and Lyon certainly would have had the happily-ever-after.

Particularly if seen as Anne's story, *Valley of the Dolls* seems a long time coming. Some version of it may even have been inevitable. Susann's novel is a screed against society's indulgent attitude toward men and the toll this indulgence takes on women; it is no mere coincidence that its major male character is not only a veteran but is a decorated captain and self-defined by his service. It is, however, equally important that the other men are not. Lyon, a veteran, is the ultimate representative of cruel, self-involved, unpredictable masculinity, but though they are less narratively significant, the other men in the novel share these qualities. Walking-on-eggshells devotion and erratic callousness are now simply women's and men's respective roles in heterosexual relationships. The tragedy of the novel, according to Peter Michelson, is that "Susann offers no exit."

I don't entirely disagree with Michelson—Susann's heterosexual relationships are, at best, miserable, and there are no lights at the end of the tunnel—except in that Anne is, in one sense, "exiting" via emotional detachment as the novel ends. After nineteen years, she unfortunately relies heavily on "dolls" to help her escape her feelings, but she also has an epiphany: he can only hurt her so much, until it hurts a little bit less each time. Her heart is hardening because she has, simply, reached her limit. Presumably, by 1966, many women had.

Anne, like many others, followed the advice of experts like sociologist Willard Waller to the letter:

> She must try to learn, as well as she can, being a woman and a civilian, what it feels like to be a veteran, and she must thoroughly realize that the boy who comes back is not the boy who went away. She must give him time to find his bearings again, to rest and recover; she must make him feel secure again, must tolerate his outbursts, and forbear to lecture him for his eccentricities and strange habits. Above all, she must give him lavish—and undemanding—affection, for part of his emotional maladjustment arises from his love-starved condition. But this love she gives him must expect no immediate return from the man whose sickness is his soul.

But Lyon told her in the first conversation all that she would need to know about him. Just as her behavior followed Waller's instructions, so did Lyon's mimic Waller's description: "Why is the soldier angry? Because he was the one singled out to fight and die and suffer and see horrors. He feels akin to everyone who has suffered as he has, even the enemy; he hates everyone who has not." Though Anne and even Neely work to break down this hatred, Lyon clings to it as he clings to his veteran identity. And his hatred of women spreads like a sickness to the novel's other male figures. Susann and other women writing in the 1960s attack this stance: time's up, we have done enough, and we are not the enemy. It is time to create a heterosexuality that works for women. Unfortunately, Susann and others realize that, for some, it may be too late for exit. For others, that is just what they are offering.

Susann was by no means the first woman writing fiction to articulate the profound disconnect between men and women in the postwar period. In fact, Lorraine Hansbury's celebrated play *A Raisin in the Sun* (1958), set "somewhere between World War II and the present," has been interpreted in thousands of ways (unlike *Valley of the Dolls*), but the relationship between Ruth and Walter, a working-class African American couple in their thirties living in Chicago, is central to any reading. Scene 1 already represents this conflict of emotional and intellectual priorities. Walter and Ruth are angry at each other; Ruth's lack of interest in the news of the world (a bomb dropped and a sick Colonel) becomes symbolic of the gulf between them. Walter is not just struggling with his marriage, but, while he claims his friends are interested in the same things as he, he is surrounded by women he is certain cannot understand him: in addition to Ruth, his mother (who controls the purse-strings at the beginning of the play), and his ambitious and "liberated" sister, Beneatha. Like *Valley of the Dolls*, the play goes so far as to intimate the possibility of abortion and cast women's empowerment in a positive light. Written almost a decade earlier, in the era of *Leave It to Beaver* and *The Donna Reed Show*, these representations are nothing short of radical.

Hansbury's conclusions are also radically different from Susann's. While critics disagree on whether or not the ending is "happy," it sees Beneatha moving to Nigeria to marry a man who has proven to her that she is not as "liberated" as she believed—this conclusion suggests the opposite of the "detachment" that white women writers would later advocate. She intends to be a doctor in her husband's home country, but whether she does is left unknown. Most importantly, the play certainly affirms Walter's place as the head of the household and it is his harnessing of his anger to stand up for his family in the face of racism which shows his growth. In the end, he exemplifies the repression-expression ethos of the postwar age.

As we have seen time and again, while there is significant overlap in the issues marriages faced after the war, the force of racism required Black couples and families to have multiple and simultaneous priorities. In order to create change and in seeking equality, the simpering wartime stereotype of Black men and the reemergence of prewar stereotypes of fearsome Black masculinity which were key to their disenfranchisement had to be dismantled. Black women were as important as the men themselves in dismantling and complicating these stereotypes, while also fighting those of their own.[4] For these reasons, while *A Raisin in the Sun* is groundbreaking, it is also breaking different ground. This fact should not dismiss the contribution Hansbury made to the literary landscape into which Susann and other women writers of fiction and nonfiction entered. Not only did she lay some of the groundwork for and gave language to concerns that were difficult to name, Hansbury also modeled a new role for women in the late 1950s and early 1960s, making her name as both an artist and public intellectual, a "serious" woman who was also willing to write and speak about the romantic and the domestic.[5]

Seemingly different in goals, process, and ability, prominent white women addressed the same concerns that Susann and Hansbury do in fiction with their nonfiction work. As I do, Michelson connects Susann to another major public woman of the 1960s, Helen Gurley Brown:

> Susann and Brown seem to be cut from the same bolt, both skillful exploiters of the tension women face in trying to reconcile feminine roles with professional careers, the ground on which much feminist argument still takes it stand. That they were exploiters rather than stateswomen in suggested in the fundamental contradiction between their positions. Brown's stance in *Cosmopolitan* was that women could and should reconcile femininity with careers, advice she gave with blithe cheeriness. Susann's plot, however, quite explicitly traces the destructive consequences of attempting this reconciliation. In the great forum of ideas this merely presents differing perspectives, but insofar as the forum becomes the marketplace, it would seem to offer the buyer opposing remedies.[6]

The fact that Susann's novel ends tragically does not mean that it offers a different remedy than Brown's "blithe cheeriness." In fact, Brown's *Sex and the Single Girl* and Susann's *Valley of the Dolls* suggest the same thing: it is time for women to get fed up with men's volatility and demands and to emotionally detach from them as much as possible. Preserve the pleasures of femininity: fashion and cosmetics, interior decorating, men's admiration, female friendships (and sometimes same-sex erotic contact too); reject the postwar version of femininity defined by caring for, protecting, fearing, needing, depending upon, and unconditionally loving a man who is, by definition, turbulent, uncaring, and selfish, if not violent.

For the most part, Brown and Susann do not yet envision the possibility of living fully without men, but Brown claims it is possible to live without a particular man. As she put it, "You do need a man, of course, every step of the way, and they are often cheaper emotionally and a lot more fun by the dozen."[7] The entire book emphasizes thrift—she carefully lists all the things on which single girls can save money—but it highlights emotional thrift above all. Having only one man in her life brings a woman emotional pain and demands because she surrenders her identity to his. Not only must the married woman care for him, even and especially when she is afraid of him or bored with him, but she must become bored and afraid in the rest of her life, reading little, cooking the same things, keeping in line.

While break-ups might be difficult for single women, surviving the ups and downs of marriage, she argues, is harder. Brown writes that her friend killed herself over her husband's infidelity and another friend is panicked over the same. Given the imperatives upon women in the 1950s to take care of their men, Brown's friends' actions are not irrational. Brown does admit that married women have all manner of responses to cheating husbands, but that it is harder on them than for women who enter relationships expecting nonmonogamy. Instead, Brown offers, try being "The Girl" to several men (she claims to have been "The Girl" to twelve). After all, "to be The Girl imposes very few obligations. You may not have to do anything but just exist" (8). Though she is courteous and fun to be around, Brown's single girl is very definitely not obligated to a man. To avoid obligation, Brown urges her reader to consider a variety of "types" of men, some of which that reader might not expect. Most famously, Brown celebrates being "the other woman" in affairs with married men. They are already attached and emotionally tended to—it might be easier not to "take them seriously" (12–13). For similar reasons, Brown suggests that single girls pause before eliminating homosexual men as prospects: the closeted ones might still be open to sex, and even the "declared" or "overt" ones can be fun otherwise (31). Brown urges women to take advantage of a series of men for flirtation, passion, and sex, gifts and money, advice and good conversation (because the single girl, unlike the busy married woman, "has the freedom to furnish her mind. She can read Proust, learn Spanish, study *Time, Newsweek,* and *The Wall Street Journal*"). What Brown realized was that, if women were marrying in order to access men's wealth, sex, or even his few hours of pleasant company, perhaps a woman could better access these outside of marriage. Her ideas about "single girlhood," then, could be about obtaining more independence. She realizes that it will be difficult if not impossible to have the money and education (and physical strength and mechanical know-how) of the men she knows; she does not need these things for herself, nor does she need a husband, in order to take advantage of them. Men's wealth and sex are less painfully accessible, she suggests, if love is not required. As if speaking directly to Jennifer, Anne, and Neely, Brown advises, "while they are 'using' you to add varnish to their egos, you 'use' *them* to add spice to your life. I say 'them' advisedly. . . . [To] fall in love is like a dope addiction—dangerous and degrading" (24). Use men, Brown suggests, only recreationally.

Brown starts the book by telling readers that she is fairly recently married at nearly forty, but she enjoyed being a single girl and is more happily married as a result of her experiences in those years. During that period of her life, she enjoyed many men, had fun with friends, pursued her interests, rose professionally, and got ready "psychologically" for marriage by becoming herself "worldly enough, relaxed enough" that she could keep herself grounded in her ultimate relationship (3–4). Brown actually prepared herself for marriage by practicing strategies for maintaining emotional detachment.

Using her own life story, Brown illustrates just how effective this detachment can be. She tells of meeting her husband years before they became an item. After their first date, he was emotionally confused as he was coming out of a (second) divorce. After their second date a year later, he was "drowning himself in starlets" After three years, Brown and her husband finally began a serious relationship. Though she was interested in David, she kept herself happily detached throughout the process, dating other men and focusing on the rest of her life. Rather than trying to pry his affection from others, desperately attempting to make him happy when she could see that he was lost, or avoiding him because he seemed so unstable, she accepted him only once he already seemed happy. She could wait because she was already pretty happy herself.

Her standards even for marriageable men, as her choice of husband belies, are relatively low, and they can be because she preaches detachment. In this way, she agrees with mainstream marriage advice: men are what they are and it is up to women to accept them. Brown extends the argument further, though, saying that a woman protects herself by holding back her emotions and expectations rather than by attempting to change the man or protect him from himself. After all, he cannot be changed. Brown makes a significant feminist leap here, arguing that, when men misbehave, women are not responsible for their behavior, so women have not failed. Having relieved women of this responsibility, she encourages women to reconsider their closely held opinions about how a good husband would behave, saying that men

> can't help themselves . . . or if they could it would be at such a severe penalty of pleasure and prestige to themselves that they couldn't take it . . . You don't *like* his being this way and neither do I. . . . But to be trite and cliché, this is the nature of the beast. Man is *not* monogamous no matter how much religion and social writ tell him he is. You don't like your adorable Persian kitty dragging a maimed, half-alive pigeon into your living room, but that's the nature of Persian kitties. (237)

If a woman can manage her expectations of men—they are beasts, after all, or choose not to forgo pleasure to act otherwise—she can enjoy them.

However, even Brown admits that it can be hard to stay entirely detached, so single women ought to be on guard for their emotions: "Affording an impossible man is very much like living beyond your means any other way—paying too much rent, taking too many taxis, wolfing too many eight-dollar, three-martini lunches. After you have overspent emotionally for a long time, you may decide that your extravagance just isn't affording you enough happiness units to justify its cost" (244). A woman must be thrifty; a relationship should not be difficult. Brown entirely dismisses the postwar definition of heterosexual relations as a struggle between dark and light, good and evil, love and lust, war and peace. She lowers the stakes on relationships in such a way that women can give up. If a woman is not getting what she needs from a relationship, she should leave. If she struggles with that, she should enlist her girlfriends, "reliable men" friends, and even psychiatrists to help her with it (241).

But most importantly, if she finds herself emotionally invested, she should not tolerate bad behavior from men in her life without speaking up for herself: she should not become what Brown snidely calls "the loving little stoic" (242). She tells of a woman who "pretended to herself that she wasn't angry because [her partner] was spoiled and unfaithful, but inside she was seething with rage"—Brown says that these emotions came out eventually but should have come out sooner. Emotional detachment is a state of mind, not a performance. In this way, Brown counters a decade and a half of relationship advice telling women to hold back their own emotions in order to leave room for men's, to playact an easygoing nature so that men can have the difficult feelings. Brown tells women that, when their emotions surface, they should be communicated.

Women who are afraid to speak up for themselves, to "use" men, or to acknowledge and indulge men's "inherent" immaturities, have Brown's example to ease their minds, she says. Having remained emotionally detached and happily single for many years, she has now married well. She says very little about David to distinguish him; he is so vacantly described that, in her 1965 profile of Brown, Joan Didion simply refers to David as "dreamboat."[8] Even though Brown describes herself as "mean and cranky," "not beautiful, or even pretty," and an uneducated woman from a poor small-town family, her marriage has brought her "two Mercedes Benzes, one hundred acres of virgin forest near San Francisco, a Mediterranean house overlooking the Pacific, a full-time maid, and a good life" (3, 54). Financial security used to be held out (in popular culture, at least) as a reward for women to push through the hard times with their husbands, to stay quiet about violence, cruelty, negligence, and infidelity, and to build their lives around meeting their husbands' needs. Brown suggests that that aspect of marriage is accessible to women even while remaining detached.

Brown is unapologetically interested in money and the trappings of the good life, but she warns against gold-digging; she also suggests that even men without money can be sexy fun. Brown's ability to distinguish her sexuality from her feelings for one particular man is in stark contrast to Anne's belief that she was frigid—and therefore not a real woman—until she found Lyon (though she was a virgin). Whereas Jennifer, Neely, and Anne often have painful sex that does not bring them pleasure and perform sex acts that make them uncomfortable or worse, Brown sees sexual pleasure as something a single girl seeks for herself. She suggests that women who do not love and accept their own bodies as both "sexy" and "worthy," are unable to enjoy sex, and women who have sex that they do not enjoy should seek psychiatric help. She is firmly against the notion that sex with one particular man will turn a woman "sexy" and believes just as strongly that women should only have the sex that they want and will enjoy.

Jennifer, Neely, and Anne were all, to varying extents, tortured by body image concerns. Jennifer, of course, commits suicide because her partner cannot imagine life without her breasts and, as a result, she cannot either. Neely's addiction to "dolls" began when she used them for quick weight loss and, when she wins Lyon's attention, the novel suggests it is because she has gotten below one hundred pounds. Anne becomes worried that her aging has led Lyon to cheat on her again. Brown highlights the importance of positive body image to female sexual pleasure in a way that completely disrupts the equation of sex appeal to men and a "sexy" female body: "A sixteen-month-old baby girl is the prototype of sexiness . . . she likes her body. It feels good when she's dried off with a terry towel. At night she may fall asleep across her doll because that feels good too. . . . [S]he touches herself with pleasure and curiosity" (65, 72). Of course, "our society" quickly disrupts this positive experience for the little girl, and she begins to feel that sex is dirty and to despise her own body (66). Brown believes deeply that the experience of the body's pleasure—not just its image—is the key to healthy sexuality. And health matters greatly. Though she instructs readers to stay slim, she takes them to task for unhealthy weight loss measures, saying, "It's silly to say you can't afford protein!" and "Eat breakfast, *you idiot!*" (167).

Instead, Brown, a self-described "health nut," offers an entire chapter on nutrition advice: "Single girls *need* lecturing. You are the world's *dumbest* about nutrition!" She includes book recommendations, supplement suggestions, basic guidelines, and a recipe for her personal favorite, "Gladys Lindberg's Serenity Cocktail" for readers who would like to "fortify your bones, blood, and beautiful outlook" (173–74). Ultimately, if "she's got it"—health, confidence, and love of her own body—even if she's "droop-shouldered, flat-chested, horse-faced, or bone-headed," she will find her orgasm. Though the "horse-faced," however sexually comfortable, would never be on the pages of *Playboy*, much of Brown's advice could be. In particular, her equation of good sex with good health brilliantly usurps the *Playboy* discourse of the girl next door—healthy and vibrant—in order to make them feel as sexy the centerfolds.

However counterintuitively, many elements of Brown's sex and love advice also dovetail nicely with Betty Friedan's insights in *The Feminine Mystique*, published the year after *Sex and the Single Girl*. Though Friedan found Brown's advice to young women "obscene and horrible," the two women share similar concerns for the women they observe and these concerns could fairly be boiled down to what Friedan calls "the forfeited self." This "self," on which women are losing out in droves, is the "positive growth tendency with the organism, which, from within, drives it to fuller development, to self-realization. . . . [I]t is the individual affirming his existence and his potentialities as a being in his own right."[9] According to Susann, Brown, and Friedan, *she* ought to affirm *her* existence and *her* potentialities as a being in *her* own right.

For both Brown and Friedan, education and work are the major means to finding this "self." Like Beneatha in the first two-thirds of *A Raisin in the Sun*, these women do not just critique other ways of women's "enlightenment," but also celebrate it as something that could be joyful in its empowerment. According to Brown, "a job gives a single woman something to *be*" (90). Friedan agrees that, "the only way for a woman, as for a man, to find herself, to know herself as a person, is by creative work of her own" and, also, it allows her to make "a commitment to the world outside the home" (341). Brown expresses her hopes for women in more colloquial terms: "a job can be your love, your happy pill, your means of finding out who you are and what you can do . . . and your means of participating, not having your nose pressed to the glass" (90). However different the prose, Friedan and Brown both agree that it is not just work that helps to build or restore the self—it is *challenging* work (a definition which differs between the texts) and work that engages with the world. Friedan, a leftist journalist who was dismissed from her job at a union newspaper when she became pregnant, and Brown, a striver born into poverty, see the value of work as multifold. Whereas women's ideal participation in the public sphere had long been vicarious—if she made life easier for her male partner, he could have a positive impact on the world in war and peace—Brown and Friedan believe women should participate directly. Since men are unreliable, so is any vicarious life through them.

In order to advance their cases, Brown and Friedan each ably point out the ways in which housewifery falls short. First of all, they claim that the life of a housewife—though so constantly discussed as a high-stakes struggle for the very lives and souls of men and children—actually has low stakes for failure. This is a powerful argument: since wartime, government and media women implored women to "rise to the challenge" of womanhood, whether as nurses or devoted wives, through letter-writing or personal grooming, unflappable tolerance or sexual availability. Endorsing a definition of "housewife" marketed to men in men's media, Friedan and Brown revoke whatever "pride" a woman might feel in her domestic role, while capitalizing on the popular discourse of "egalitarianism."

Friedan makes this case around the issue of efficiency, arguing that, "Housewifery Expands to Fit the Time Available," such that women take six hours on a chore that would take a man only one (380). A woman is killing time, convincing herself that she is doing a good job, when she easily could have accomplished exponentially more. Brown argues that a job, more so than marriage, offers the imperative to meet a standard. An employee can be "summarily fired! [But a] wife can be a lousy housekeeper, indifferent cook, lackluster bedmate, self-centered mother, dull-as-grime companion, and the law protects her! When she finally *is* dismissed, the men who served her papers often has to pay her half her salary. *Quelle* severance pay!" Much of Brown's rant here could have come out of a sexist editorial in *Playboy*, and the same is true for some of Friedan's argument: "There are, of course, many reasons for divorce, but chief among them seems to be the growing aversion and hostility that men have for the feminine millstones hanging around their necks." Friedan goes on: "Sometimes his aversion to his wife finally makes him seek sex in an object totally divorced from any human relationship. Sometimes, in phantasy more often than in fact, he seeks a girl-child, a

Lolita, as sexual object—to escape that grownup woman who is devoting all her aggressive energies, as well as her sexual energies, to living through him" (381). He becomes so disgusted that he begins "sex-seeking . . . motivated simply by the need to escape his devouring wife." Brown and Friedan implicitly endorse the critiques of women as "dependent" (Friedan) and "parasites" (Brown) that are rampant in media marketed to men, and explain why men feel this way. When women are devouring and dependent, Friedan and Brown argue, they are definitely unsexy. And, Friedan continues, they may not just be cheated on, but may well be abandoned: "the rate of 'separations' increased a wild 100 percent during the 1950s, as the able, ambitious men kept on growing in the city while their wives evaded growth in vicarious living" (417). In later years, many feminists came to regret this denigration of the housewife, but Brown and Friedan had an enormous amount to resist.

Stephanie Coontz argues that Brown and Friedan are different because "Brown's strategy ultimately pitted working women against one another in competition for the favor of men rather than uniting them for collective goals."[10] In fact, both Brown and Friedan had programs to bring women, collectively, into the workforce, pitting the women who were not there yet against the ones who were as, effectively, a marketing campaign. Brown and Friedan knew that in order to attract women to the lives they suggested they should live, they needed to make women feel bad for the women who made the other, the "wrong" choices. Susann made her readers feel bad for those women, too, through a tragic novel: no woman would willingly put herself in Anne's, or Jennifer's, or Neely's shoes. Brown and Friedan also found their own ways to create "characters," including Brown's suicidal married friend and Friedan's new mother who had a nervous breakdown and, also like Susann, they express a great deal of sympathy for the women they both portray and address. To present some women as "bad examples"—and victims of widespread societal pressures at that—is not to "pit some women against each other" so much as to force them to learn from each other, if to learn the lessons that Brown and Friedan want them to learn.

All three of them had one major lesson in mind. Like Susann and Brown, Friedan suggests that, in the vast majority of cases, a woman's detaching emotionally, sexually, and intellectually from her husband and family may actually lead to a happier home life. Friedan urges her readers "to see marriage as it really is, brushing aside the veil of over-glorification imposed by the feminine mystique." She quotes a woman who now feels contented that she can look at her family "as though they were a sunset, something outside me, separate." *Sex and the Single Girl* and *The Feminine Mystique* are both advice books by women who would proudly attach themselves to—and see themselves as pioneers of—"women's liberation." The latter more than the former suggested that societal shifts were critical; the former more than the latter argued that such shifts were already in motion and the reader should allow herself to get swept up in and make the most of them. Both use personal anecdotes and research to bolster their claims for "the right way" to be an American woman in the early 1960s, but they share one more thing in common: they have learned from the war and they are ready to take that knowledge for themselves.

Friedan advocates for "a national education program, similar to the GI Bill, for women who seriously want to continue or resume their education—and who are willing to commit themselves to its use in a profession. . . . The GIs, matured by war, needed education to find their identity in society. In no mood for time-wasting, they astonished their teachers and themselves by their scholastic performance. Women who matured during the housewife moratorium can be counted on for similar performance." Friedan believes that World War II caused a generation's problems, problems manifested in everything from Betty Grable to the suburb. For Friedan, the GI Bill fixed parts of the problems that the war started and, in fact, worsened others. She says, unequivocally, that the "problem" she identifies is specific to and new to the postwar era. Before the war, she claims, feminism was vigorous.

On the other hand, Brown feared for her sisters, not herself. She began her "single girl" life in wartime and continued it through the 1950s. According to her biographer, "During World War II, she danced at USO dances at various Army, Navy, and Marine camps along the coast of Southern California and later jokingly claimed to have danced with 'approximately three thousand, four hundred and seventy-five GIs.'" Cheerful detachment from men became her way of life at a time when other women were clinging ever more tightly. But she acknowledges that it was not always easy to be single once the women around her had fled with their husbands to the suburbs. She found her way and is better for it. She hopes other women will too, and she wants to give them the strength to do it:

> In a World War II book, *The Battle is the Payoff* (Harcourt, Brace), war correspondent Ralph Ingersoll said that the early rugged training of the

GI—the toughening of muscle, sleeping out in the rain, walking ten miles under a thirty-pound pack—although drudgery, was often the difference between life and death for a foot soldier when he got home from battle. Five fewer obstacle courses run might have kept him from making the foxhole when he jumped for it. I believe the same principle applies to single women. The unglittery, unglamorous, sound-pitiful-when-you-tell-anybody-about-them things you do when you're alone can be the difference between an interesting job assignment or a love affair with a fabulous man and getting absolutely passed over by both.

Susann's treatment of the veteran, Friedan's concurrent blame and appropriation of the GI Bill, and Brown's breezy analogy between boot camp and single womanhood may be offensive, and they may be so intentionally. Like the "cool" stance so many men were taking elsewhere, this irreverence may have been a grasp for true detachment. For women exhausted by years of managing and catering to men, even in the face of abuse and neglect, while refusing themselves sexual pleasure, intellectual satisfaction, or even fun, it may have been refreshing—liberating—to read these three women refusing to put veterans on a pedestal. Women may also have relished seeing Susann conquer Spillane in 1966, Brown's *Cosmopolitan* tackle *Playboy* in 1965, and Doris Day beat John Wayne at the box office in 1962, the same year that Lucille Ball returned to CBS and the Nielsen Top-10 with *The Lucy Show* (1962–68) . . . playing a working widow.

Registering the importance of *The Feminine Mystique,* Coontz writes: "Authors have labeled the older members of this group [adults in the early 1960s] as 'the greatest generation.' Other have called it 'the silent generation.' Both these labels apply to the collective experiences of the men, as soldiers in World War II or as citizens during the Cold War and Korean War; they have little relevance to the collective experiences of the women of the era. The women who found solace in Friedan's ideas would not have called themselves, or their mothers, members of the greatest generation." They wouldn't have called themselves "the silent generation" either. And now, by the 1960s, they finally weren't.

NOTES

INTRODUCTION

1. Kozloff, "Wyler's Wars."
2. Thomson, *The New Biographical Dictionary of Film*, 949.
3. Beidler, *The Good War's Greatest Hits*, 23.
4. Giddins, *Bing Crosby: A Pocketful of Dreams*, 6.
5. Bennett, *When Dreams Came True*, 26.
6. See also Kenneth Jackson, *Crabgrass Frontier*; and Rosalyn Baxandall and Elizabeth Ewen, *Picture Windows: How the Suburbs Happened*. On racial issues of suburbanization, see "'The House I Live In': Race, Class, and African American Suburban Dreams in the Postwar United States" in Kruse and Sugrue, *The New Suburban History*.
7. Wynn, *The African American Experience in World War II*, 69.
8. Glover, "The Stuff That Dreams Are Made Of," 74.
9. Herman, *The Romance of American Psychology*, 87.
10. Casey, *Cautious Crusade*, 72.
11. Franklin D. Roosevelt: "Fireside Chat," May 2, 1943.
12. Dower, *War Without Mercy*, 9.
13. Terkel, *The Good War*, 61.
14. Ibid, 110.
15. Birdwell, *Celluloid Soldiers*, 178.
16. Koppes and Black, *Hollywood Goes to War*, 283.
17. Roosevelt, "State of the Union Address," January 6, 1942.
18. Blum, *V Was for Victory*, 8.
19. See Lisio, *The President and Protest*; and Dickson and Allen, *The Bonus Army*.

20. Waller, *The Veteran Comes Back*; Wechter, *When Johnny Comes Marching Home*. Further citations in text.
21. Wechter, *When Johnny Comes Marching Home*, 552; Waller, *The Veteran Comes Back*, 110.
22. Tuck, "You can sing and punch," 118.
23. Ellison, *Shadow and Act*, 274.
24. See Knauer, *Let Us Fight as Free Men: Black Soldiers and Civil Rights*; Morehouse, *Fighting in the Jim Crow Army*; White, "Building a Church in the Army: Chaplain Robert Boston Dokes, Religious Resistance to Racial Segregation, and Black Troops in World War II."
25. Fleming, *Black Patience, Performance, Civil Rights, and the Unfinished Project of Emancipation*.
26. See Wynn's definitive *The African American Experience in World War II* and the essays in Kruse and Tuck, eds, *Fog of War*.
27. Rodriguez, Heilig, and Prochnow, "Higher Education, the GI Bill, and the Postwar Lives of Latino Veterans," 60.
28. See Hata and Hata, *Japanese Americans and World War II*.
29. Jarvis, *The Male Body at War*, 138–40.
30. Petigny, *The Permissive Society*, 4
31. Kinsey, *Sexual Behavior in the Human Male*, 285.
32. Reumann, *American Sexual Character*, 10.
33. Menand, "Freud, Anxiety, and the Cold War," 189.
34. Freud, "Group Psychology and the Analysis of the Ego," 122.
35. Fenichel, *The Psychoanalytic Theory of Neurosis*, 109–13.
36. Fenichel, *The Psychoanalytic Theory of Neurosis*, 121.
37. Ibid., 124.
38. Douglas, *Terrible Honesty*, 31.
39. "Quentin Reynolds Talks on Terrific Job Big and Little Showbiz is Doing Overseas," *Billboard*, Oct. 30, 1943, p. 4.
40. Herman, *The Romance of American Psychology*, 98.
41. Claireday, *Postcards from World War II*, 4.
42. Yellin, *Our Mothers' War*, 86. These women included Helen Gurley Brown. See Epilogue.
43. Yellin, *Our Mothers' War*, 87.
44. Nouryeh, "The Stage Door Canteen," 256–73.
45. Weaks-Baxter, Bruun, and Forslund, *We Are a College at War: Women Working for Victory in World War II*, 105.
46. Cohan, *The Road Movie Book*, 113.
47. Marcus, *Double Trouble*, 209.

48. Halpern, *Norman Rockwell*, x.
49. Roosevelt, "State of the Union Address," January 6, 1945.
50. See May, "Rosie the Riveter Gets Married," 129; Kennedy, *Freedom from Fear*, 777; McEuen, *Making War, Making Women*, 2; Sorel, *The Women Who Wrote the War*, prologue.
51. Wynn, *The African American Experience in World War II*, 68.
52. See Brock, *Beyond Rosie*, 122; Monahan and Neidel-Greenlee, *And If I Perish*; Threat, *Nursing Civil Rights*.
53. Litoff and Smith, *American Women in a World at War*, 150.
54. Knauer, 306.
55. McEuen, *Making War, Making Women*, 179.
56. Celello, *Making Marriage Work*, 44–67; Lingeman, *Don't You Know There's a War On?*, 28–60.
57. See May, "Rosie the Riveter Gets Married," 129; Kennedy, *Freedom from Fear*, 777; McEuen, 2; Sorel, *The Women Who Wrote the War*, prologue.
58. See Coontz, *A Strange Stirring*, 13–14; on marital rape 9–10. For more on how women were told to treat returning veterans, see Hartmann, "'Prescriptions for Penelope.'"
59. Published in book form under this title in 1958.
60. See Gilbert, *Men in the Middle*, 62–73; and Osgerby, *Playboys in Paradise*, 70–71.
61. Roth, *Memory, Trauma, History*, xvii.
62. Coleman, *Flashback*, 51.
63. Herman, *The Romance of American Psychology*, 82–120.
64. MacNair, *Perpetration-Induced Traumatic Stress*, v. Further citations in text.
65. Coleman, *Flashback*, 50.
66. Childers, *Soldier from the War Returning*, 5.
67. Affron and Affron, *Best Years*.
68. Beidler, *The Good War's Greatest Hits*, 9.
69. Ibid., 91–92
70. Dick, *The Star-Spangled Screen*, 142.
71. Zerubavel, *Hidden in Plain Sight*, 60.
72. Dickstein, *Leopards in the Temple*, 9.
73. For examples, see May, Paul Boyer, Alan Nadel, Stephen Whitfield.
74. Meyerowitz, "Women and Gender in Postwar America, 1945–1960."
75. Taylor, *Every Citizen a Soldier*, 143–71; Tuttle, *Daddy's Gone to War*, 260–61.
76. Schlesinger, *The Vital Center*, 255. Further citation in text.

PROLOGUE

1. Popkin, *History, Historians, and Autobiography*, 71.
2. Fussell, *Wartime*, 147.
3. Stringer and Stringer, *Letters of Love and War*, 292. Further citations in text.
4. Elevitch, *Dog Tags Yapping*, 201.
5. Carroll, *War Letters*, 302–3. Some further citations in text.
6. Mock collection.
7. A similar linguistic deflection: "it's no picnic."
8. Masuda and Masuda, *Letters from the 442nd*, 18. Further citations in text.
9. Carroll, *War Letters*, 193.
10. "My Dear Wife, I Love You: Charles Lewis in World War II," National Underground Railroad Freedom Center.
11. Carroll, *War Letters*, 204.
12. Ibid., 215–17.
13. Ibid., 244.

1. "IT WAS EASY"

1. Nishikawa, *Street Players*, 6.
2. Brier, *A Novel Marketplace*, 56.
3. O'Brien, *Hardboiled America*, 25.
4. Sutherland, *Bestsellers*, 65.
5. Barson, "Just a Writer Working for a Buck," 296.
6. Spillane, *I, the Jury*, 1. Further citations in text.
7. May, *Homeward Bound*, 27. Further citations in text.
8. McGirr, *Suburban Warriors*, 21, 25–26.
9. Cohen, *A Consumer's Republic*, 56–62.
10. Dietze, "Gender Topography of the Fifties," 646.
11. Spillane, *My Gun Is Quick*, 1–2. Further citations in text.
12. Nyman, *Men Alone*, 181.
13. Cassuto, *Hardboiled Sentimentality*, xviii.
14. Johnston, "Death's Faired-Haired Boy," 92.
15. Porter, *The Pursuit of Crime*, 14.
16. Whiting, "Bodies of Evidence," 156–57.
17. Freedman, "'Uncontrolled Desires,'" 96. Further citations in text.
18. Simpson, *Psycho Paths*, xii.

19. Breu, "Radical Noir," 208.
20. Blades, "The Returning Vet's Experience in *A Streetcar Named Desire*," 18.
21. Biskind, *Seeing Is Believing*, 37.

2. "DO WE BECOME WHAT WE DO?"

1. Cassady, *Impact of the Paramount Decision*.
2. Gomery, *The Hollywood Studio System*, 185–96.
3. Prindle, *The Politics of Glamour*, 68; Nielson and Mailes, *Hollywood's Other Blacklist*.
4. Wojcik, *Movie Acting*, 169.
5. Davis, *Van Johnson*, 84. Further citations in text.
6. "The Lion Reigns Supreme."
7. Deane, *James Edwards*, 3. Next citation in text.
8. O'Brien, *The Color of the Law*, 1–58.
9. Deane, 7. Further citations in text.
10. Bogle, *Toms, Coons, Mulattoes, Mammies, and Bucks*, 129.
11. McCann, *Rebel Males*, 6.
12. Palmer, "Stardom in the 1950s," 4.
13. Braudy, *The World in a Frame*, 245.
14. Naremore, *Acting in the Cinema*, 19.
15. Maltby, *Hollywood*, 380–84.
16. Parish and DeCarl, *Hollywood Players: The Forties*, 14.
17. Bingham, Acting Male, 49.
18. Thomas, *King Cohn*, 17.
19. Gomery, 165.
20. Lawrence, "James Mason," 97.
21. Hansberry, 307.
22. Hansbery, 305, "Movie of the Week," 103.
23. Cohan, *Masked Men*, 36.
24. Dyer, *Queers*, 113.
25. Ibid., 104.
26. Dyer, "Homosexuality and Film Noir."
27. Basinger, *The World War II Combat Film*, 8.
28. Farber, "Violence and the Bitch Goddess," 48–49.
29. Bruzzi, *Bringing Up Daddy*, 51.

3. GETTING COMFORTABLE

1. Leder, *Thanks for the Memories*, 31; Yellin, *Our Mothers' War*, 86; Bloomfield, *Duty, Honor, Applause*, 184.
2. Merrill, *Esky*, 93.
3. Pendergast *Creating the Modern Man*, 221.
4. Merrill, *Esky*, 93.
5. Despite this association, *Stars and Stripes* is proudly editorially independent.
6. McGurn, *YANK: The Army Weekly*, ix.
7. Pendergast, *Creating the Modern Man*, 208.
8. Gunelias, *Building Brand Value the Playboy Way*, 15.
9. Brady, *Hefner*, 36–37
10. Ibid., 3.
11. Sumner, *The Magazine Century*, 134.
12. Editorial, December 1953.
13. "Model Folio," December 1952.
14. Watts, *Mr. Playboy*, 64.
15. Just which member among this party of three came up with *Playboy* is disputed (Ibid., 59; Weyr, 14).
16. I have never seen it mentioned elsewhere by scholars or in interviews with Hefner, Paul, Sellers, or other early *Playboy* staff, but my research uncovered *The Playboy's Handbook: The Bedside Reader for Men*, edited by William Allen Brooks. It was published in 1946 by Knickerbocker Publishing, predominantly a magazine and pulp paperback publisher at the time. *The Playboy's Handbook* includes: "Some of My Best Friends are Lechers," by Leonard Hall; "The 99 and 44/100% Puritans," by Duncan Underhill; "On Sleeping with Women," by Roger Lawson; "Women Are Also Wolves," by Lou Linnett; and "The Technique of Seduction," a tongue-in-cheek advice piece by Stephen Moore. The other pieces, too, would have been entirely at home on the pages of *Playboy*, as would any of the featured cartoons, and the cover. Interestingly, nearly half of the content is printed with the permission of Fawcett, which, in addition to comic books and paperbacks including Spillane's *I, the Jury*, published the magazines *Captain Billy's Whiz Bang* and *True*, in which Hefner's cartoons appeared. Finally, I cannot confirm that the cover artist is Norman Saunders, but the style and his contract at the time suggest that he may have been. Saunders would later illustrate for *Playboy*, but also cultivated the colorful illustrations in men's adventure magazines. If nothing else, *The Playboy Reader*'s existence and content suggest that the term "Playboy" was not entirely out of circulation after the war, nor would Hefner's use of the word constitute any sort of reinvention.

17. Weyr, *Reaching for Paradise*, 13.
18. Beggan and Allison, "An Analysis of Stereotype Refutation in *Playboy*," 341.
19. Saraccino and Scott, *The Porning of America*, 73. Further citations in text.
20. Collins and Hagenauer, *Men's Adventure Magazines*, 16.
21. Saraccino and Scott, 72.
22. Parfrey, *It's a Man's World*, 4.
23. Saraccino and Scott, 72.
24. Hegarty, *Victory Girls, Khaki-Wackies, and Patriotutes*, 14–15.
25. Ibid., 93.
26. Brandt, *No Magic Bullet*, 104.
27. Hegarty, 101.
28. Ibid., 88, 107.
29. Ibid., 88.
30. May, *Homeward Bound*, 109; Neuhaus, "The Importance of Being Orgasmic," 72.
31. Strausbaugh, *Victory City*, 299–300.
32. Bailey and Farber, *First Strange Place*, 99.
33. McEnloe, *Let the Good Times Roll: Prostitution and the US Military in Asia*, 22.
34. Hegarty, 98.
35. Ibid., 124.
36. Ibid., 122; Westbrook, "'I Want a Girl, Just Like the Girl that Married Harry James," 603; Buzsek, 222.
37. Merrill, *Esky*, 95.
38. Knauer, 170.
39. Buszek, *Pin-up Grrrls*, 187.
40. Ibid., 198.
41. Pendergast, *Creating the Modern Man*, 221; Merrill, *Esky*, 87.
42. Quoted in Merrill, 90.
43. Buszek, *Pin-up Grrrls*, 205–6. Further citations in text.
44. Pendergast, 221.
45. Westbrook, 596.
46. Ibid.; Buzcek, 224.
47. McEuen, *Making War, Making Women*, 56.
48. Cushman, *Constructing The Self*, 188; Reumann, *American Sexual Character*, 128; Robinson, *The Modernization of Sex*, 101.
49. Petigny, *The Permissive Society*, 58–59.
50. Bailey, *Sex in the Heartland*, 260.
51. Adams, *Preparing for Marriage*, 16–17. Further citations in text.
52. "Mike Wallace Interviews Playboy," 83.
53. Banner, *American Beauty*, 285; Lukas, "The Alternative Lifestyle of Playboys and Playmates," 72.

54. Quoted in Pitzulo, *Bachelors and Bunnies*, 47.
55. Dines, *Pornland*, 1–2; Rutherford, *World Made Sexy*, 105.
56. Berman, *Hugh Hefner*.
57. Broege, "Technology and Sexuality in Science Fiction," 118.
58. November 1955, 6.
59. D'Emilio and Freedman, *Intimate Matters*, 62.
60. November 1955, 6.
61. Pitzulo, *Bachelors and Bunnies*, 104; Rutherford, *World Made Sexy*, 108.
62. Pitzulo, 35.
63. Moore, "Love in the Dark," February 1957; 55–58, 76.
64. Osgerby, *Playboys in Paradise*, 139.
65. *Playboy*, December 1956.
66. Halberstam, *The Fifties*, 574.
67. Vince Tajiri, quoted in Miller, *Bunny*, 35.
68. Brady, *Hefner*, 138.
69. See Preciado, "Pornotopia," *Cold War Hothouses*.
70. Gunelias, *Building Brand Value the Playboy Way*, 30.
71. Dinerstein, *The Origins of Cool in Postwar America*, 272–73.
72. Nadel, *Containment Culture*, 131.
73. Fraterrigo, *Playboy and the Making of the Good Life*, 143
74. Ibid.
75. Ehrenreich, *The Hearts of Men*. 42–51.

4. THE HORROR OF "HONEY, I'M HOME!"

1. Marc, *Comic Visions*, 44.
2. Hamamoto, *Nervous Laughter*, 26.
3. Halberstam, *The Fifties*, 512; Coontz, *The Way We Never Were*, 29; Douglas, *Where The Girls Are*, 143.
4. Bodroghkozy, Equal Time; Mellencamp, "Situation Comedy, Feminism, and Freud," 54; Doty, "The Cabinet of Lucy," 9; Landay, TV *Milestones: I Love Lucy*; Dalton and Linder, The Sitcom Reader; Scott, "From Blackface to Beulah."
5. Celello, *Making Marriage Work*, 7–8.
6. Lasch, *Haven in a Heartless World*, 172; Lassonde, "Age and Authority," 95–105.
7. Fontaine, "Raise Your Boy to Be a Soldier," 484.
8. McCarthy, *Ambient Television*, 40.
9. Marc, *Comic Visions*, 27.
10. Watson, Nash, and Etulain, *Defining Visions*, 106.

11. Becker, "Glamour Girl"; Von Schilling, *The Magic Window*, 140–41; Baughman, *Same Time, Same Station*, 27. Chunovic treats many similar controversies in *One Foot on the Floor*, 27–32. Herman Gray also addresses the controversy involving *Amos 'n' Andy* and the NAACP in *Watching Race*.
12. Baughman, *Same Time, Same Station*, 25.
13. Murray, *Hitch Your Antenna*, 80.
14. Watson, Nash, and Etulain, *Defining Visions*, 106.
15. Baughman, *Same Time, Same Station*, 27.
16. Ibid., 25.
17. Murray, *Hitch Your Antenna*, 80.
18. Yoggy, *Back in the Saddle*, 5.
19. Kackman, *Citizen Spy*, 43.
20. Hough, "Trials and Tribulations," 205; Hamamoto, *Nervous Laughter*, 5; Leibman, *Living Room Lectures*, 7; Smith, *Visions of Belonging*, 106.
21. Mellencamp, "Situation Comedy, Feminism, and Freud," 54; Doty, "The Cabinet of Lucy," 9; Landay, *TV Milestones: I Love Lucy*.
22. Chambers, *Representing the Family*, 73.
23. Spigel 172
24. See Beltrán, *Latina/o Stars in U.S. Eyes*; Desjardins, "Lucy and Desi"; and Perez, *On Becoming Cuban*.
25. Tucker, 123.
26. Mintz, "Situation Comedy," 43.
27. Castleman and Podrazik, *Watching TV*, 66.
28. Ellis, "Stars as a Cinematic Phenomenon," 313.
29. "P.S.," 21.
30. Weisblat, "Will the Real George and Gracie and Ozzie and Harriet and Desi and Lucy Please Stand Up?," 14.
31. Lester, "Ask Her Anything About Desi, Sr.," 33, 54.
32. Sher, "The Cuban and the Redhead"; Parsons, "Lucy and Desi Say: Laugh and Be Happily Married"; Carini, "Love's Labors Almost Lost," 48; Arnaz, *A Book*, 267.
33. Ellis, "Stars as a Cinematic Phenomenon," 314.
34. *Confidential*'s circulation was 4 million, surpassing the *Saturday Evening Post* and *Look*, so this article was very much a part of the public's knowledge of Ball and Arnaz (Harris, *Lucy and Desi*, 210).
35. Sanders and Gilbert, *Desilu*, 117–18; Kanfer, *Ball of Fire*, 181; Brady, *Lucy*, 227.
36. See Desjardins, "Lucy and Desi: Sexuality, Ethnicity, and TV's First Family."
37. Ibid., 64.
38. Doty, "The Gay Straight Man," 63.

39. Jones, *Honey, I'm Home!*, 101; Denis and Denis, *Favorite Families of TV*, 48.
40. Brokaw, *The Greatest Generation*, xxix.

CONCLUSION

1. Black Women's Blueprint, "An Open Letter to Playboy from Black Women," https://msmagazine.com/2019/07/08/an-open-letter-to-playboy-from-black-women/.
2. Steinem, "A Bunny's Tale," *Show*, May 1, 1963: 90, 92, 94, 114.
3. Susann, *Valley of the Dolls*, 19. Future citations in text.
4. See Flood, "'They Didn't Treat Me Good': African American Rape Victims and Chicago Courtroom Strategies During the 1950s," 38–54.
5. For more on Hansbury as a model of "cool," see Dinerstein 403–36.
6. Michelson, *Speaking the Unspeakable*, 197.
7. Brown, *Sex and the Single Girl*, 30. Future citations in text.
8. Didion, 38.
9. Friedan, *The Feminine Mystique*, 429. Future citations in text.
10. Coontz, *A Strange Stirring*, xx–xxi.

BIBLIOGRAPHY

Abrams, Nathan, and Julia Hughes, eds. *Containing America: Cultural Production and Consumption in 50s America*. Birmingham, UK: University of Birmingham, 2000.

Adams, Clifford Rose. *Preparing for Marriage: A Guide to Marital and Sexual Adjustment*. New York: E. P. Dutton and Company, Inc., 1951.

Adams, Michael C. C. *The Best War Ever*. Baltimore, MD: Johns Hopkins University Press, 1994.

Affron, Charles, and Mirella Jona Affron, *Best Years: Going to the Movies, 1945–1946*. New Brunswick, NJ: Rutgers University Press, 2009.

Aichinger, Peter. *The American Soldier in Fiction, 1880–1963: A History of Attitudes toward Warfare and the Military Establishment*. Ames, IA: Iowa State University Press, 1975.

Appy, Christian. *Working-Class War: American Combat Soldiers and Vietnam*. Chapel Hill: University of North Carolina Press, 1993.

Arnaz, Desi. *A Book*. Chutchogue, NY: Buccaneer Books, 1976.

Ashby, LeRoy. *With Amusement for All: A History of American Popular Culture since 1830*. Knoxville, KY: University of Kentucky Press, 2006.

Axelrod, Alan. *Patton: Lessons in Leadership*. New York: Palgrave, 2006.

Bailey, Beth L. *Sex in the Heartland*. Cambridge, MA: President and Fellows of Harvard College, 1999.

Bailey, Beth L., and David Farber. *The First Strange Place: The Alchemy of Race and Sex in World War II Hawaii*. New York: Free Press, 2012.

Banner, Lois. *American Beauty: A Social History. Through Two Centuries of the American Idea, Ideal, and Image of the Beautiful Woman*. Los Angeles: Figueroa Press, 2006.

Baral, Robert. *Revue: A Nostalgic Reprise of the Great Broadway Period*. New York: Fleet Publishing, 1962.

Barson, Michael. "Just a Writer Working for a Buck." *The Armchair Detective* 12 (1979): 293–99.

Basinger, Jeanine, *The World War II Combat Film: Anatomy of a Genre*. Middletown, CT: Wesleyan University Press, 2003.

Baxandell, Rosalyn, and Elizabeth Ewen. *Picture Windows: How the Suburbs Happened*. New York: Basic Books, 2000.

Baughman, James. *Same Time, Same Station: Creating American Television, 1948–61*. Baltimore, MD: Johns Hopkins University Press, 2007.

Becker, Christine. "'Glamour Girl Classed as a TV Show Brain': The Body and Mind of Faye Emerson." *Journal of Popular Culture* 4, no. 2 (Summer 2004): 242–60.

———. *It's the Pictures That Got Small: Hollywood Film Stars on Fifties Television*. Middletown, CT: Wesleyan University Press, 2008.

Beggan, James K., Patricia Gagne, and Scott Allison, "An Analysis of Stereotype Refutation in *Playboy* by Editorial Voice: The Advisor Hypothesis." *The Journal of Men's Studies* 9, no. 1 (Fall 2000): 1–21.

Beidler, Philip. *The Good War's Greatest Hits: World War II and American Remembering*. Athens, GA: University of Georgia Press, 1998.

Belken, Aaron. *Bring Me Men: Military Masculinity and the Benign Façade of American Empire, 1898–2001*. New York: Columbia University Press, 2012.

Beltrán, Mary. *Latina/o Stars in U.S. Eyes: The Making and Meanings of Film and TV Stardom*. Urbana, IL: University of Illinois Press, 2009.

Bennett, Michael. *When Dreams Came True: The GI Bill and the Making of Modern America*. Dulles, VA: Potomac Books, 1999.

Bess, Michael. *Choices Under Fire: Moral Dimensions of World War II*. New York: Knopf, 2006.

Bingham, Dennis. *Acting Male: Masculinities in the Films of James Stewart, Jack Nicholson, and Clint Eastwood*. New Brunswick, NJ: Rutgers University Press, 1994.

Birdwell, Michael E. *Celluloid Soldiers: The Warner Brothers Campaign Against Nazism*. New York: New York University Press, 2001.

Black, Cheryl, and Jonathan Shandell, eds. *Experiments in Democracy: Interracial and Cross-Cultural Exchange in American Theatre, 1912–1945*. Carbondale, IL: Southern Illinois University Press, 2016.

Blades, Larry. "The Returning Vet's Experience in *A Streetcar Named Desire*: Stanley as the Decommissioned Warrior under Stress." *The Tennessee Williams Annual Review* 10 (2009). http://www.tennesseewilliamsstudies.org/journal/work.php?ID=89.

Blair, Sara, Joseph B. Entin, and Franny Nudelman. *Remaking Reality: US Documentary Culture After 1945*. Chapel Hill, NC: University of North Carolina Press, 2018.

Bloomfield, Gary L., and Stacie L. Shain. *Duty, Honor, Applause: American Entertainers in World War I*. Augusta, GA: Globe Pequot, 2004.

Blum, John Morton. *V Was for Victory: Politics and American Culture During World War II*. New York: Harcourt Brace, 1976.

Bodner, John E. *The "Good War" in American Memory*. Baltimore, MD: Johns Hopkins University Press, 2010.

Bodroghkozy, Aniko. *Equal Time: Television and the Civil Rights Movement*. Chicago, IL: University of Illinois Press, 2012.

Bogle, Donald. *Primetime Blues: African-Americans on Network Television*. New York: Farrar, Strauss, and Giroux, 2001.

Boucher, Diane. *The 1950s American Home*. Oxford, UK: Shire Publications, 2013.

Bourke, Joanna. *An Intimate History of Killing: Face-to-Face Killing in Twentieth Century Warfare*. New York: Basic Books, 1999.

Boyer, Paul. *By the Bomb's Early Light: American Thought and Culture at the Dawn of the Atomic Age*. Chapel Hill, NC: 1985.

Brady, Frank. *Hefner*. New York: Macmillan, 1974.

Brady, Kathleen. *Lucy: The Life of Lucille Ball*. New York: Hyperion Books, 1994.

Brandt, Allan M. *No Magic Bullet: A Social History of Venereal Disease in the United States*. Oxford, UK: Oxford University Press, 1987.

Braudy, Leo. *The World in a Frame: What We See in Films*. Chicago: University of Chicago Press, 1976.

Breines, Wini. *Young, White, and Miserable: Growing Up Female in the Fifties*. Boston, MA: Beacon Press, 1992.

Brier, Evan. *A Novel Marketplace: Mass Culture, the Book Trade, and Postwar American Fiction*. Philadelphia: University of Pennsylvania Press, 2010.

Brock, Julia, Jennifer W. Dickey, Richard J. W. Harker, and Catherine M. Lewis, eds. *Beyond Rose: A Documentary History of Women and World War II*. Fayetteville, AR: University of Arkansas Press, 2015.

Broege, Valerie. "Technology and Sexuality in Science Fiction: Creating New Erotic Interfaces." In *Erotic Universes: Sexuality and Fantastic Literature*, edited by Donald Palumbo, 103–29. New York: Greenwood Press, 1986.

Brokaw, Tom. *The Greatest Generation*. New York: Random House, 1998.

Brown, Helen Gurley. *Sex and the Single Girl*. New York: Bernard Geis Associates, 1962.

Bruzzi, Stella. *Bringing Up Daddy: Fatherhood and Masculinity in Postwar Hollywood*. London, UK: British Film Institute, 2006.

Burnham, John, ed. *After Freud Left: A Century of Psychoanalysis in America*. Chicago: University of Chicago Press, 2012.

Busch, Andrew E. *Truman's Triumphs: The 1948 Election and the Making of Postwar America*. Lawrence, KS: Kansas University Press, 2012.

Buszek, Maria. *Pin-up Grrrls: Feminism, Sexuality, Popular Culture*. Durham, NC: Duke University Press, 2006.

Cahir, Linda Costanzo. "The Artful Rerouting of *A Streetcar Named Desire*." *Literature/Film Quarterly*, 22, no. 2 (1994): 72–77.

Caputi, Mary. *A Kinder, Gentler America: Melancholia and the Mythical 1950s*. Minneapolis, MN: University of Minnesota Press, 2005.

Carini, Susan M. "Love's Labors Almost Lost: Managing Crisis during the Reign of *I Love Lucy*." *Cinema Journal* 43, no. 1 (Autumn 2003): 44–62.

Carroll, Andrew. *War Letters: Extraordinary Correspondence from American Wars*. New York: Simon and Schuster, 2008.

Cassady, Ralph. *Impact of the Paramount Decision on Motion Picture Distribution and Price Making*. Los Angeles, CA: University of Southern California Press, 1958.

Casaregola, Vincent. *Theaters of War: America's Perceptions of World War II*. New York: Macmillan, 2009.

Casey, Richard Gardiner. *The Washington Diaries of R. G. Casey 1940–1942*. Edited by Carl Bridge. Sydney: National Library of Australia, 2002.

Casey, Steven. Cautious Crusade: Franklin D. Roosevelt, American Public Opinion, and the War Against Nazi Germany. Oxford, UK: Oxford University Press, 2001.

Cassuto, Leonard. *Hard-boiled Sentimentality: The Secret History of American Crime Stories*. New York: Columbia University Press, 2008.

Castleman, Harry, and Walter J. Podrazik. *Watching TV: Six Decades of American Television*. 2nd ed. Syracuse, NY: Syracuse University Press, 2003.

Cawelti, John. *Adventure, Mystery and Romance: Formula Stories as Art and Popular Culture*. Chicago, IL: University of Illinois Press, 1977.

Celello, Kristin. *Making Marriage Work: The History of Marriage and Divorce in the Twentieth Century United States*. Chapel Hill, NC: University of North Carolina Press, 2009.

Chambers, Deborah. *Representing the Family*. London, UK: Sage Publications, 2001.

Childers, Thomas. *Soldier from the War Returning: The Greatest Generation's Troubled Homecoming From World War II*. New York: Houghton Mifflin Harcourt, 2009.

Christiansen, Erik. *Channeling the Past: Politicizing History in Postwar America*. Madison, WI: University of Wisconsin Press, 2013.

Chunovic, Louis. *One Foot on the Floor: The Curious Evolution of Sex on Television*. New York: TV Books, 2000.

Christianson, Scott R. "Tough Talk and Wisecracks: Language as Power in American Detective Fiction." *Journal of Popular Culture* 23, no. 2 (Fall 1989): 151–62.

Claireday, Robynn. *Postcards from World War II*. Garden City, NY: Square One Publishers, 2001.

Clarke, Alison J. *Tupperware: The Promise of Plastic in 1950s America*. Washington, DC: Smithsonian Institution, 1999.

Cohan, Steven. *The Road Movie Book*. New York: Routledge, 1997.

Cohen, Lizabeth. *A Consumer's Republic: The Politics of Mass Consumption in Postwar America*. New York: Knopf Doubleday, 2008.

Cohen, Paula Marantz. *Alfred Hitchcock: The Legacy of Victorianism*. Lexington: University Press of Kentucky, 1995.

Coleman, Penny. *Flashback: Posttraumatic Stress Disorder, Suicide, and the Lessons of War*. Boston: Beacon Press, 2006.

Collins, Max Allan. Introduction to *The Mike Hammer Collection, Vol. 1*. New York: New American Library, 2001.

Collins, Max and George Hagenauer. Introduction to *Men's Adventure Magazines in Postwar America*, edited by Collins, Hagenauer, Rich Oberg, and Steven Heller. New York: Taschen Press, 2008.

Colomina, Beatriz, AnnMarie Brennan and Jeannie Kim, eds. *Cold War Hothouses: Inventing Postwar Culture from Cockpit to Playboy*. New York: Princeton Architectural Press, 2004.

Conway-Lanz, Sahr. *Collateral Damage: Americans, Noncombatant Immunity, and Atrocity after World War II*. New York: Routledge, 2006.

Cooke, James J. *Chewing Gum, Candy Bars, and Beer: The Army PX in World War II*. Columbia, MO: University of Missouri Press, 2009.

Coontz, Stephanie. *The Way We Never Were: American Families and the Nostalgia Trap*. New York: Basic Books, 2000.

———. *A Strange Stirring: The Feminine Mystique and American Women at the Dawn of the 1960s*. New York: Basic Books, 2011.

Cott, Nancy F. *Public Vows: A History of Marriage and the Nation*. Cambridge, MA: Harvard University Press, 2000.

Cox, Jim. *The Great Radio Sitcoms*. Jefferson, NC: McFarland, 2007.

Creadick, Anna G. *Perfectly Average: The Pursuit of Normality in Postwar America*. Amherst, MA: University of Massachusetts Press, 2010.

Culbert, David. "'Why We Fight': Social Engineering for a Democratic Society at War." In *Film and Radio Propaganda in World War II*, edited by K. R. M. Short. Knoxville: University of Tennessee Press, 1983.

Cushman, Philip. *Constructing The Self, Constructing America: A Cultural History of Psychotherapy*. Boston, MA: Da Capo Press, 1996.

Danesi, Marcel. *Forever Young: The Teen-aging of American Culture*. Toronto: University of Toronto Press, 2003.

Davis, Kenneth C. *Two-bit Culture: The Paperbacking of America*. New York: Houghton Mifflin, 1984.

Davis, Rebecca L. *More Perfect Unions: The American Search for Marital Bliss*. Cambridge, MA: Harvard University Press, 2010.

Davis, Ronald. *The Glamour Factory: Inside Hollywood's Big Studio System*. Dallas: Southern Methodist University Press, 1993.

———. *Van Johnson: MGM's Golden Boy*. Jackson, MS: University Press of Mississippi, 2001.

Day, Marele. "'Cold Hard Bitch': The Masculinist Imperatives of the Private-Eye Genre." *The Journal of Narrative Technique* 21, no. 1 (Winter 1991): 121–35.

Deane, Pamala. *James Edwards: African American Hollywood Icon*. Jefferson, NC: McFarland, 2009.

D'Emilio, John and Estelle Freedman. *Intimate Matters: A History of Sexuality in America*. Chicago, IL: University of Chicago Press, 1988.

Delton, Jennifer A. *Rethinking the 1950s: How Anticommunism and the Cold War Made America Liberal*. New York: Cambridge University Press, 2013.

Denis, Christopher Paul and Michael Denis. *Favorite Families of TV*. New York: Carol Publishing, 1991.

Dervin, Daniel. "The Absent Father's Presence in Modern and American Gay Drama." *American Imago* 56, no. 1 (1999): 53–74.

Desjardins, Mary. "Lucy and Desi: Sexuality, Ethnicity, and TV's First Family." In *Television, History, and American Culture: Feminist Critical Essays,* edited by Mary Beth Haralovich and Lauren Rabinovitz, 56–74. Durham, NC: Duke University Press.

Dick, Bernard F. *The Star-Spangled Screen: The American World War II Film*. Knoxville: University of Kentucky Press, 1985.

Dickson, Paul and Thomas B. Allen. *The Bonus Army: An American Epic*. New York: Walker and Company, 2004.

Dickstein, Morris. *Dancing in the Dark*. New York: W. W. Norton, 2009.

———. *Leopards in the Temple: The Transformation of American Fiction, 1945–1970*. Cambridge, MA: Harvard University Press, 2002.

Didion, Joan. "Bosses Make Lousy Lovers," *Saturday Evening Post,* January 30, 1965.

Dietze, Gabriele. "Gender Topography of the Fifties: Mickey Spillane and the Post–World War II Masculinity Crises." *Amerikastudien / American Studies* 43, no. 4 (1998): 645–56.

Dinerstein, Joel. *The Origins of Cool in Postwar America*. Chicago, IL: University of Chicago Press, 2017.

Dines, Gail. *Pornland: How Porn Has Hijacked Our Sexuality*. Beacon, NY: Beacon Press, 2010.

Doherty, Thomas. *Cold War, Cool Medium: Television, McCarthyism, and American Culture*. New York: Columbia University Press, 2003.

Donaldson, Gary. *Modern America: A Documentary History since 1945.* Armonk, NY: M. E. Sharpe, 2007.

Doty, Alexander. "The Cabinet of Lucy Ricardo: Lucille Ball's Star Image." *Cinema Journal* 29, no. 4 (Winter 1990): 3–22.

———. "The Gay Straight Man: Jack Benny and *The Jack Benny Program*." In *Making Things Perfectly Queer: Interpreting Mass Culture,* edited by Alexander Doty, 63–80. Minneapolis: University of Minnesota Press, 1993.

Douglas, Ann. *Terrible Honesty: Mongrel Manhattan in the 1920s.* New York: Farrar, Strauss, and Giroux, 1995.

Douglas, Susan. *Where The Girls Are: Growing Up Female with the Mass Media.* New York: Times Press, 1994.

Douglas, George H. *Postwar America: 1948 and the Incubation of Our Times.* Malabar, FL: Krieger Publishing, 1998.

Dower, John. *The Violent American Century: War and Terror Since World War II.* Chicago, IL: Haymarket Books, 2018.

———. *War Without Mercy: Race and Power in the Pacific War.* New York: Pantheon Press, 1986.

Dunak, Karen M. *As Long as We Both Shall Love: The White Wedding in Postwar America.* New York: New York University Press, 2013.

Dunn, Frederick S. *War and the Minds of Men.* Washington, DC: Council on Foreign Relations, Inc, 1950.

Dunne, Matthew W. *A Cold War State of Mind: Brainwashing and Postwar American Society.* Amherst, MA: University of Massachusetts Press, 2013.

Ehrenreich, Barbara. *The Hearts of Men: American Dreams and the Flight from Commitment.* New York: Anchor Books, 1983.

Ehrenreich, Barbara, Hess, Elizabeth, and Gloria Jacobs. *Re-making Love: The Feminization of Sex.* New York: Anchor Books, 1986.

Eislet, Benita. *Private Lives: Men and Women of the Fifties.* New York: Franklin Watts, 1986.

Elevitch, Morton D. *Dog Tags Yapping: The World War II Letters of a Combat GI.* Carbondale, IL: Southern Illinois University Press, 2003.

Ellis, John. "Stars as a Cinematic Phenomenon." In *Star Texts: Image and Performance in Film and Television,* edited by Jeremy G. Butler, 300–315. Detroit, MI: Wayne State University Press, 1991.

Ellison, Ralph. *Shadow and Act.* New York: Random House, 1964.

Ellwood, Robert S. *The Fifties Spiritual Marketplace: American Religion in a Decade of Conflict.* New Brunswick, NJ: Rutgers University Press, 1997.

Epstein, Lawrence Jeffrey. *Mixed Nuts: America's Love Affair with Comedy Teams: From Burns and Allen to Belushi and Ackroyd.* New York: PublicAffairs, 2004.

Field, Douglas, ed. *American Cold War Culture*. Edinburgh, UK: Edinburgh University Press, 2005.

Finler, Joel Waldo. *The Hollywood Story*. London, UK: Wallflower Press, 2003.

Fagelson, William Friedman. "'Nervous out of the Service': 1940s American Cinema, World War II Veteran Readjustment, and Postwar Masculinity." *Dissertation Abstracts International, Section A: The Humanities and Social Sciences* 65, no. 8 (Feb 2005).

Farber, David. *The Age of Great Dreams: America in the 1960s*. New York: Hill and Wang, 1994.

Farber, David, and Beth L. Bailey. *The First Strange Place: The Alchemy of Race and Sex in World War II Hawaii*. New York: Free Press, 2012.

Fass, Paula S. and Michael Grossberg, eds. *Reinventing Childhood After World War II*. Philadelphia, PA: University of Pennsylvania Press, 2012.

Feifer, George. *The Battle of Okinawa: Blood and the Bomb*. New York: Houghton Mifflin, 1992.

Fenichel, Otto. *The Psychoanalytic Theory of Neurosis*. London: Kegan Paul, Trench, Trubner & Co., 1946.

Fontaine, Andre, "Raise Your Boy to Be a Soldier," In *The Children's Culture Reader*, ed. Henry Jenkins. New York: NYU Press, 1998: 483–84.

Foster, Verna. "Desire, Death, and Laughter: Tragicomic Dramaturgy in A Streetcar Named Desire." In *Bloom's Modern Critical Views: Tennessee Williams*, updated edition, edited by Harold Bloom, 111–22. New York: Infobase, 2007.

Fratterigo, Elizabeth. *Playboy and the Making of the Good Life in Modern America*. New York: Oxford University Press, 2011.

Freedman, Estelle. "'Uncontrolled Desires': The Response to the Sexual Psychopath, 1920–1960." *Journal of American History* 74, no. 1 (June 1987): 83–106.

Freud, Sigmund. *Beyond the Pleasure Principle*. Translated by C. J. M. Hubback. London: International Psychoanalytical, 1922.

———. "Group Psychology and the Analysis of the Ego." Translated by James Strachey, *International Psychoanalytical Library No. 6* (1949).

Frey-Wouters, Ellen, and Robert S. Laufer. *Legacy of War: The American Soldier in Vietnam*. New York: M. E. Sharpe, 1986.

Fried, Richard M. *The Russians Are Coming! The Russians Are Coming!: Pageantry and Patriotism in Cold War America*. Oxford, UK: Oxford University Press, 1998.

Friedan, Betty. *The Feminine Mystique*. New York: W. W. Norton, 1963.

Fussell, Paul. *Wartime: Understanding and Behavior in the Second World War*. New York: Oxford University Press, 1989.

Gambone, Michael D. *The Greatest Generation Comes Home: The Veteran in American Society*. College Station, TX: Texas A&M University Press, 2005.

Giddins, Gary. *Bing Crosby: A Pocketful of Dreams: The Early Years 1903–1940*. New York: Back Bay Books, 2002.

Gilbert, James. *A Cycle of Outrage: America's Reaction to the Juvenile Delinquent in the 1950s*. New York: Oxford University Press, 1986.

———. *Men in the Middle: Searching for Masculinity in the 1950s*. Chicago: University of Chicago Press, 2005.

Glick, Ira and Sidney Levy. *Living with Television*. Washington, DC: Social Research Inc, 1962.

Glover, David. "The Stuff That Dreams Are Made of: Masculinity, Femininity, and the Thriller." In *Gender, Genre, and Narrative Pleasure*, edited by Derek Longhurst. London: Unwin Hyman, 1989.

Gomery, Douglas. *The Hollywood Studio System: A History*. London, UK: Bloomsbury Academic, 2005.

Gooden, Phyllis. "The Secret Lucy Kept from Desi," Clippings: Lucille Ball, pre-1955.14, 6–8. New York Public Library of the Performing Arts.

Gray, Herman. *Watching Race: Television and the Struggle for "Blackness."* Minneapolis, MN, University of Minnesota Press, 1995.

Green, Michael Cullen. *Black Yanks in the Pacific: Race in the Making of American Military Empire after World War II*. Ithaca, NY: Cornell University Press, 2010.

Grote, David. *The End of Comedy: The Sit-Com and the Comedic Tradition*. Hamden, CT: Archon Books, 1983.

Gunelias, Susan. *Building Brand Value the Playboy Way*. New York: Palgrave Macmillan, 2009.

Haggett, Ali. *Desperate Housewives, Neuroses and the Domestic Environment, 1945–1970*. New York: Routledge, 2015.

Hall, Simon. *1956: The World in Revolt*. New York: Pegasus Books, 2015.

Halberstam, David. *The Fifties*. New York: Random House, 1996.

Halliwell, Martin. *American Culture in the 1950s*. Edinburgh: Edinburgh University Press, 2007.

Halpern, Richard. *Norman Rockwell: The Underside of Innocence*. Chicago: University of Chicago Press, 2006.

Hamamoto, Darrell Y. *Nervous Laughter: Television Situation Comedy and Liberal Democratic Ideology*. New York: Praeger, 1989.

Hansbury, Lorraine. *A Raisin in the Sun*. New York: Random House, 1958.

Haralovich, Mary Beth. "Sitcoms and Suburbs: Positioning the 1950s Homemaker." In *Private Screenings: Television and the Female Consumer*, edited by Lynn Spigel and Denise Mann, 111–40. Minneapolis: University of Minnesota Press, 1992.

Harris, Warren G. *Lucy and Desi: The Legendary Love Story of Television's Most Famous Couple*. New York: Simon and Schuster, 1991.

Hartmann, Susan M. "'Prescriptions for Penelope': Literature on Women's Obligations to Returning World War II Veterans." *Women's Studies* 5, no. 3 (1978): 223–39.

Hass, Dorothy B. "Lucille Ball." Clippings: Lucille Ball, pre-1955. New York Public Library of the Performing Arts.

Hata, Donald Teruo and Nadine Ishitani Hata. *Japanese Americans and World War II: Mass Removal, Imprisonment, and Redress.* Wheeling, IL: Harlan Davidson, 1974.

Hauser, Brooke. *Enter Helen: The Invention of Helen Gurley Brown and the Rise of the Modern Single Woman.* New York: Harper Collins, 2016.

Hegarty, Marilyn E. *Victory Girls, Khaki-Wackies, and Patriotutes: The Regulation of Female Sexuality during World War II.* New York: New York University Press, 2010.

Hendershot, Cyndy. *Anticommunism and Popular Culture in Mid-Century America.* Jefferson, NC: Macfarland, 2003.

Herbert, Thomas Walter. *Sexual Violence and American Manhood.* Cambridge, MA: Presidents and Fellows of Harvard College, 2002.

Herman, Ellen. *The Romance of American Psychology: Political Culture in the Age of the Experts.* Berkeley, CA: University of California Press, 1995.

Himes, Chester. *If He Hollers Let Him Go.* New York: Doran Press, 1945.

Himmelstein, Hal. *Television Myth and the American Mind.* New York: Praeger Publishers, 1984.

Hirshey, Gerri. *Not Pretty Enough: The Unlikely Triumph of Helen Gurley Brown.* New York: Farrar, Straus & Giroux, 2016.

Hollinger, David A., ed. *The Humanities and the Dynamics of Inclusion since World War II.* Baltimore, MD: Johns Hopkins University Press, 2006.

Hollings, Ken. *Welcome to Mars: Politics, Pop Culture, and Weird Science in 1950s America.* Berkeley, CA: North Atlantic Books, 2008.

Holm, Tom. *Code Talkers and Warriors: Native Americans in World War II.* New York: Infobase Publishers, 2007. Holt, Marilyn Irvin. *Cold War Kids: Politics and Childhood in Postwar America, 1945–1960.* Lawrence, KS: University of Kansas Press, 2014.

Hough, Arthur. "Trials and Tribulations—Thirty Years of Sitcom." In *Understanding Television: Essays on Television as a Social and Cultural Force,* edited by Richard P. Adler, 201–23. New York: Praeger, 1981.

Huebner, Andrew J. *The Warrior Image: Soldiers in American Culture from the Second World War to the Vietnam Era.* Chapel Hill, NC: University of North Carolina Press, 2008.

Hughes, Dorothy. *In a Lonely Place.* New York: Duell, Sloane, and Pierce, 1947.

Humes, Edward. *Over Here: How the GI Bill Transformed the American Dream.* Orlando, FL: Harcourt Inc, 2006.
Igo, Sarah E. *The Averaged American: Surveys, Citizens, and the Making of a Mass Public.* Cambridge, MA: Harvard University Press, 2007.
———. *The Known Citizen: A History of Privacy in Modern America.* Cambridge, MA: Harvard University Press, 2018.
Illouz, Eva. *Saving the Modern Soul: Therapy, Emotions, and the Culture of Self-Help.* Berkeley, CA: University of California Press, 2008.
Jackson, Kenneth. *Crabgrass Frontier: The Suburbanization of the United States.* New York: Oxford University Press, 1987.
Jacobs, Robert A. *The Dragon's Tail: Americans Face the Atomic Age.* Amherst, MA: University of Massachusetts Press, 2010.
Jarvis, Christina F. *The Male Body at War: American Masculinity during World War II.* Dekalb, IL: Northern Illinois University Press, 2004.
Jenkins, Henry. "The Sensuous Child: Benjamin Spock and the Sexual Revolution," in *The Children's Culture Reader,* ed. Jenkins. New York: NYU Press, 1998: 231–40.
Jewell, Richard B. *The Golden Age of Cinema: Hollywood 1929–1945.* Malden, MA: Blackwell Publishing, 2007.
Jezer, Marty. *The Dark Ages: Life in the United States, 1945–60.* Brooklyn, NY: South End Press, 1982.
Johns, Michael. *Moment of Grace: The American City in the 1950s.* Berkeley, CA: University of California Press, 2003.
Johnston, Richard W. "Death's Fair-Haired Boy: Sex and Fury Sell 13 Million Gory Books for Mickey Spillane." *Life* magazine. June 23, 1952.
Jones, Gerard. *Honey, I'm Home!: Sitcoms and the Selling of the American Dream.* New York: Grove Press, 1992.
Jurca, Catherine. *White Diaspora: The Suburb and the Twentieth Century American Novel.* Princeton, NJ: Princeton University Press, 2001.
Kackman, Michael. *Citizen Spy: Television, Espionage, And Cold War Culture.* Minneapolis, MN: University of Minnesota Press, 2005.
Kaminsky, Stuart M. with Jeffrey H. Mahan. *American Television Genres.* Chicago: Nelson Hall Publishers, 1985.
Kanfer, Stefan. *Ball of Fire: The Tumultuous Life and Comic Art of Lucille Ball.* New York: Knopf, 2003.
Kaplan, Fred. *1959: The Year Everything Changed.* Hoboken, NJ: Wiley and Sons, 2009.
Karol, Michael A. *Lucy in Print.* Lincoln, NE: iUniverse, 2003.
Kassel, Michael B. "Mass Culture, History, and Memory and the Image of the American Family in *Leave It to Beaver.*" PhD diss., Michigan State University, 2005.

Keith, Thomas. "Pulp Williams: Tennessee in the Popular Imagination." In *Ten at One Hundred: The Reputation of Tennessee Williams*, edited by David Kaplan. East Brunswick, NJ: Hansen Publishers, 2011.

Kelley, N. Megan. *Projections of Passing: Postwar Anxieties and Hollywood Films, 1947–1960*. Jackson, MS: University of Mississippi Press, 2016.

Kennedy, David. *Freedom from Fear: The American People in Depression and War, 1929–1945*. New York: Oxford University Press, 2001.

Kercher, Stephen E. *Revel with a Cause: Liberal Satire in Postwar America*. Chicago: University of Chicago Press, 2006.

Kerouac, Jack. *On the Road*. New York: Viking Press, 1957.

Kinsey, Alfred P. *Sexual Behavior in the Human Male*. Philadelphia: Saunders, 1948.

Kiszely, Philip. *Hollywood through Private Eyes: The Screen Adaptations of the "Hard-boiled" Private Detective Novel in the Studio Era*. New York: Peter Lang, 2006.

Knauer, Christine. *Let Us Fight as Free Men: Black Soldiers and Civil Rights*. Philadelphia, PA: University of Pennsylvania Press, 2014.

Knight, Peter, ed. *Conspiracy Nation: The Politics of Paranoia in Postwar America*. New York: New York University Press, 2002.

Kolin, Philip C. "The Family of Mitch: (Un)suitable Suitors in Tennessee Williams." In *Magical Muse: Millennial Essays on Tennessee Williams*, edited by Ralph F. Voss, 131–46. Tuscaloosa, AL: University of Alabama Press, 2002.

Kompare, Derek. "I've Seen This Before: The Construction of 'Classic TV' on Cable Television." In *Small Screens, Big Ideas: Television in the 1950's*, edited by Janet Thumin, 22–27. London: I. B. Tauris & Company, 2002.

Koppes Clayton R. and Gregory D. Black. *Hollywood Goes to War: Patriotism, Movies, and the Second World War*. London: I.B. Tauris, 1987.

Kozloff, Sarah. "Wyler's Wars." *Film History: An International Journal* 20, no. 4 (2008): 456–73.

Kruse, Kevin M., and Steven Tuck, eds. *Fog of War: The Second World War and the Civil Rights Movement*. Oxford, UK: Oxford University Press, 2012.

Kutulas, Judy. "Who Rules the Roost?: Sitcom Family Dynamics from the Cleavers to the Osbournes." In *The Sitcom Reader: America Viewed and Skewed*, edited by Mary M. Dalton and Laura R. Linder, 49–60. Albany, NY: SUNY Press, 2005: 49–60.

Laham, Nicholas. *Currents of Comedy on the American Screen: How Film and Television Deliver Different Laughs for Changing Times*. Jefferson, NC: McFarland and Company, 2009.

Landay, Lori. *TV Milestones: I Love Lucy*. Detroit, MI: Wayne State University Press, 2010.

———. *Madcaps, Screwballs, and Con Women: The Female Trickster in American Culture*. Philadelphia: University of Pennsylvania Press, 1998.

Lasch, Christopher. *Haven in a Heartless World: The Family Besieged*. New York: Basic Books, 1977.

Lassonde, Stephen. "Age and Authority: Adult-Child Relations During the Twentieth Century in the United States." *Journal of the History of Childhood and Youth* 1, no. 1 (2008): 95–105.

Lawrence, Amy. "James Mason: A Star is Born Bigger than Life." In *Larger Than Life: Movie Stars of the 1950s*, edited by R. Barton Palmer. New Brunswick, NJ: Rutgers University Press, 2010.

Lears, T. J. Jackson. "Making Fun of Popular Culture." *The American Historical Review* 97, no. 5 (December 1992): 1417–26.

Leibman, Nina C. *Living Room Lectures: The Fifties Family in Film and Television*. Austin, TX: University of Texas Press, 1995.

Leder, Jane Mersky. *Thanks for the Memories: Love, Sex, and World War II*. Portsmouth, NH: Greenwood Press, 2006.

Levine, Alan J. *Bad Old Days: The Myth of the 1950s*. New Brunswick, NJ: Transaction Publishers, 2008.

Lhamon, W. T. *Deliberate Speed: The Origins of a Cultural Style in the American 1950s*. Cambridge, MA: Harvard University Press, 2002.

Lingeman, Richard. *Don't You Know There's a War On?: The American Homefront, 1941–1945*. New York: G. P. Putnam and Sons, 1970.

Lisio, Donald J. *The President and Protest: Hoover, Conspiracy, and the Bonus Riot*. Columbia, MO: University of Missouri Press, 1974.

Litoff, Judy B. and David Clayton Smith., *Since You Went Away World War II Letters from American Women on the Home Front*. Lawrence: University Press of Kansas, 2009.

Luddington, Peter. *Why the Good War Was Good: Roosevelt's New World Order*. Los Angeles: University of California Press, 2008.

Lukas, J. Anthony. "The Alternative Lifestyle of Playboys and Playmates." *New York Times*. June 11, 1972.

Maier, Thomas. *Dr Spock, An American Life*. New York: Harcourt Brace, 1998.

Maltby, Richard. *Hollywood*. 2nd ed. Oxford, UK: Blackwell Publishing, 2003.

Marc, David. *Comic Visions: Television Comedy and American Culture*. 2nd ed. Malden, MA: Blackwell, 1997.

Marc, David, and Robert J. Thompson. *Prime Time, Prime Movers: From I Love Lucy to L.A. Law—America's Greatest TV Shows and the People Who Created Them*. Syracuse, NY: Syracuse University Press, 1995.

Marcus, Greil. *Double Trouble: Bill Clinton and Elvis Presley in a Land of No Alternatives*. New York: Henry Holt and Company, 2000.

MacDonnell, Francis. *Insidious Foes: The Axis Fifth Column and the American Home Front*. New York: Oxford University Press, 1995.

MacNair, Rachel. *Perpetration-Induced Traumatic Stress: The Psychological Consequences of Killing.* Santa Barbara, CA: Praeger Press, 2002.

Macpherson, Myra. *A Long Time Passing: Vietnam and the Haunted Generation.* Bloomington: Indiana University Press, 1984.

Masuda, Minoru and Tano Masuda. *Letters from the 442nd: The World War II Correspondent of a Japanese American Combat Medic.* Seattle, WA: University of Washington Press, 2008.

Matheson, Calum L. *Desiring the Bomb: Communication, Psychoanalysis, and the Atomic Age.* Tuscaloosa, AL: University of Alabama Press, 2019.

May, Elaine Tyler. *Homeward Bound: American Families in the Cold War Era.* New York: Basic Books, 1990.

———. "Rosie the Riveter Gets Married." In *The War in American Culture: Society and Consciousness During World War II,* edited by Lewis A. Erenberg and Susan E. Hirsch, 128–43. Chicago: University of Chicago Press, 1996.

McArthur, Colin. *Underworld U.S.A.* New York: Viking Press, 1972.

McCann, Graham. *Rebel Males: Clift, Brando, and Dean.* New Brunswick, NJ: Rutgers University Press, 1991.

McCarthy, Anna. *Ambient Television.* Durham, NC: Duke University Press, 2001.

McEnloe, Cynthia, "Introduction." In *Let the Good Times Roll: Prostitution and the US Military in Asia,* ed. Saundra Pollock Sturdevant and Brenda Stoltzfus. New York: The New Press, 1992.

McEuen, Melissa. *Making War, Making Women: Femininity and Duty on the Homefront.* Athens: University of Georgia Press, 2010.

McGirr, Lisa. *Suburban Warriors: The Origins of the New American Right.* Princeton, NJ: Princeton University Press, 2001.

McGurn, Barrett. *YANK: The Army Weekly—Reporting the Greatest Generation.* London: Fulcrum Press, 2004.

McManus, John. *The Deadly Brotherhood: The American Combat Soldier in World War II.* New York: Random House, 1998.

Mellencamp, Patricia. "Situation Comedy, Feminism, and Freud: Discourses of Gracie and Lucy." Reprinted in *Critiquing the Sitcom: A Reader,* edited by Joanne Morreale, 41–55. Syracuse, NY: Syracuse University Press, 2003.

Melley, Timothy. *Empire of Conspiracy: The Culture of Paranoia in Postwar America.* Ithaca, NY: Cornell University Press, 2000.

Menand, Louis. "Freud, Anxiety, and the Cold War." In *After Freud Left: A Century of Psychoanalysis in America,* edited by John Burnham. University of Chicago Press, 2012.

Merrill, Hugh. *Esky: The Early Years of Esquire.* New Brunswick, NJ: Rutgers University Press, 1995.

Mettler, Suzanne. *Soldiers to Citizens: The GI Bill and the Making of the Greatest Generation.* Oxford, UK: Oxford University Press, 2005.

Meyerowitz, Joanne, ed. *Not June Cleaver: Women and Gender in Postwar America, 1945–1960.* Philadelphia: Temple University Press, 1994.

Miller, Russell. *Bunny: The Real Story of Playboy.* New York: Henry Holt & Co, 1985.

Mintz, Lawrence. "Situation Comedy." In *TV Genres,* edited by Brian Rose, 105–29. Westport, CT: Greenwood Press, 1985.

Mock, Lewis. Personal Collection of the Author.

Monahan, Evelyn M. and Rosemary Neidler-Greenlee. *And If I Perish: Frontline US Army Nurses in World War II.* New York: Anchor Books, 2003.

Moore, Deborah Dash. *GI Jews: How World War II Changed a Generation.* Cambridge, MA: Belknap Press, 2006.

Morehouse, Maggi M. *Fighting in the Jim Crow Army: Black Men and Women Remember World War II.* Lanham, MD: Rowan and Littlefield Press, 2000.

Morley, David. *Family Television: Cultural Power and Domestic Leisure.* London: Psychology Press, 1995.

Mosse, George L. *Fallen Soldiers: Reshaping the Memory of the World Wars.* Oxford, UK: Oxford University Press, 1990.

Murray, Susan. *Hitch Your Antenna to the Stars: Early Television and Broadcast Stardom.* New York: Routledge, 2005.

Naremore, James. *Acting in the Cinema.* Berkeley, CA: University of California Press, 1988.

Nelson, Deborah L., ed. "Gender and Culture in the 1950s." Special issue, *Women's Studies Quarterly* 33, nos. 3–4.

Newcomb, Horace. "The Opening of America: Meaningful Difference in 1950s Television." In *The Other Fifties: Interrogating Midcentury Icons,* edited by Joel Foreman, 103–23. Urbana: University of Illinois Press, 1997.

Neuhaus, Jessamyn. "The Importance of Being Orgasmic: Sexuality, Gender, and Marital Sex Manuals in the United States, 1920–1963." *Journal of the History of Sexuality* 9, no. 4 (2000): 447–73.

Nielson, Mike and Gene Mailes. *Hollywood's Other Blacklist: Union Struggles in the Studio System.* Bloomington, IN: Indiana University Press, 1995.

Nishikawa, Kinohi. "Race, Respectability, and the Short Life of *Duke Magazine.*" *Book History* 15 (2012): 152–82.

Nouryeh, Andrea. "The Stage Door Canteen: The American Theatre Wing's Experiment in Integration." In *Experiments in Democracy: Interracial and Cross-Cultural Exchange in American Theatre, 1912–1945,* edited by Cheryl Black and Jonathan Shandell, 256–73. Carbondale, IL: Southern Illinois University Press, 2016.

Nyman, Jopi. *Men Alone: Masculinity, Individualism, and Hardboiled Fiction.* Atlanta, GA: Rodopi Editions, 1997.

O'Brien, Gail Williams. *The Color of the Law: Race, Violence, and Justice in the Post–World War II South.* Chapel Hill, NC: University of North Carolina Press, 1999.

O'Brien, Geoffrey. *Hardboiled America: The Lurid Years of Paperbacks,* expanded ed. Cambridge, MA: Da Capo Press, 1997.

O'Meally, Robert, ed. *New Essays on Invisible Man.* Cambridge, UK: Cambridge University Press, 1998.

O'Neill, Eithne. "Kazan's *Streetcar:* Film Noir, Woman's Film or Noir Woman's Film?" *Cercles* 10 (2004): 169–76.

Oren, Tasha G. "Domesticated Dads and Double-Shift Moms: Real Life and Ideal Life in 1950s Domestic Comedy." *Cercles* 8 (2003): 78–90.

Osgerby, Bill. *Playboys in Paradise: Masculinity, Youth, and Leisure-Style in Modern America.* London: Berg Press, 2001.

Palmer, R. Barton. "Stardom in the 1950s." Introduction to *Larger Than Life: Movie Stars of the 1950s,* edited by R. Barton Palmer. New Brunswick, NJ: Rutgers University Press, 2010.

Parish, James Robert, and Lennard DeCarl. *Hollywood Players: The Forties.* New Rochelle, NY: Arlington House, 1976.

Parfrey, Adam. *It's a Man's World: Men's Adventure Magazines—The Postwar Pulps.* Los Angeles, CA: Feral House, 2003.

Parsons, Louella. "Lucy and Desi Say: Laugh and Be Happily Married." *International News Service.* Clippings: Lucille Ball, pre-1955. New York Public Library of the Performing Arts.

Paul, Christopher, and Michael Denis. *Favorite Families of TV.* New York: Carol Publishing, 1991.

Pauwel, Jacques R. *The Myth of the Good War: America in the Second World War.* Ontario, CA: Lorimer and Company, 2002.

Pendergast, Tom. *Creating the Modern Man: American Magazines and Consumer Culture 1900–1950.* Columbia: University of Missouri Press, 2000.

Perez, Louis. *On Becoming Cuban: Identity, Nationality, and Culture.* Chapel Hill: University of North Carolina Press, 2007.

Peterson, Marva. "Living on Wheels." Clippings: Lucille Ball, pre-1955. New York Public Library of the Performing Arts.

Petigny, Alan. *The Permissive Society: 1941–1965.* Cambridge, UK: Cambridge University Press, 2009.

Piehler, G. Kurt, ed. *The United States in World War II: A Documentary Reader.* Malden, MA: Wiley Blackwell Publishing, 2013.

Pitzulo, Carrie. *Bachelors and Bunnies: The Sexual Politics of Playboy*. Chicago: University of Chicago Press, 2011.

Playboy magazine, edited by Hugh Hefner, 1953–62.

Popkin, Jeremy P. *History, Historians, and Autobiography*. Chicago: University of Chicago Press, 2005.

Popp, Richard K. *The Holiday Makers: Magazines, Advertising, and Mass Tourism in Postwar America*. Baton Rouge, LA: Louisiana State Press, 2012.

Porter, Dennis. *The Pursuit of Crime: Art and Ideology in Detective Fiction*. New Haven, CT: Yale University Press, 1981.

Prindle, David F. *The Politics of Glamour: Ideology and Democracy in the Screen Actors Guild*. Madison: University of Wisconsin Press, 1988.

Pyle, Ernie. *Brave Men*. Lincoln: University of Nebraska Press, 1944.

———. *Ernie's War: The Best of Ernie Pyle's War Dispatches*, edited by David Nichols. New York: Simon and Schuster, 1987.

Radner, Hilary. *Shopping Around: Feminine Culture and the Pursuit of Pleasure*. New York: Routledge, 1995.

Ramsay, Debra. *American Media and the Memory of World War II*. London, UK: Routledge, 2015.

Reumann, Miriam. *American Sexual Character: Sex, Gender, and National Identity in the Kinsey Reports*. Berkeley: University of California Press, 2005.

Riesman, David. *The Lonely Crowd: A Study of the Changing American Character*. New Haven, CT: Yale University Press, 1950.

Ritzenberg, Aaron. *The Sentimental Touch: The Language of Feeling in the Age of Managerialism*. New York: Fordham University Press, 2013.

Rivas-Rodriguez, Maggie. *A Legacy Greater than Words: Stories of US Latinos and Latinas of the World War II Generation*. Austin: University of Texas Press, 2006.

Robinson, Paul A. *The Modernization of Sex: Havelock Ellis, Alfred Kinsey, William Masters, and Virginia Johnson*. New York: Harper and Row, 1976.

Roeder Jr., George H. *The Censored War: American Visual Experience During World War II*. New Haven, CT: Yale University Press, 1993.

Roosevelt, Franklin D. "Fireside Chat." May 2, 1943. Available online at Gerhard Peters and John T. Woolley, The American Presidency Project. https://www.presidency.ucsb.edu/documents/fireside-chat-0.

———. "State of the Union Address." January 6, 1945. Available online at Gerhard Peters and John T. Woolley, The American Presidency Project. https://www.presidency.ucsb.edu/documents/state-the-union-address.

Rose, Lisle. *Farewell to Prosperity: Wealth, Identity, and Conflict in Postwar America*. Columbia, MO: University of Missouri Press, 2014.

Rose, Kenneth D. *Myth and the Greatest Generation: A Social History of Americans in World War II*. New York: Routledge, 2008.

Ross, Gary. "Gary Ross breathes his life into 'Pleasantville.'" Interview by Jamie Allen. *CNN Interactive*, October 12, 1998, http://www.cnn.com/SHOWBIZ/Movies/9810/12/austin.ross/.

Rotskoff, Lori. *Love on the Rocks: Men, Women, and Alcohol in Post–World War II America*. Raleigh, NC: University of North Carolina Press, 2002.

Roth, Michael. *Memory, Trauma, History: Essays on Living with the Past*. New York: Columbia University Press, 2011.

Rubin, Joan Shelley. *The Making of Middlebrow Culture*. Chapel Hill: University of North Carolina Press, 1992.

Rutherford, Paul. *World Made Sexy: Freud to Madonna*. Toronto: University of Toronto Press, 2007.

Sanders, Coyne S. and Tom Gilbert. *Desilu: The Story of Lucille Ball and Desi Arnaz*. New York: Quill, 1993.

Sake, Robert Francis. *Settling Down: World War II Veterans' Challenge to the Postwar Consensus*. New York: Palgrave Macmillan, 2007.

Sarracino, Carmine and Kevin Scott. *The Porning of America: The Rise of Porn Culture, What It Means, and Where We Can Go from Here*. Beacon, NY: Beacon Press, 2009.

Savran, David. *Communists, Cowboys, and Queers: The Politics of Masculinity in the Work of Arthur Miller and Tennessee Williams*. Minneapolis: University of Minnesota Press, 1992.

———. *Taking It Like a Man: White Masculinity, Masochism, and Contemporary American Culture*. Princeton, NJ: Princeton University Press, 1998.

Scanlon, Jennifer. *Bad Girls Go Everywhere: The Life of Helen Gurley Brown*. New York: Oxford University Press, 2009.

Scheibach, Michael. *Atomic Narratives and American Youth*. Jefferson, NC: Macfarland Publishers, 2003.

Schlesinger, Arthur. *The Vital Center: The Politics of Freedom*. Boston: Houghton Mifflin, 1949.

Schryer, Stephen. *Fantasies of the New Class: Ideologies of Professionalism in Post–World War II American Fiction*. New York: Columbia University Press, 2011.

Scott, Mack. "From Blackface to Beulah: Subtle Subversion in Early Black Sitcoms." *Journal of Contemporary History* 49 no. 4 (Oct. 2014): 743–69.

Scott, Wilbur J. *Vietnam Veterans Since the War: The Politics of PTSD, Agent Orange, and the Veterans Memorial*. Oklahoma City: University of Oklahoma Press, 1993.

Sebestyen, Victory. *1946: The Making of the Modern World*. New York: Vintage Books, 2014.

Server, Lee. *Over My Dead Body: The Sensational Age of the American Paperback, 1945–1955*. New York: Chronicle, 1994.

Shackleford, Dean. "Is There a Gay Man in this Text?: Subverting the Closet in *A Streetcar Named Desire*." In *Literature and Homosexuality*, edited by Michael J. Meyer. Amsterdam: Rodopi Press, 1994.

Shales, Tom and James Andrew Miller. *Live from New York: An Uncensored History of Saturday Night Live*. New York: Little, Brown, 2005.

Shapiro, Laura. *Something from the Oven: Reinventing Dinner in 1950s America*. New York: Penguin, 2004.

Sher, Jac. "The Cuban and the Redhead." Clippings: Lucille Ball, pre-1955. New York Public Library of the Performing Arts.

Simpson, Phillip. *Psycho Paths: Tracking the Serial Killer Through Contemporary American Film and Fiction*. Carbondale, IL: Southern Illinois University Press, 2000.

Sklar, Robert. *City Boys: Cagney, Bogart, Garfield*. Princeton, NJ: Princeton University Press, 1992.

———. *Prime-Time America: Life on and Behind the Television Screen*. New York: Oxford University Press, 1980.

Specter, Ronald. *Eagle against the Sun: The American War with Japan*. New York: Random House, 1985.

Smith, Judith E. *Visions of Belonging: Family Stories, Popular Culture, and Postwar Democracy*. New York: Columbia University Press, 2004.

Smith, R.J. *The Great Black Way: LA in the 1940s and the Lost Harlem Renaissance*. New York: Public Affairs, 2006.

Sochen, June. "Slapsticks, Screwballs, and Bawds: The Long Road to the Performing Talents of Lucy and Bette." In *Women's Comic Visions*, edited by June Sochen, 141–57. Detroit, MI: Wayne State University Press, 1991.

Sorel, Nancy Caldwell. *The Women Who Wrote the War: The Riveting Saga of World War II's Daredevil Women Correspondents*. New York: Arcade Publishing, 1999.

Spigel, Lynn. *Make Room for TV: Television and the Family Ideal in Postwar America*. Chicago: University of Chicago Press, 1992.

Spillane, Mickey. *I, the Jury*. New York: E. P. Dutton, 1947.

———. *My Gun Is Quick*. New York: E. P. Dutton, 1950.

———. *Vengeance Is Mine*. New York: E. P. Dutton, 1950.

———. *One Lonely Night*. New York: E. P. Dutton, 1951.

Stanfield, Peter and Richard Maltby. *Maximum Movies-Pulp Fictions: Film Culture and the Worlds of Samuel Fuller, Mickey Spillane, and Jim Thompson*. New Brunswick, NJ: Rutgers University Press, 2011.

Stanley, Liz. *Sex Surveyed 1949–1994: From Mass-Observations 'Little Kinsey' to the National Survey and the Hite Reports*. London, UK: Taylor and Francis, 1995.

Stark, Steven D. *Glued to the Set: The Sixty Television Shows and Events That Made Us Who We Are Today.* New York: Bantam Doubleday Dell, 1997.

Stewart, Patrick (host). "The Lion Reigns Supreme." *MGM: When the Lion Roars.* March 23, 1992.

Strausbaugh, John. *Victory City: A History of New York and New Yorkers During World War II.* New York: Hachette Book Group, 2018.

Stringer, Helen D., and Sydney Walter Stringer. *Letters of Love and War: A World War II Correspondence.* Syracuse, NY: Syracuse University Press, 1997.

Sumner, David E. *The Magazine Century: American Magazines since 1900.* New York: Peter Lang, 2010.

Susann, Jacqueline. *Valley of the Dolls.* New York: Bernard Geis Associates, 1966.

Sutherland, John. *Bestsellers: A Very Short Introduction.* New York: Oxford University Press, 2007.

Taylor, Anthea. *Celebrity and the Feminist Blockbuster.* New York: Springer Publishing, 2017.

Taylor, William A. *Every Citizen a Soldier: The Campaign for Universal Military Training After World War II.* College Station, TX: Texas A&M University Press, 2012.

Terkel, Studs. *"The Good War": An Oral History.* New York: The New Press, 1984.

Thomson, David. *The New Biographical Dictionary of Film.* London: Little, Brown, 2002.

Thompson, Jim. *The Killer Inside Me.* New York; Faucett Publications, 1952.

Thorne, Christopher. *Allies of a Kind: The United States, Britain, and the War Against Japan, 1941–1945.* London: Oxford University Press, 1978.

Threat, Charissa J. *Nursing Civil Rights: Gender and Race in the Army Nurse Corps.* Urbana, IL: University of Illinois Press, 2015.

Tithecott, Richard. *Of Men and Monsters: Jeffrey Dahmer and the Construction of the Serial Killer.* Madison, WI: University of Wisconsin Press, 1997.

Tobin, James. *Ernie Pyle's War: America's Eyewitness to World War II.* New York: Free Press, 1997.

Torgovnick, Mariana. *The War Complex: World War II in Our Time.* Chicago, IL: University of Chicago Press, 2005.

Trask, Michael. *Camp Sites: Sex, Politics, and Academic Style in Postwar America.* Stanford, CA: Stanford University Press, 2013.

Trilling, Lionel. *The Liberal Imagination: Essays on Literature and Society.* New York: New York Review of Books, 1950.

Tucker, Sherrie. *Dance Floor Democracy: The Social Geography of Memory at the Hollywood Canteen.* Durham, NC: Duke University Press, 2014.

Tuck, Stephen. "'You can sing and punch . . . but you can't be a soldier or a man': African American Struggles for a New Place in Popular Culture." In *Fog of War:*

The Second World War and the Civil Rights Movement, edited by Kevin M. Kruse and Stephen Tuck, 103–25. Oxford, UK: Oxford University Press, 2012.

Tuttle Jr., William M. *Daddy's Gone to War: The Second World War in the Lives of American Children.* Oxford, UK: Oxford University Press, 1993.

TV Guide. "Honest, She's My Wife! But Most TV Viewers Are Still Baffled." November 20–26, 1954.

———. "P. S. We Want 'Father'!: Letters from Viewers Bring Back a Show—At the Expense of a Higher Rated Program." September 3–9, 1955, 20–21.

———. "Situation Comedies Galore: Funny Families Replace Fast-Patter Comedians." September 18–24, 1953, 4–5.

Twitchell, James B. *Carnival Culture: The Trashing of Taste in America.* New York: Columbia University Press, 1992.

Van Den Oever, *Mama's Boy: Momism and Homophobia in Postwar American Culture.* New York: Palgrave Macmillan, 2012.

Van Ells, Mark. *To Hear Only Thunder Again: American's World War II Veterans Come Home.* Lanham, MD: Lexington Books, 2001.

Von Schilling, James Arthur. *The Magic Window: American Television, 1939–1953.* Binghamton, NY: Haworth Press, 2003.

Waller, Willard. *The Veteran Comes Back.* New York: The Dryden Press, 1944.

Watson, Mary Ann, Gerald D. Nash and Richard W. Etulain. *Defining Visions: Television and The American Experience Since 1945.* Belmont, CA: Wadsworth Press, 1997.

Watts, Steven. *Mr. Playboy: Hugh Hefner and the American Dream.* Hoboken, NJ: John Wiley and Sons, 2009.

Weaks-Baxter, Mary, Christine Bruun, and Catherine Forslund, *We Are a College at War: Women Working for Victory in World War II.* Carbondale: Southern Illinois State University Press, 2010.

Wecter, Dixon. *When Johnny Comes Marching Home.* New York: Houghton Mifflin, 1944.

Weinstein, Deborah. *The Pathological Family: Postwar America and the Rise of Family Therapy.* Ithaca, NY: Cornell University Press, 2013.

Weisblat, Tinky. "Will the Real George and Gracie and Ozzie and Harriet and Desi and Lucy Please Stand Up?: The Functions of Popular Biography in 1950s Television." PhD diss., University of Texas, Austin, 1991.

Weiss, Jessica. *To Have and to Hold: Marriage, the Baby Boom, and Social Change.* Chicago, IL: University of Chicago Press, 2000.

Wertheim, Albert. *Staging the War: American Drama and World War II.* Bloomington, IN: Indiana University Press, 2004.

Westbrook, Robert B. "'I Want a Girl, Just Like the Girl that Married Harry James': American Women and the Problem of Political Obligation in World War II." *American Quarterly* 42 no. 4 (Dec. 1990): 587–614.

Weyr, Thomas. *Reaching for Paradise: The Playboy Vision of America*. New York: New York Times Books, 1978.

White Jr., George. "'Building a Church in the Army': Chaplain Robert Boston Dokes, Religious Resistance to Racial Segregation, and Black Troops in World War II," *International Journal of Africana Studies* 20, no. 1 Spring/Summer 2019: 43–65.

White, Hayden. *Figural Realism: Studies in the Mimesis Effect*. Baltimore, MD: Johns Hopkins University Press, 1999.

Whiting, Frederick. "Bodies of Evidence: Post-War Detective Fiction and the Monstrous Origins of the Sexual Psychopath." *Yale Journal of Criticism* 18, no. 1 (2005): 149–78.

Whyte, William. *The Organization Man*. New York: Simon and Schuster, 1956.

Wilde, Larry. *The Great Comedians Talk About Comedy*. New York: Citadel Press, 1968.

Wiese, Andrew. "'The House I Live In': Race, Class, and African American Suburban Dreams in the Postwar United States." In *The New Suburban History*, edited by Kevin M. Kruse and Thomas J. Sugrue, 101–2. Chicago, IL: University of Chicago Press, 2006.

Williams, Tennessee. *A Streetcar Named Desire*. New York: Dramatists Play Service, 1947.

Wills, Charles A. *America in the 1950s*. New York: Chelsea House, 2005.

Wilson, Sloan. *The Man in the Gray Flannel Suit*. New York: Simon and Schuster, 1955.

Winkler, Allan M. *Home Front USA: America during World War II*. Wheeling, IL: Harlan Davidson Inc, 1986.

———. *Life Under a Cloud: American Anxiety about the Atom*. Urbana, IL: University of Illinois Press, 1993.

Wood, Linda Sargent. *A More Perfect Union: Holistic Worldviews and the Transformation of American Culture After World War II*. Oxford, UK: Oxford University Press, 2010.

Wojcik, Pamela Robertson, ed. *Movie Acting: The Film Reader*. New York: Routledge, 2004.

Wright, Mike. *What They Didn't Teach You About World War II*. New York: Random House, 2009.

Wright, Richard. *Native Son*. New York: Harpers and Bros, 1940.

Wynn, Neil. *The African American Experience in World War II*. Lanham, MD: Rowan and Littlefield, 2010.

Walker, Nancy. *A Very Serious Thing: Women's Humor and American Culture*. Minneapolis: University of Minnesota Press, 1988.

Yellin, Emily. *Our Mothers' War: American Women at Home and at the Front During World War II*. New York: Simon and Schuster, 2005.

Yoggy, Gary A, ed. *Back in the Saddle: Essays on Western Film and Television Actors.* Jefferson, NC: Macfarland and Co, 1998.

Young, Kay. *Ordinary Pleasures: Couples, Conversation, and Comedy.* Columbus, OH: Ohio State University Press, 2001.

Zerubavel, Eviatar. *Hidden in Plain Sight: The Social Structure of Irrelevance.* Oxford, UK: Oxford University Press, 2015.

INDEX

acting, 98–101
Act of Violence, 31, 116–19, 207
Actors' Equity, 21
Adams, Clifford, 152–53, 161
Adventures of Augie March, The (Bellow), 33
Adventures of Ozzie and Harriet, The, 172–73, 181, 188, 193, 195–97, 199–200
Afghanistan War, 3, 30, 36, 208
African Americans, 4, 12–15, 21–22, 24, 51, 60, 96–99, 119–21, 145–47, 150, 168–70, 176, 181, 209–10, 216–17
alcohol, 1, 22, 27, 47, 50–51, 71, 89, 106, 138, 167, 170, 174, 211
All My Sons (Miller), 33
American Theatre Wing (Stage Door Canteen), 21–22
Andrews, Dana, 103
Andrews Sisters, the, 21
Armed Services Editions, 22–23
Arnaz, Desi. See *I Love Lucy*
Arthur, Jean, 122–23
Astaire, Fred, 21
Astor, Mary, 118
atomic anxiety, 36, 144

Baby Boom, 25, 171
baby boomers, 172, 205–8
Bacall, Lauren, 148
Bad Day at Black Rock, 31, 207
Baldwin, James, 33, 139
Ball, Lucille. See *I Love Lucy*
Band of Brothers, 37
Battle Cry, 121
Battleground, 30, 96
Battle Hymn, 98
Beaumont, Charles: "The Crooked Man," 157–61, 163, 165; "The Hunger," 161–64, 166
Beaumont, Hugh. See *Leave It to Beaver*
beauty, 25, 59, 63, 111, 130, 148–50, 154, 164, 168, 196, 210, 212, 215, 221–22
Bellow, Saul, 33
Benny, Jack, 21, 202
Bergen, Edgar, 203
Best Years of Our Lives, The, 1–2, 61, 208
Beulah, 176, 181
Beyond the Pleasure Principle. See Freud, Sigmund
Big Heat, The, 101, 113, 121, 125–27, 131
Birth of a Nation, The, 14
bisexuality. *See* same-sex intimacy

Black Americans. *See* African Americans
Blackboard Jungle, 117, 119–21
Black Widow, 121
Black Women's Blueprint, 209–10
Blood and Steel, 99
Blue Dahlia, The, 31, 207
Bob Hope Chevy Show, The, 201–2
Bogart, Humphrey, 59, 72, 99, 105
Bradbury, Ray, 33
Brando, Jocelyn, 126
Brando, Marlon, 99–101
"Brave Men, Brave Men" (Pyle), 5–10, 14
Breen, Joe, censorship by, 91, 115
Bridges, Lloyd, 98
Bright Victory, 98
Brodie, Steve, 98
Brooks, Richard, 119–21
Brown, Helen Gurley, 206, 210–27
Buchanan, Edgar, 108
Burns and Allen, 181
Burroughs, William, 33

Caine Mutiny, The: film, 96, 99; novel, 32
"Can This Marriage Be Saved?," 178–79
Capote, Truman, 33
Carter, Jimmy, 208
Case, Kathleen, 111
Catch-22 (Heller), 32
Catholics. *See* religion
censorship, 2, 41, 48–49, 148, 151, 181; by Joe Breen, 91, 115
Chapin, Lauren, 205
class, 4–5, 14–15, 32, 38–39, 52, 54, 63, 80, 86, 119, 134, 136–38, 141–47, 165–71, 173, 186, 208, 216

Cleaver, Eldridge, 168
Clift, Montgomery, 100–101, 103
Cold War, 36, 227
Columbia Pictures, 103–4, 108, 115
Columbia race riots, 97
combat films, 30–31, 66, 96, 98–99, 105, 109, 207–8
Command Decision, 96
communism, anticommunism, 36–38
Confidential magazine, 201–3
conformity, 36–37, 39, 60, 182
consensus, 39
containment, 36, 68, 83
Cooper, Gary, 103, 106
Cosmopolitan magazine, 200, 218, 227
Crawford, Broderick, 113
Crawford, Joan, 110–11
Crosby, Bing, 21

Dana, Leora, 128–31
Dangling Man, The (Bellow), 33
Danny Thomas Show, The. *See Make Room for Daddy/The Danny Thomas Show*
Daves, Delmer, 30; *3:10 to Yuma*, 99, 102, 104, 105, 127–32
Day, Doris, 227
Dean, James, 100–101
"Decline of the American Male, The" (Moskin), 26
Deep Are the Roots, 96–97
de Havilland, Olivia, 95
De Havilland Law, 95
del Rio, Dolores, 148
Denning, Richard, 121
depression, the, 5, 13, 21, 144, 165
de Wilde, Brandon, 122–23
Dietrich, Marlene, 148

Dmytryk, Edward, 96
Donna Reed Show, The, 35, 181, 182, 189, 192–96, 203, 205
Don't Go Near the Water, 132
Drew, Ellen, 108
Duke magazine, 169, 171

Easy to Get, 146
Ebony magazine, 150, 169
Edwards, James, 96–99, 119
Ellis, Havelock, 152
Ellison, Ralph, 14, 33
Emerson, Faye, 180
Esquire magazine, 134–40, 144, 147–50, 157, 165–69, 171
Ethel and Albert, 189
ethnicity, 4–5, 7, 15–16, 21–22, 39, 149–50, 170, 193–94

Farr, Felicia, 128
Father Knows Best, 35, 173, 181, 182–86, 188–90, 192–200, 204–6
Feminine Mystique, The (Friedan), 206, 210, 223–27
feminism, 39, 60, 76, 176, 181, 208, 210, 217–18, 220, 225–26
Fenichel, Otto, 19–20
Fenton, Leslie, 109
film noir, 31, 78, 104, 106–7, 109–13, 115–19, 121, 125–27, 207–8
Fireside Chats. *See* Roosevelt, Franklin D.
Fitzgerald, Ella, 159
Fleming, Victor, 1, 95–96
"Flying Home" (Ellison), 14, 33
Ford, Glenn, 94–132
Forever Darling, 202

4F status, 16, 51, 96, 103, 105
Francis, Anne, 120–21
Freud, Sigmund, 5, 17–19, 34, 78, 152, 156, 166
Friedan, Betty, 206, 210, 223–27
Fuller, Samuel, 98

Gable, Clark, 102
Garland, Judy, 21
genre, 31, 61–62, 109–10, 157, 175–82. *See also* film noir; sitcom/situation comedy; western
GI Bill, 3, 8, 13, 15, 65–66, 96, 133, 138, 143, 166, 226, 227
Gilda, 103, 105–7
Gingrich, Arnold, 138, 144, 148, 157
Ginsburg, Allen, 33
Go for Broke!, 96
Gone with the Wind, 1, 95
Grable, Betty, 148–51, 155, 226
Grahame, Gloria, 111, 113, 126–27
Grand Central Murder, 104
Gravity's Rainbow (Pynchon), 32
Gray, Billy, 205–6
Great Depression, the, 5, 13, 21, 144, 165
Greatest Generation, the, 28, 171, 206, 227
Green Dolphin Street, 104
"Group Psychology and the Analysis of the Ego." *See* Freud, Sigmund
Guadalcanal Diary, 30
Gunman's Walk, 132
Guy Named Joe, A, 96

Hammett, Dashiell, 60, 69, 72
Hansbury, Lorraine, 33, 210, 216–17, 223

Hawaii, 146
Hayes, Margaret, 120–21
Hayworth, Rita, 103, 106–7, 140, 148–50
Heflin, Van, 99–132
Hefner, Hugh. See *Playboy*
Heller, Joseph, 32
Himes, Chester, 13, 33, 60, 69
Hitler, Adolf. *See* nazis
Holden, William, 108
Hollywood, 1, 4, 21–22, 30–31, 50, 52, 59, 94–132, 134, 148, 150, 200–203, 207, 209, 211
Hollywood Canteen, 22, 30, 105
Home of the Brave, 30, 97–98, 119
homosexuality. *See* same-sex intimacy
Honeymooners, The, 176, 206
Hope, Bob, 21, 134, 201–2
Horne, Lena, 21, 149–50
"Howl" (Ginsburg), 33
Hughes, Dorothy, 34, 59–62, 66–67, 75–85, 91–92
Hughes, Langston, 96
Human Desire, 111–13, 117
Hunters, The (Salter), 33

I, the Jury (Spillane), 59–64, 66–74, 77, 84, 91–93
I Love Lucy, 34–35, 172–78, 181, 185, 188–89, 194–96, 199–207
I Married Joan, 181, 196, 199
In a Lonely Place (Hughes), 34, 59–62, 66–67, 75–85, 91–92
Inner Ring, the. *See* psychoanalysis
I've Got a Secret, 201–3
Invisible Man (Ellison), 14, 33
Iraq War, 3, 28, 36, 208
Ireland, John, 114

Jackson, Jennifer, 169
Jaffe, Rona, 169–70
Japanese, 6–8, 12, 16, 111
Japanese Americans, 15
Jewish, 15–16, 21, 103
Johnny Eager, 104–7
Johnson, Nunnally, 121
Johnson, Van, 96, 98–99, 103
Jolson, Al, 21
Jones, James, 32, 210

Kazan, Elia, 96, 101
Kerouac, Jack, 32–33
Keyes, Evelyn, 113–16
Kid Glove Killer, 104
Killer Inside Me, The, 77–78
Kinsey, Alfred, 16, 31, 152, 156, 161
Kiss Me Deadly, 92
Klein, Melanie, 19

labor unions, 21, 95
Ladd, Alan, 122–25. See also *Blue Dahlia, The*
Ladies' Home Journal, 178, 188
Lamour, Dorothy, 52, 150
Lang, Fritz, 101, 111–13, 121, 125–27, 131
Latino/as, 116, 150, 193, 201
Laurel and Hardy, 21
Leave It to Beaver, 35, 173, 175, 176, 181, 182–90, 196–97, 199, 203–5, 217
Lee, China, 169
Leigh, Janet, 117–19
LeRoy, Mervyn, 96, 104, 106
letters, 24–25, 41–57
Life magazine, 74, 168
Life with Elizabeth, 181

literary fiction, 31–33, 142, 155
Lonely Crowd, The (Riesman), 37–38
Look magazine, 26, 168
Losey, Joseph, 115–16
Lost Generation. *See* World War I
"Love in the Dark" (Moore), 37–38
Lovejoy, Frank, 91, 98
Lucille Ball, 34–35
lynchings, 13, 97

Macready, George, 106
Madame Bovary, 104
magazines
Mailer, Norman, 32, 169
Make Room for Daddy/The Danny Thomas Show, 173, 181, 183–93, 195–96, 199, 204
Malcolm X, 168
MAMs/men's adventure magazines, 142–44, 165
Man from Colorado, The, 107–9
Man in the Gray Flannel Suit (Wilson), 31–32, 37, 143
Mann, Anthony, 98–99
man who does/man who doesn't, 31, 99, 105, 208
Marcus, Greil, 23
marriage, 16, 25, 38–39, 46, 68–72, 78–80, 83, 85–90, 105–7, 113–15, 118–19, 121, 123–24, 126–27, 129, 133, 147, 151–53, 162, 165–66, 168, 177–79, 181–204, 216, 218–25
Marvin, Lee, 126
Marx Brothers, the, 21
Mason, James, 104
Mating of Millie, The, 114–16
McCarthy, Mary, 33
Mead, Shepherd, 167

Men in War, 98–99
#MeToo, 209
Meyer, Emile, 122–25
MGM Studios (Metro Goldwyn Mayer), 2, 103–4, 106
middle class. *See* class
Milestone, Lewis, 99, 104
Milland, Ray, 103
Miller, Arthur, 33
Minelli, Vincente, 104
Modern Man, 140–41
Monroe, Marilyn, 140, 155
Moore, Pamela, 163–65
morale, 5, 9, 20–27, 42, 49–50, 54–55, 134–37, 145, 147, 151
Morrow, Vic, 120–21
Moskin, J. Robert, 26
Movie Life magazine, 200
Mr. Soft Touch, 114
Murrow, Edward R., 204
My Favorite Husband, 181
My Gun Is Quick (Spillane), 69–74

NAACP, 14–15, 147
Naked and the Dead, The (Mailer), 32, 169
Native Son (Wright), 13
nazis, 7–8, 29, 45, 103, 211–12
Negulesco, Jean, 121
Nelson, Ozzie and Harriet. *See Adventures of Ozzie and Harriet, The*
Nelson, Ricky, 172–74, 205. *See also Adventures of Ozzie and Harriet, The*
New Sentimentality, 171
New Yorker magazine, 148
Nine Stories (Salinger), 33
Nixon, Richard, 207
nostalgia, 33, 63, 66

O'Connor, Flannery, 33
Office of War Information, 6, 22–23
On the Road (Kerouac), 32–33
Organization Man, The (Whyte), 31–32, 36–37

Pacific, The, 37
Palance, Jack, 122–23
Paramount Pictures, 104; *United States v. Paramount Pictures, Inc.*, 94, 103
patriotism, 5, 14–15, 23, 25, 53, 62, 135, 145–46
Pearl Harbor, 5, 106
Peck, Gregory, 103
performance. *See* acting
perpetration-induced trauma stress (PITS). *See* trauma
Person to Person, 204
Petty, George, Petty Girls, 148
Pilgrim, Janet, 156
pin-ups, 23–25, 34, 68, 135–38, 147–55, 159, 164–65
Playboy, 30, 34, 132–71, 179, 206–8, 209–10, 223, 224, 227
Players, 169–71
Playmates. *See Playboy*
Poitier, Sidney, 98, 119–21
Pork Chop Hill, 99
Possessed, 109–11, 113
post-traumatic stress disorder. *See* trauma
Powell, William, 125
Preparing for Marriage (Clifford), 152–53, 161
primal horde. *See* Freud, Sigmund
Protestants. *See* religion
Prowler, The, 115–16

psychoanalysis, 75–77. *See also* Fenichel, Otto; Freud, Sigmund; Simmel, Ernst
pulp fiction, 31–33, 59–94, 179
Pyle, Ernie, 5–10, 14
Pynchon, Thomas, 32

race, 4, 5, 12–15, 21–22, 24, 51, 60, 96–99, 119–21, 145–47, 149–50, 168–70, 176, 181, 209–10, 216–17
Raisin in the Sun, A (Hansbury), 33, 210, 216–17, 223
Rat Pack, the, 170
Reagan, Ronald, 96
Redhead and the Cowboy, The, 109
religion, 4, 14, 15–16, 21, 38, 220
"Remembering, Repeating, and Working Through." *See* Freud, Sigmund
repetition-compulsion. *See* Freud, Sigmund
repression-expression conundrum, 17, 20–42, 151–54, 217
Reynolds, Quentin, 20
Riesman, David, *The Lonely Crowd*, 37–38
RKO Pictures, 104
Rockwell, Norman, 23
Roosevelt, Franklin D., 6–7, 21, 23, 38, 145
Rosie the Riveter, 23
Russell, Jane, 140, 148, 156
Ryan, Robert, 98, 117

Salinger, J. D., 33
Salter, James, 32
same-sex intimacy, 16, 39, 88, 90, 105–7, 157–61, 175, 201–2, 218
Sands of Iwo Jima, 30
Saturday Night Live, 172–74

Saving Private Ryan, 37
Schlesinger, Arthur, 39
Scott, Lizabeth, 110
Screen Actors Guild (SAG), 21, 95, 115
Sex and the Single Girl (Brown), 206, 210–27
sexual assault, 53–54, 75–78, 89, 91, 94, 115, 120–21, 147, 162–64, 209–10
Sexual Behavior in the Human Male (Kinsey), 16, 31, 152, 156, 161
sex work, 16, 54, 74, 77, 85–87, 118, 142, 145–48, 154
Shane, 101, 105, 121–25, 127, 132
Shaw, Irwin, 32
shellshock. *See* trauma
Simmel, Ernst, 17, 19
Sinatra, Frank, 21, 103, 170
Sirk, Douglas, 98, 121
sitcom/situation comedy, 34–35, 172
Slaughterhouse Five (Vonnegut), 32
Smart, David, 135, 144, 148
So Ends Our Night, 103
Spillane, Mickey, 34, 59–64, 66–75, 84, 85, 91–93, 166, 210, 227; *I, the Jury*, 59–64, 66–74, 77, 84, 91–93; *My Gun Is Quick*, 69–74
Spock, Benjamin, 179, 188
Stage Door Canteen, 21–22
Stag magazine, 142–43, 165
Stag Party magazine, 141
Stanwyck, Barbara, 104, 110, 148
Stars and Stripes, 136–37, 139
star studies, 102–5
State of the Union. *See* Roosevelt, Franklin D.
Steel Helmet, The, 98
Steinem, Gloria, 164, 210
Stewart, James, 103
Stimson, Henry L., 21–22, 136

Strange Love of Martha Ivers, The, 109–10, 111, 117
Streetcar Named Desire, A (Williams), 33–34, 59–62, 66, 85–91
suburbanization. *See* suburbs
suburbs, 3–4, 38–39, 65–66, 118–19, 159, 168, 173, 226
superego. *See* Freud, Sigmund
Susann, Jacqueline, 210–18, 222, 225
sweats, 142–44, 165

Tap Roots, 104
Taylor, Robert, 104–6
Tennessee Johnson, 104
Texas, 103, 105, 108–9
Thin Red Line, The, 32
Thirty Seconds Over Tokyo, 96
Thomas, Danny. See *Make Room for Daddy/The Danny Thomas Show*
Thompson, Jim, 77–78
Three Musketeers, The, 104
3:10 to Yuma, 99, 102, 104, 105, 127–32
Till the Clouds Roll By, 104
Time magazine, 219
Tracy, Spencer, 125
trauma, 17–31, 44, 84–85, 92, 107–9, 144, 191–92
Trilling, Lionel, 16–17
Trouble with Father, The (*The Stu Erwin Show*), 189
Truman, Harry, 36
TV Guide magazine, 199–200, 205
Twelve O'Clock High, 30

United Artists, 21
United Services Organization (USO), 21–23, 105, 134, 145, 148–50, 226

United States v. Paramount Pictures, Inc., 94, 103
Universal Pictures, 104
Updike, John, 33

Valley of the Dolls (Susann), 210–18, 222, 225
Vance, Vivian, 175, 199, 201
Vargas, Alberto, Varga Girls, 147–50, 154, 156
Vaughn, Sarah, 159
Veteran Comes Back, The (Waller), 9–12, 23, 26, 30, 35
Victim, The (Bellow), 33
Vidor, Charles, 106–7
Vietnam War, 2–3, 15, 29–30, 37, 208
Vital Center, The (Schlesinger), 39
Vonnegut, Kurt, 32, 147

Wallace, Mike, 153–54, 156, 165
Waller, Willard, 9–12, 16–17, 23, 25–26, 30, 35, 37, 216
Walsh, Raoul, 121
War, The, 37
war films, 30–31, 66, 96, 98–99, 105, 109, 207–8
Warner Bros., 21
Wayne, John, 103, 227
Wechter, Dixon, 9–12, 16–17, 35
Weekend with Father, 121
West, Dorothy, 33
western, 31, 109, 138, 142, 180, 206, 207
When Johnny Comes Marching Home (Wechter), 9–12, 16–17, 35
White, Walter. See NAACP
whiteness, 4, 12–15, 22, 24, 38–39, 52, 59–60, 65, 94, 97–99, 119, 133, 142, 145–47, 150, 168–70, 181, 193, 208, 210, 215, 217–18
white women, 13, 22, 24, 38–39, 52, 59–60, 97, 142, 145–47, 150, 169–70, 208, 210, 215, 217
Whyte, William, 31–32, 36–37
Williams, Tennessee, 33–34, 59–62, 66, 85–91
Wilson, Sloan, 31–32, 37, 143
Wise Blood (O'Connor), 33
Woman's World, 121
women's liberation. See feminism
working class. See class
World War I, 8–10, 27, 30, 32, 33, 136, 148
Wouk, Herman, 32, 96, 99
Wright, Richard, 13
Wyler, William, 1–2

YANK: The Army Weekly, 22, 136–37
Young, Robert, 199–200, 204–5
Young Lions, The (Shaw), 32

Zinneman, Fred: *Act of Violence*, 31, 116–19, 207; *Kid Glove Killer*, 104

CULTURAL FRAMES, FRAMING CULTURE

We, Us, and Them: Affect and American Nonfiction from Vietnam to Trump
DOUGLAS DOWLAND

Criminal Cities: The Postcolonial Novel and Cathartic Crime
MOLLY SLAVIN

Skimpy Coverage: Sports Illustrated *and the Shaping of the Female Athlete*
BONNIE M. HAGERMAN

Institutional Character: Collectivity, Agency, and the Modernist Novel
ROBERT HIGNEY

Walk the Barrio: The Streets of Twenty-First-Century Transnational Latinx Literature
CRISTINA RODRIGUEZ

Fashioning Character: Style, Performance, and Identity in Contemporary American Literature
LAUREN S. CARDON

Neoliberal Nonfictions: The Documentary Aesthetic from Joan Didion to Jay-Z
DANIEL WORDEN

Dandyism: Forming Fiction from Modernism to the Present
LEN GUTKIN

Terrible Beauty: The Violent Aesthetic and Twentieth-Century Literature
MARIAN EIDE

Women Writers of the Beat Era: Autobiography and Intertextuality
MARY PANICCIA CARDEN

Stranger America: A Narrative Ethics of Exclusion
JOSH TOTH

Fashion and Fiction: Self-Transformation in Twentieth-Century American Literature
LAUREN S. CARDON

American Road Narratives: Reimagining Mobility in Literature and Film
ANN BRIGHAM

The Arresting Eye: Race and the Anxiety of Detection
JINNY HUH

Failed Frontiersmen: White Men and Myth in the Post-Sixties American Historical Romance
JAMES J. DONAHUE

Composing Cultures: Modernism, American Literary Studies, and the Problem of Culture
ERIC ARONOFF

Quirks of the Quantum: Postmodernism and Contemporary American Fiction
SAMUEL CHASE COALE

Chick Lit and Postfeminism
STEPHANIE HARZEWSKI

American Iconographic: "National Geographic," Global Culture, and the Visual Imagination
STEPHANIE L. HAWKINS

Wanted: The Outlaw in American Visual Culture
RACHEL HALL

Male Armor: The Soldier-Hero in Contemporary American Culture
JON ROBERT ADAMS

www.ingramcontent.com/pod-product-compliance
Lightning Source LLC
Chambersburg PA
CBHW021657230426
43668CB00008B/650